CW00558047

AFTER THE FIRE

London Churches in the Age of Wren, Hooke, Hawksmoor and Gibbs

AFTER THE FIRE

London Churches in the Age of Wren, Hooke, Hawksmoor and Gibbs

Angelo Hornak

Foreword by The Right Reverend Stephen Platten

PIMPERNEL
PRESS LTD
www.pimpernelpress.com

CONTENTS

For Laura

www.pimpernelpress.com

AFTER THE FIRE
London Churches in the Age of Wren, Hooke, Hawksmoor
and Gibbs
© Pimpernel Press Limited 2016
Text © Angelo Hornak 2016
Photographs © Angelo Hornak 2016
Except as noted on page 384

All rights reserved. No part of this publication may be
reproduced, stored in a retrieval system or transmitted,
in any form, or by any means, electronic, mechanical,
photocopying, recording or otherwise, without prior
permission in writing from the publisher or a licence
permitting restricted copying. In the United Kingdom such
licences are issued by the Copyright Licensing Agency,
Saffron House, 6–10 Kirby Street, London, EC1N 8TS.

A catalogue record for this book is available from the
British Library.

Designed by Anne Wilson
Typeset in Caslon, Centaur and Vaud

ISBN 978-1-910258-08-8
Printed and bound in China
by C&C Offset Printing Company Limited

9 8 7 6 5 4 3 2 1

ENDPAPERS St Mary-le-Strand, 1714–17,
by James Gibbs. The ceiling.

HALF TITLE St Vedast-alias-Foster. *Dove in Glory*,
1690s, carved by Edward Strong.

TITLE PAGE St Stephen Walbrook, *c*.1672–1715,
by Sir Christopher Wren.

RIGHT Detail from *A Prospect of the City of
London*, by Johannes Kip. This engraving of 1724
shows the City as rebuilt after the Great Fire.

OPPOSITE St Mary Woolnoth, 1716–27,
by Nicholas Hawksmoor. The ceiling.

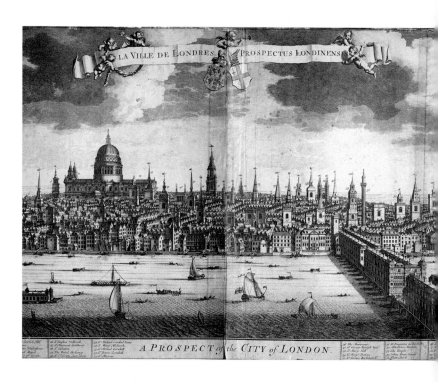

LA VILLE DE LONDRES — PROSPECTUS LONDINENSIS

A PROSPECT of the CITY of LONDON.

FOREWORD

Stephen Platten
Rector of St Michael on Cornhill
and Assistant Bishop in the Diocese of London

THE CITY OF LONDON is an architectural palimpsest. Written over the straight lines of Roman streets and city walls are the patterns of medieval life; these too are overwritten with Baroque, Georgian and Victorian patterns of buildings; the twentieth and twenty-first centuries have added their own towering structures in different modern styles. Angelo Hornak's richly illustrated book of London's Baroque churches focuses on one important architectural strand in this remarkable palimpsest.

The period covered here owes almost everything to the devastating impact of the Great Fire of London of 1666. Ironically, that fire offered a unique opportunity to the burgeoning capital in a number of different ways. First it opened up the possibility for a fairly late flowering of the Baroque in England, with the work of Wren, Hooke, Hawksmoor and others. It did so at a particularly intriguing time both religiously and intellectually. English religion was in the midst of tumultuous change. The Restoration of the Monarchy under Charles II was accompanied by the publication of the Book of Common Prayer in 1662. This presaged the 'Great Ejection' of hundreds of Presbyterian divines which would be followed only twenty five years later with the beginnings of toleration in the Glorious Revolution and the accession of William III to the throne.

Evidence of so much of this history is there in the extraordinary period of church building in the fifty years following the Great Fire, the apotheosis of which was the completion of Christopher Wren's great Cathedral of St Paul. Other more modest churches, however, also tell something of this unfolding story, writing still more layers into this architectural palimpsest.

Take, for example, St Michael on Cornhill. Tucked discreetly behind the frontages of Victorian and Edwardian buildings, this church tells its own tale of the City. The church stands directly over the basilica of the forum of the Roman city of Londinium – so there has probably been worship on this site for two thousand years. That worship would originally have been of the Emperor, of Caesar. Following the Roman retreat *c.*AD 400, it is most likely that the basilica was converted into a Christian church; that was the advice Pope Gregory the

Great gave to Augustine and his fellow missionaries some two centuries later: 'Do not destroy pagan temples, but inhabit them with the Christian gospel.' Already a new script was written over the Roman base.

We have definite evidence of a continuous stream of clergy from the twelfth century onwards. The medieval church which they served was burnt down, save for the tower, in the Great Fire. In the 1670s a classical Baroque church rose up; forty years later a new tower was added, the upper section being the design of Nicholas Hawksmoor. One hundred and fifty years on and Sir George Gilbert Scott 'restored' the church again, writing over the ancient architectural manuscript with his recognizable Gothic Revival style.

This is but one example of the multitude of churches which survive from the unique period of church building that followed the Fire. Angelo Hornak tells the story, deciphers the palimpsest, with his outstandingly rich set of photographs and accompanying text. His interpretation helps this great treasury of ecclesiastical architecture to speak to another and very different age.

Stephen Platten

INTRODUCTION

The Fire and the Coal Tax

THIS BOOK is about the London Baroque churches built in the sixty years after the Great Fire of 1666, when the City of London was almost totally destroyed. The losses included St Paul's Cathedral and eighty-seven parish churches, as well as many important secular buildings. The catastrophe provided an opportunity for Christopher Wren and his colleagues, notably Robert Hooke, to create a new style of church architecture inspired by the Baroque churches of Rome, Paris and the Netherlands.

Most books on Wren's City churches are just that – they deal with those built by Wren within the City of London, often leaving out St Paul's Cathedral, his masterpiece. This approach also ignores the continuity between Wren's churches and those built in the second wave of Baroque church construction during the reign of Queen Anne, the so-called Fifty New Churches (of which only twelve were built). Although Wren did not design any of these, he was one of the Commissioners responsible for the programme, and six were built by his brilliant pupil Nicholas Hawksmoor in his own highly individual Baroque style.

Besides the stylistic continuity, another reason for considering these churches together is the fact that they were all funded by the Coal Tax. In 1667, within months of the Fire, Parliament passed the Rebuilding Act, which authorized a tax to be levied on all coal arriving in the City of London. The coal unloaded here was not only for Londoners, it also provided much of the fuel used in the hole of the Thames estuary, ensuring a large tax base. In 1670, three-quarters of the Coal Tax revenue was allocated to rebuilding the parish churches and St Paul's. It also provided money for the Monument to the Fire of London. In 1711 another Act of Parliament extended the tax to pay for the Fifty New Churches.

Three years later the Hanoverians succeeded to the throne; George I and his Whig supporters were less enthusiastic about church building, and the Coal Tax was not extended beyond the 1720s. This coincided with a change in taste which saw Wren and Hawksmoor's Baroque replaced by the new Palladianism of Lord Burlington and William Kent, and such churches as were built were in a more restrained and sober style. But before the Coal Tax money came to an end it had provided most of the funding for London's Baroque churches.

The crossing and nave of St Paul's Cathedral, seen from the Whispering Gallery.

THE GREAT FIRE OF LONDON

'LONDON WAS, BUT IS NO MORE!' In these words John Evelyn summed up the destruction of the City of London in the Great Fire. Evelyn's diary entry for 3 September 1666 reads

> Oh the miserable and calamitous spectacle! . . . All the skie was of a fiery aspect, like the top of a burning oven, and the light seene above 40 miles round about for many nights . . . the noise and cracking and thunder of the impetuous flames, the shreiking of women and children, the hurry of people, the fall of Towers, Houses and Churches, was like an hideous storme.[1]

The Fire started in the early hours of Sunday 2 September in Thomas Farriner's bakery in Pudding Lane, in the east of the City. Small outbreaks of fire were a common enough event, and when the Lord Mayor, Sir Thomas Bludworth, was roused to deal with the fire, he dismissed it with the contemptuous phrase 'a woman might piss it out!'[2] and went back to bed.

But once the fire got going, a fierce easterly wind quickly spread the flames to neighbouring houses. Samuel Pepys, Evelyn's friend and fellow-diarist, wrote how he had 'seen the fire rage every way . . . and the wind mighty high and driving it into the city, and everything, after so long a drought, proving combustible, even the very stones of churches.'[3]

Many of the houses on both sides of the narrow streets were built with thatched roofs and overhanging jetties, whose upper storeys projected out over the street so their eaves were almost touching; in these conditions the fire could spread easily from one side of the street to the other.

It was bad enough that the closely packed timber-framed houses were all tinder-dry after a long hot summer; but soon the fire found more fuel in the warehouses along the river Thames, as Pepys explains: 'the houses too, so very thick thereabouts, and full of matter for burning, as pitch and tar, in Thames Street – and warehouses of oyle and wines and brandy and other things.'

London Bridge, packed with shops and houses like the Ponte Vecchio in Florence today, was the only fixed river crossing, and led into the City close to Pudding Lane, where the fire had started. The bridgehead, and the nearby

[1] John Evelyn, *Diary*, 3 September 1666
[2] James Peller Malcolm, *London Redivivum*, vol. iv, page 74
[3] Samuel Pepys, *Diary*, 2 September 1666

church of St Magnus the Martyr, were soon consumed by the fire, although most of the bridge survived.

The City of London, mostly built within the walls of Roman Londinium, occupied an area of about one square mile.[4] The river Thames along its southern border, with its quays and warehouses, gave the City easy access to the sea and maritime trade, so it had become the principal port and trading centre for the whole region. The population of about eighty thousand lived for the most part in cramped and squalid housing conditions, with sewage and butchers' offal running down open drains to the river. Even the air was foul: John Evelyn attacked the 'pernicious Smoake' from the coal burnt by *'Brewers, Diers, Lime-burners, Salt, and Sope-boylers*, . . . Whilst these are belching it forth . . . the City of London resembles . . . the Suburbs of *Hell.*'[5]

It was in these conditions that an epidemic of bubonic plague had struck London the previous year. The death toll in the summer of 1665 was on a terrifying scale, with 7,165 deaths recorded in one week in September.

The Great Fire of London, as imagined by the French artist Philippe-Jacques de Loutherbourg, (1740–1812).

[4] Today a small – but important – part of the metropolis we call London, or Greater London.
[5] John Evelyn, *Fumifugium,* pages 5–6

Those who could afford to left the City, and the streets fell silent: 'no rattling coaches, no prancing horses, no calling in customers, nor offering wares; no London Cries sounding in the ears: if any voice be heard, it is the groans of dying persons, breathing forth their last.'[6]

Within less than a year, one Londoner in five had died, leaving a weakened population less able to fight the fire when it broke out.

At the time fire-fighting techniques involved cutting into the pipes supplying water from the New River reservoir at Clerkenwell to the north, while to the south water was pumped up from the Thames by waterwheels at London Bridge. These waterwheels, however, were soon put out of action when the bridgehead caught fire. There were a few fire engines with powerful pumps, but they were cumbersome and unwieldy in the narrow streets of London. One even fell into the Thames as it attempted to fill its reservoir. Hand-held 'squirts' were not much better, being capable of delivering only four pints at a time.

John Dryden's *Annus Mirabilis* describes how:

Some run for buckets to the hallow'd quire:
Some cut the pipes, and some the engines play;
And some more bold mount ladders to the fire.[7]

The 'hallow'd quire' refers to St Paul's Cathedral. The only really effective method of fire-fighting was to create fire-breaks by removing houses in the path of the fire, either pulling them down with hooks on long poles, or blowing them up with gunpowder. But home-owners were – not unnaturally – reluctant to allow their houses to be sacrificed as fire-breaks. As Evelyn explains: 'this some tenacious and avaritious men, aldermen &c. would not permitt, because their houses must have ben of the first.'

Only King Charles had the authority to order houses to be pulled down – Pepys tells how he went to the King to report on the fire and told him that:

unless his Majesty did command houses to be pulled down, nothing could stop the fire . . . and the King commanded me to go to my Lord Mayor from him and command him to spare no houses but to pull down before the fire every way . . . at last met my Lord Mayor in Canning Streete, like a man spent, with a hankercher about his neck. To the King's message, he cried like a fainting woman, 'Lord, what can I do? I am spent! People will not obey me. I have been pulling down houses. But the fire overtakes us faster then we can do it.'

[6] Thomas Vincent, *God's Terrible Voice in the City*
[7] John Dryden, *Annus Mirabilis*, verse 229, lines 914-916. The 'hallow'd quire' refers to St Paul's Cathedral.

Wenceslaus Hollar's engraving of Old St Paul's burning, inscribed 'Even the ruins perished'.

Poor Lord Mayor Bludworth – he had cause to regret his earlier dismissive remark about how to extinguish the fire. A contemporary account tells how 'Everyone condemned the Lord Mayor, as a person delighting more in drinking and dancing than is necessary for such a magistrate.'[8]

The King appointed his brother James, Duke of York (later King James II) to take charge of the fire-fighting, and together they visited the front line and set an example by taking a hand in the operations. James was particularly active: John Rushworth wrote to a friend that he had seen him 'handing Bucketts of water with as much diligence as the poorest man that did assist.'[9]

But Charles pitched in too, as Evelyn commented: 'how extraordinary the vigilance and activity of the King and the Duke was, even labouring in person, and being present to command, order, reward or encourage workmen.'

The 'workmen' were rounded up by the Duke of York's press gangs, like those used to provide manpower for the navy. William Denton, a physician, tells how two of his servants had been taken: 'I dare not send a man out of doors for feare of being pressed to work att the fier. James and Jack were both pressed this morning.'[10]

And it wasn't only men who were at risk – women and children were also pressed into fire-fighting. But while fire-breaks were being created to the west, to protect the Strand and Whitehall, and in the east to save the Tower of London, fire raged on in the centre of the City. By Tuesday, the third night of the Fire, flames were seen coming out of the roof of St Paul's Cathedral. A schoolboy, William Taswell, recorded in his memoir how: 'About eight o'clock it broke out on the top of St Paul's Church, already scorched up by the violent heat of the air.'[11]

[8] Malcolm, *London Redidivum*, vol iv, page 80
[9] John Rushworth, *A Letter Giving Account of that Stupendious Fire which consumed the City of London, 1666*
[10] Margaret M. Verney, *Memoirs of the Verney family from the restoration to the revolution, 1660 to 1696*, page 141
[11] William Taswell, *Autobiography, 1651–1682*

View of Part of LONDON as it appeared in the Dreadful Fire in 1666.

Walter Harrison's 'View of Part of LONDON as it appeared in the Dreadful Fire in 1666' shows Londoners escaping from the Fire.

[12] But he did recover the wine. Ten days later he wrote: 'got my wine out of the ground again, and set it in my cellar; but with great pain to keep the porters that carried it in from observing the money-chests there.'

The medieval cathedral had suffered badly from neglect and abuse in the recent Civil War, when the south transept roof had fallen in. It was being repaired with wooden scaffolding and a temporary timber roof, and embers blown from the nearby properties set the timber boards and poles on fire. Evelyn tells how the policy of pulling down nearby houses backfired: 'the demolition had stopp'd all the passages, so that no help could be applied.'

The fire engines themselves got caught, as Taswell explains: 'In my way home I saw several engines . . . all on fire, and those concerned with them escaping with great eagerness from the flames.'

Evelyn describes how the very stones of the old cathedral exploded in the intense heat: 'the stones of Paules flew like granados, the mealting lead running downe the streetes in a streame, and the very pavements glowing with fiery rednesse.'

By Wednesday morning, when St Paul's was a smouldering heap of ruins, the wind had finally eased up. The fire's progress to the west was stopped at the Temple, sparing the twelfth-century church of the Knights Templar. In the east, the flames threatened the Tower of London, with its massive magazine of gunpowder. If that had caught fire there would have been a catastrophic explosion. Instead, the gunpowder was used to create firebreaks by blowing up the neighbouring houses, and the fire got no further than the parsonage of All Hallows by the Tower. The church itself escaped. Close by in Seething Lane was the Navy Office complex, where Samuel Pepys lived and worked. Pepys, fearing the worst, decided 'about 4 a-clock in the morning [to use] a cart to carry away all my money and plate and best things to W. Riders at Bednall Greene; which I did, riding myself in my nightgown in the car.'

He wasn't alone. Although profiteering carters charged what they could get, anybody who could afford to rent a cart was trying to get their goods to safety: 'Lord, to see how the streets and highways are crowded with people, running and riding and getting of carts at any rate to fetch away things.'

But not everything could be got safely away, so with the help of a friend Pepys dug a pit in the garden and 'put our wine in it and I my parmezan cheese'.

To his surprise and relief, Seething Lane escaped. He doesn't say what happened to the cheese.[12]

By Wednesday afternoon the gales had dropped away, and by Thursday morning the fire was effectively out. King Charles, alarmed at rumours that it had been deliberately started by dissident Roman Catholics or foreign agents, rode to the camp at Moorfields where many thousands had taken refuge, to announce that the fire was an accident and not the work of Papists or foreigners. Suspicion of foreigners was particularly high. This was the period of the Second Anglo-Dutch War: in 1665 Charles had declared war on the Dutch, and in August 1666, only weeks before the Fire, Robert Holmes led an attack on the island of Terschelling in what became known as Holmes's Bonfire. The English destroyed some 130 Dutch merchant ships and sacked the island, setting fire to many warehouses. Louis XIV of France had entered the war on the side of the Dutch, so the streets of London just after the Fire were a dangerous place to be taken for a foreigner, as vigilante groups roamed the streets hunting for scapegoats. According to Taswell, 'The ignorant and deluded mob . . . vented forth their rage against the Roman Catholics and Frenchmen . . . A blacksmith in my presence, meeting an innocent Frenchman walking along the street, felled him instantly to the ground with an iron bar.' When Robert Hubert, a hapless French watchmaker of unsound mind, insisted against all the evidence that he had started the fire, he was sent to the gallows at Tyburn.

It was time to take stock of the damage. The recorded human death toll was remarkably low: fewer than ten people are known to have died, including Thomas Farriner's maid, who failed to escape when his bakery caught fire. But this is probably an underestimate, as any bodies would have been cremated in the intense heat, and poorer Londoners' deaths would have gone unrecorded. Many more would have succumbed to disease after the Fire, as tens of thousands had to face the harsh winter in makeshift refugee camps on Moorfields and Islington, and as far north as Highgate.

On the other hand, the destruction of overcrowded buildings infested with plague-carrying rats and fleas probably helped put an end to the epidemic that had killed so many only the year before.

The damage to property was immense. Over 400 acres of land and 13,000 houses were destroyed. The Guildhall, the Sessions House, the Royal Exchange and the Customs House, the City's civic judicial and commercial centres, were gone. As were the halls of some fifty livery companies, representing the interests of the different trades in the City. Quays and warehouses along the Thames, vital to London's commercial survival, were badly damaged. St Paul's Cathedral was a smoking ruin and eighty-seven parish churches were destroyed. The full extent of the devastation is shown in Wenceslaus Hollar's 'Exact Surveigh of the Ruins of the City of London', commissioned by the King immediately after the Fire and produced a few months later.

OVERLEAF Wenceslaus Hollar's 'Exact Surveigh of the Streets Lanes and Churches contained within the Ruines of the City of London', 1666–67.

The Prospect of this Citty, as it appeared from the opposite Southwarke side, in the fire time.

Hatton Garden

Long lane

Smith Field

Aldersgate

Newgate

162

Cripli...

Guild Hall

Alde Street

Libertie of S. Mar...

le Grand

Cheapside

Chepe

Pauls Churchyard

X

W

ZZ

Ludgate

Ludgate hill

W

Z

Fleet Street

Bridewell

The Ward robe

Doctors Commons

Y

Thames Street

Thames Street

a Scale of Feet,

THE   R I V E R

Published with the description of the Wards, by the care Industrie
and Charge of Nathanaell Brooke Stationer, and are to be Sould
at his shop at the Angel, in the second Yard of Gresham Colledge
leading from Bishopsgate street.

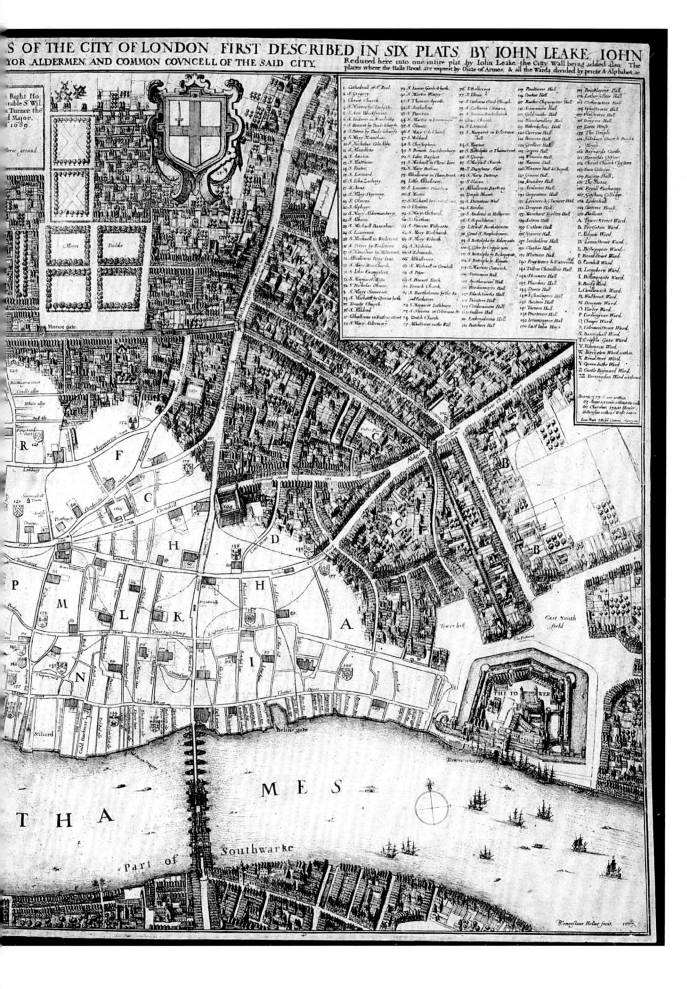

RISING FROM THE ASHES

Christopher Wren

Sir Godfrey Kneller's portrait of Sir Christopher Wren, painted in 1711 when Wren was seventy-nine. He is shown holding a pair of dividers, with his arm resting on the plan of St Paul's Cathedral.

WITHIN DAYS OF THE FIRE GOING OUT, the King was presented with several ambitious plans for rebuilding London. The first came from Christopher Wren, who beat his friend John Evelyn by a couple of days: 'Everybody brings in his idea, amongst the rest I presented his Majestie my owne conceptions . . . within dayes after the Conflagration: But Dr Wren had got the start of me.'

Wren, although not a courtier like Evelyn, was in a position to access the King because he came from a staunchly Royalist family. Both his father, also Christopher, and his uncle Matthew were high-ranking clergymen in the Church of England who had been loyal to King Charles I during the Civil War. At different times they both held the position of Dean of St George's Chapel, attached to the royal castle at Windsor. Matthew had been Charles I's personal chaplain before he became King. The two Wren brothers were followers of Archbishop Laud, whose brand of anti-Calvinist Anglicanism, enforced by the King, had driven the Puritans to rebellion and Civil War. Both Charles and Laud paid with their heads. Matthew, who had been promoted to Bishop of Ely, was accused of 'idolatry and superstition' and spent eighteen years in the Tower of London for refusing to accept the Puritan version of the Protestant liturgy. Christopher lost his position at Windsor in 1643, and some six years later had to go to live with his daughter Susan and son-in-law William Holder at their rectory at Bletchingdon near Oxford. He took with him his son Christopher, then a young teenager.

The sketchy information we have about Christopher's early education comes from *Parentalia, or, Memoirs of the family of the Wrens*[1] compiled after the great architect's death by his son, yet another Christopher. Designed to establish Wren's reputation, and in the process downplaying the contributions of others, such as Robert Hooke, *Parentalia* provides a mass of useful, if not always accurate, information. According to *Parentalia*, Wren was born in 1632 and 'by reason of a Tender health' was first educated at home by a 'Domestick Tutor'. At about the age of nine he was sent to Westminster School, where he would have learnt Latin and Greek. Later, when the family moved to Bletchingdon, Christopher was taught mathematics by his brother-in-law William: 'In the

[1] *Parentalia, or, Memoirs of the family of the Wrens . . . Now Published by Stephen Wren, 1750*

Principles of Mathematicks, upon the early Appearance of an uncommon Genius, he was initiated by Dr William Holder.' Holder 'was a great Virtuoso and a person of many accomplishments', including writing a treatise on music theory: *The Natural Grounds and Principles of Harmony*. He was also interested in the science of chronology and timekeeping, which involved astronomical observations of 'the Natural Day, Lunar Month and Solar Year'. The young Christopher was an exceptional student: 'At the Age of Thirteen this young Mathematician had invented a new Astronomical Instrument, of general Use' which he dedicated to his father, also a keen astronomer. He demonstrated a theoretical brilliance combined with great practical skill at making things: 'He contrived also a peculiar Instrument of Use in Gnomonicks', a new form of sundial designed to 'shew the equal Hours of the Day'.

This was a period of great importance in the development of science. The political revolution that, in questioning the authority of the King, had brought about the Civil War had its counterpart in the revolutionary theories of Galileo and Copernicus, who dared to suggest that the earth revolved around the sun, contrary to the orthodox view that the earth was the centre of the universe. Galileo died in 1642, when Wren would have been at Westminster. Astronomy, and the empirical observations being made possible by the new sciences of optics and lens-making, were crucial to this revolution. The 'Virtuoso', in the seventeenth-century sense of a man with a wide range of interests including the arts as well as the sciences, would naturally take a keen interest in astronomy and would prefer to base his views of the world on empirical experiments rather than superstition or received wisdom. So young Christopher was brought up in a world of clergymen who were also amateur 'natural philosophers' – or scientists, as we would say.

Parentalia goes on to tell us that in 1646, at the age of fourteen, Wren was admitted to Wadham College, Oxford, 'where he soon attracted the Friendship, & Esteem of the two most celebrated Virtuosi and Mathematicians of their Time'. These were 'Dr John Wilkins, Warden of Wadham and Dr Seth Ward, Savilian Professor of Astronomy'. He also made the acquaintance of 'the incomparable Anatomist, Physician and Mathematician' Dr Charles Scarburgh, whose assistant he became in 'anatomical Preparations and Experiments, especially upon the Muscles of human Bodies'. Despite his Royalist connections, Wren's abilities brought him early academic recognition during the rule of Cromwell and the Commonwealth. Having graduated in 1650, three years later he became a Fellow of All Souls at Oxford, where his career included a spell as Bursar. His scientific interests were very wide-ranging and included the perennial problem of finding longitude at sea, as well as astronomy, optics (for both telescopes and microscopes), meteorology, surveying, and anatomy. Following Harvey's discovery (published in 1628) of the circulation of blood, Wren undertook pioneering work on intravenous injections, including experiments on dogs, as he wrote to a friend, William Petty: 'I have injected Wine and ale in a living Dog into the Mass of Blood by a Veine, in good Quantities, till I have made him extremely drunk, but soon after he Pisseth it out.'

Parentalia gives a long list of over sixty 'Theories, Inventions, Experiments, & Mechanick Improvements exhibited by Mr. Wren' at his time in Oxford, which include

Weather-Clock,
Strainer of the Breath, to make the same Air serve in Respiration
Artificial Eye with the humours truly and dioptically made
To write in the Dark
To write double by an Instrument
To grind Glasses
New Ways of Sailing
Ways of submarine Navigation
Easier Ways of Whale-fishing
New Designs tending to Strength, Convenience & Beauty in Building
To Build in the Sea, Forts, Moles &c

In 1657 he was appointed Professor of Astronomy at Gresham College in London, and in 1660 he returned to Oxford as Savilian Professor of Astronomy. With the Restoration of the monarchy in the same year, Wren's fortunes continued to prosper. It was after one of his lectures at Gresham College that a group of like-minded 'natural philosophers' agreed to form a 'colledge for the Promoting of Physico-Mathematicall Experimentall Learning' which, with the granting of a Royal Charter in 1662, became the Royal Society, dedicated to advancing the cause of scientific enquiry and the experimental method. It took as its motto 'Nullius in Verba' – which can be roughly translated as 'Take nobody's word for it'. Besides Wren, the early members included his Oxford colleagues John Wilkins and Seth Ward, as well as the distinguished scientists Robert Boyle and Robert Hooke.

In spite of the emphasis on 'Experimentall Learning', Wren was not above superstition when it came to medical matters: in August 1677 Hooke's diary tells us that 'Sir Christopher told me . . . of curing his Lady of a thrush by hanging a bag of live boglice about her neck.'[2] Hooke doesn't say what boglice were, nor does he tell us how long the treatment lasted, nor what Lady Wren thought of this. In fact we know little about the personality of either of Wren's wives. His first wife was Faith Coghill: they married in 1669 and their two children were Gilbert,

[2] Robert Hooke, *Diary*, 16 August 1677

Sir Christopher Wren, Architect. Chiaroscuro woodcut by E. Kirkall after J. Closterman, 1695. In the background is the south portico of St Paul's Cathedral.

[3] John Aubrey, *Brief Lives*, Section 219: Sir John Denham

[4] Quoted in H.M. Colvin, *A Biographical Dictionary of British Architects 1600–1840*

[5] Colvin, ibid.

who died in infancy, and Christopher, the author of *Parentalia*. Faith died of smallpox in 1675. The Lady Wren in Hooke's anecdote was Jane Fitzwilliam, Wren's second wife. They married in February 1677, and had two children: a daughter, also Jane, and a son, William, referred to by Wren as 'poor Billy' because of his mental incapacity. Jane died of tuberculosis in 1680, leaving Wren a widower for the last forty-three years of his long life.

It's not clear when Wren first took an interest in architecture and building, but his skill in mathematics and geometry, combined with his model-making abilities, gave him a natural talent. His theoretical work in 'building in the Sea, Forts, Moles &c.' was probably known to the King when, in 1661, he offered Wren 'a Commission to Survey and direct the Works of the Mole, Harbour and Fortifications of the Citadel and Town of Tangier' (recently acquired through Charles's marriage to the Portuguese Catherine of Braganza). This offer carried with it a promise to make Wren the King's Surveyor General when the office became free. This post, once held by Inigo Jones, was the most important architectural job in the country, with a large staff, a generous salary and overall responsibility for the royal palaces.

The current Surveyor General was Sir John Denham, a courtier with little architectural experience. John Aubrey tells how he suffered 'a distemper of madnesse' after marrying his second wife, who was 'a very beautiful young lady; Sir John was ancient and limping. The duke of Yorke fell deeply in love with her though (I have been morally assured) he never had carnall knowledge of her.'[3] Denham's 'madnesse' took the form of being convinced he was the Holy Ghost, and announcing this to the King.

Whatever Wren's skill as a geometrician, there were more experienced candidates for the Surveyorship among the gentleman virtuosi at Charles's court. Hugh May, described by Pepys as 'a very ingenious man' was the Paymaster of the Works and even acted as Surveyor General during Denham's 'madnesse'. Roger Pratt was a pioneer of Renaissance architecture in England: his Clarendon House was described by Evelyn as 'the best contrived, the most usefull, gracefull and magnificent house in England'.[4] Both were a generation older than Wren, and both had avoided the Civil War by travelling in Europe.

May had joined the exiled court of Charles II in Holland, while Pratt had spent six years travelling in France, Italy and the Low Countries, 'to give myself some convenient education'.[5] Wren lacked their first-hand experience of the latest architectural developments on the continent.

Parentalia says that, despite the offer of the reversion of the Surveyor Generalship, Wren declined the Tangier job on the grounds of the work 'being not then consistent with his health'. Two years later he did accept a commission nearer home, from his uncle Matthew, now released from the Tower and restored to the bishopric of Ely. During his long imprisonment he had vowed, if ever released, to pay for 'some holy and pious employment'. This took the form of building a new chapel for his old Cambridge college, Pembroke Hall. Apart from St Paul's Church at Covent Garden by Inigo Jones, and the same architect's refacing of St Paul's Cathedral in the 1630s, Pembroke Chapel is the first completely classical church or chapel built in England.

Although the chapel lacks the originality and subtlety of his later City churches, Wren already

The Chapel at Pembroke College, Cambridge, Wren's first architectural commission.

shows a more than competent grasp of the classical vocabulary of architecture. The west front facing the street has giant Corinthian pilasters, enclosing a round-headed window and round-headed niches, supporting a pediment filled with garlands of flowers, topped off by a small lantern. These are all elements that would recur in Wren's City churches. The interior was originally a simple rectangular box, without aisles (the marble columns and separate chancel are later additions); it has high elegantly carved wainscotting and pews arranged in the collegiate fashion, facing each other across the nave, rather than facing the altar. Light floods in from round-headed windows, below a sumptuously ornate plaster ceiling.

In 1663 Wren's next commission, this time in Oxford, came from an even higher-ranking churchman. Gilbert Sheldon, Archbishop of Canterbury, wanted to provide the university with a secular venue for its graduation and degree ceremonies (which had apparently become too rowdy for their current setting, the University Church of St Mary the Virgin).

For the Sheldonian Theatre Wren produced a design consciously rooted in classical antiquity. He took as his model the Theatre of Marcellus in Rome,

a D-shaped building. The open roof of the Roman original was hardly suited to the Oxford climate, so Wren demonstrated his ingenuity by designing an intricate and sophisticated system of trusses to support the seventy-foot ceiling from above, providing unobstructed sightlines in the theatre below.

In July 1665, as the plague raged in London, Wren paid an eight-month visit to Paris, to meet fellow scientists and to study the latest architectural developments in the capital city of Louis XIV. *Parentalia* quotes a letter to a friend: 'I have busied myself in surveying the most esteem'd Fabricks of Paris, & the Country round.'

He was impressed by the great sculptor-architect Gian Lorenzo Bernini, currently working in Paris. Bernini was one of the most successful of the Italian Baroque architects employed by the papacy to embody the message of the Counter-Reformation in stone. The Italian Baroque reinvented the static classical vocabulary of Renaissance architecture by giving it movement and volume, using three-dimensional forms, light and shadow, bold projections and undulating curved surfaces to achieve dramatic effects. It reinforced the image of the papacy, and by extension that of a Catholic monarch like Louis XIV, as a legitimate absolutist authority. The message would not be acceptable in Protestant England, but the style would be attractive to the late Stuart monarchs and to their architect, Christopher Wren.

Bernini's great curving colonnades enclosing St Peter's Square in Rome were his architectural masterpiece, and his fame led Louis XIV to invite him to work at the Louvre palace. Wren became a regular visitor:

> The Louvre for a while was my daily Object, where no less than a thousand Hands are constantly employ'd in the Works; some in laying mighty Foundations, some in raising the Stories, Columns, Entablements, &c., with vast Stones, by great and useful Engines; others in Carving, Inlaying of Marbles, Plaistering, Painting, Gilding, &c. Which altogether make a School of Architecture, the best probably, at this Day in Europe.

He goes on to tell how he was introduced to the Italian master:

> Bernini's Design of the Louvre I would have given my Skin for, but the old reserv'd Italian gave me but a few Minutes view; it was five little Designs in Paper, for which he hath receiv'd as many thousand Pistoles; I had only Time to copy it in my Fancy and Memory.

The reference to the artist's fee suggests that Wren was becoming aware of the rewards a successful architect could expect.

Bernini's curving colonnades enclosing St Peter's Square in Rome.

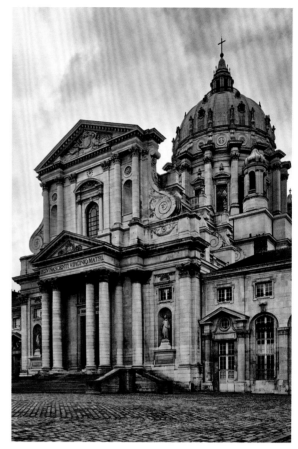

ABOVE LEFT Michelangelo's
dome of St Peter's in
Rome, designed in 1547.

ABOVE RIGHT The church
of the Val-de-Grâce in
Paris, built in the 1640s.
The facade was designed
by François Mansart, the
dome added by Jacques
Lemercier.

[6] William Dugdale, *History
of Saint Paul's Cathedral, in
London*, page 118

Although they are not mentioned in *Parentalia*, the revolutionary domed churches of Paris must also have had an effect on Wren. The builders of the great Gothic cathedrals had never attempted a dome. Ancient Rome had the Pantheon, Byzantium had Hagia Sophia, Florence had Brunelleschi's Duomo, and modern Rome had Michelangelo's St Peter's. An oval dome crowns Borromini's baroque jewel of San Carlo alle Quattro Fontane, also in Rome. Palladio, the revered authority on classical design, had built a dome over the central hall of his secular Villa Rotonda and two domed churches in Venice, the Redentore and San Giorgio Maggiore. Paris already had three recent domed churches by François Mansart and Jacques Lemercier: the Sorbonne, the Val-de-Grace and the Temple du Marais.

Within months of his return from Paris, Wren found himself in a position to propose building a dome of his own. In 1663 Charles II, concerned about the state of St Paul's Cathedral, had set up a Royal Commission to investigate 'repairing and upholding that magnificent structure . . . which hath so much suffered by the iniquity of the late times.'[6]

The church of the Sorbonne in Paris, designed by Jacques Lemercier and completed in 1635. The dome has only eight ribs dividing it into sections; St Peter's and the Val-de-Grâce have sixteen, whereas Wren used thirty-two ribs in the dome of St Paul's.

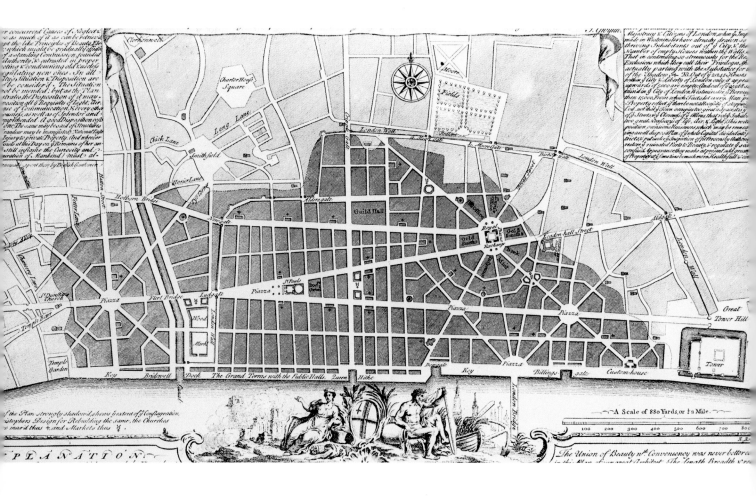

Wren's grand plan proposed replacing medieval London with a new geometric grid, with grand avenues converging on the piazza at St Paul's.

Wren's response was to propose rebuilding it 'with a noble cupola, a forme of church-building not as yet known in England'. So Wren already had plans to make St Paul's the first domed church in the country. Then, less than a week later, these discussions were overtaken by the Great Fire. And, in Evelyn's words, 'within dayes . . . Dr Wren had got the start of me'[7] and had presented the King with a grand and ambitious plan for rebuilding the whole City.

Just as he had wanted a radical modern solution to the problem of St Paul's, so his plan for the City swept away the old medieval street plan. He replaced this with a bold new geometric design of grand vistas and radiating avenues interconnecting at a series of piazzas. One was at the bridgehead of London Bridge, another in the west between the Temple and the river Fleet, itself to be turned into a navigable canal. The grandest piazza was to be built in the east, around the Royal Exchange and other vital commercial offices: the Bank, the Mint, the Excise Office, the Post Office and the Goldsmiths' Hall. From this a dead-straight avenue leads east to another piazza in front of a new St Paul's. Wren's plan clearly shows St Paul's with a dome, revealing his

[7] John Evelyn, *Diary*, 26 August 1666

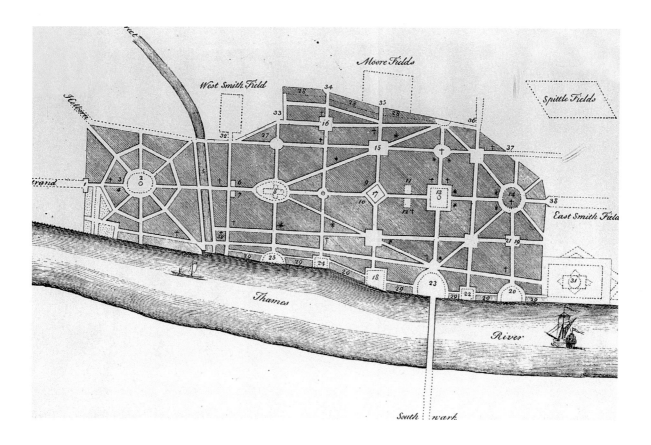

continuing determination to build a dome over the cathedral. Before the Fire there had been over ninety churches in the City of London. Wren proposed reducing this to a mere nineteen: how different the City of London would have looked if this had happened.

Wren may have been the first to come up with a new plan for London, but he wasn't alone. John Evelyn's own plan, submitted shortly afterwards, is similar enough to Wren's to suggest they had discussed it together before the Fire. They share the radiating avenues converging on piazzas, but Evelyn's plan has a more rigid grid and fewer streets.

Evelyn's grand plan for rebuilding London. Like Wren he proposed a new rational geometric plan with piazzas and avenues; but his plan is more rigid.

Robert Hooke

ANOTHER PLAN, now lost, was presented to the City authorities by Robert Hooke, and was well received by them. Apparently this was also based on a grid, and it allowed for only fifteen churches in the rebuilt City. Hooke's friend and biographer, Richard Waller, says:

> What this model was, I cannot so well determine, but I have heard that it was design'd in to it have all the chief Streets . . . lie in an exact strait Line, and all the other cross Streets turning out of them at right Angles, all the Churches, publick Buildings, Market-places, and the like in proper and convenient places, which no doubt, would have added much to the Beauty and Symmetry of the whole.[1]

The story of Robert Hooke begins on the Isle of Wight. He was born in Freshwater, in the west of the Island, in 1635. Like Wren, he was the son of a Royalist clergyman, but his background was humbler. Lacking Wren's family connections, Hooke had to make his own way in the world. After his death Waller recalled Hooke's uncompleted autobiography, which told how he had been 'very infirm and weakly and therefore Nurst at Home' and that 'his Parents had very little hopes of his life'. His father at first 'took some pains to instruct him'. But as the young boy was 'often subject to the Head-ach which hindered his learning', his father 'laid aside all Thoughts of breeding him a Scholar' and, as his own health declined, 'wholly neglected his farther Education. Being thus left to himself [he] spent his time in making little mechanical Toys' and on one occasion, using 'such Tools as he could procure, seeing an old Brass Clock taken to pieces he attempted to imitate it, and made a wooden one that would go.' We aren't told how old he was when he made his working wooden clock, but 'Much about the same time he made a small Ship about a Yard long, fitly shaping it, adding its Riggings of Ropes, Pullies, Masts &c. with a contrivance to make it fire off some small guns, as it was Sailing.' Added to these 'Indications of a Mechanick Genius' he showed artistic flair: 'He had also a great fancy for drawing, having much about the same Age Copied several Prints with a Pen, that Mr Hoskins (a court painter) . . . much admired one not instructed could so well imitate them.'

We're not told how it happened, but this artistic ability led Hooke to spend time in the studio of the great portrait painter of the day: 'I understand he was for some time with Sir Peter Lely, how long I am not certain: I suppose but a short time; for I have heard that the smell of the Oil Colours did not agree with his Constitution, increasing his Head-ach.'

[1] Robert Hooke & R. Waller, *The Posthumous Works of Robert Hooke*, page xiii

He left Lely's studio to attend Westminster School, living in the house of Dr Busby (Wren's headmaster), where 'he fell seriously upon the study of the Mathematicks, the Dr. encouraging him therein' and afterwards to 'Mechanicks, his first and last Mistress'. Both subjects were outside the normal curriculum for gentleman scholars at the time, and his encouragement of Hooke's special talents shows Busby's open-minded approach to education. (Busby was also a fierce disciplinarian who flogged his pupils at the least provocation: he once claimed that sixteen schoolboys he had caned with his 'little rod' went on to become bishops in the Church of England.)

In 1653 Hooke went from Westminster to Oxford University, attending Christ Church College. But, as his 'Circumstances . . . were but mean', he had to act as 'Servitor to one Mr Goodman', and didn't take his degree until 'several Years later, about 1662 or 1663'. So it took him about ten years to get his degree, while Wren got his in four.

While at Oxford, 'about the year 1655, he began to shew himself to the World . . . for there being a Concourse at that time of extraordinary Persons at Oxford . . . he was soon taken notice of, and for his Facility in Mechanick Inventions much priz'd by them.' These 'extraordinary Persons' included John Wilkins (Wren's mentor at Wadham) and Robert Boyle, whose famous 'Boyle's Law' (that at a constant temperature the volume of a body of gas varies inversely to the pressure exerted on it) was formulated as the result of his experiments on the properties of air and air pressure. Some of these were carried out with a pump for creating a vacuum, which Hooke developed for him: 'in 1658 or 9 I contriv'd and perfected the Air-pump for Mr Boyle.' Pepys tells how, a few years later, Charles II was unimpressed with these experiments: 'Gresham College he mightily laughed at for spending time only in the weighing of ayre.'[2]

For the next few years Hooke became Boyle's paid assistant, living in his rooms and working with him in his laboratory in Oxford High Street. He also collaborated with Seth Ward on his work with telescopes, and with Wren on barometers and microscopes. In 1662 Hooke had joined the Royal Society, as its paid Curator of Experiments, and in 1665 he became Professor of Geometry at Gresham College. He lived in rooms at the College for the rest of his life. Gresham was between Bishopsgate and Old Broad Street, on the site of what is now Tower 42 (formerly the NatWest Tower).

In 1661 Wren was using microscopes to study the anatomy of fleas and other insects, but he was too busy to spend time on the project, so Hooke took over the work: 'I came to it with much Reluctancy because I was to follow the footsteps of so eminent a Person as Dr. Wren . . . there scarce ever met in one man, in so great a perfection, such a Mechanical Hand, and so Philosophical a Mind.'[3]

[2] Pepys, *Diary*, 1 February 1664
[3] Robert Hooke, *Micrographia*

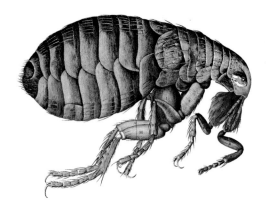

ABOVE Hooke's
engraving of a flea, from
Micrographia.

OPPOSITE Hooke's drawing
of 'snake-stones'
(fossilized ammonites),
published as an engraving
in Hooke's *Posthumous
Works* (1705). His
study of fossils led him
to speculate on the
extinction of species.

The result was the published work for which Hooke is still revered. In his book *Micrographia: or Some Physiological Descriptions of Miniature Bodies Made by Magnifying Glasses*, published in 1665, he combined his artistic skill, his mechanical genius and his scientific knowledge in an extraordinary volume describing the results of his microscopic observations. Pepys hailed *Micrographia* as 'the most ingenious book that I ever read in my life'. Hooke's drawing of the anatomy of a flea ('adorn'd with a curiously polish'd suite of sable Armour, neatly jointed') is a stunning piece of work, taking two full pages of the book, a folio volume 12 inches in height. (Little did Hooke know that this small insect, carried by rats, was responsible for the spread of bubonic plague devastating London at the moment of publication.) The list of Hooke's other achievements and inventions is as impressive as it is varied. He defined elasticity with his 'Law of Springs' (that the extension of a spring is proportional to the force applied), the theoretical basis for spring balances and weighing machines. He was the first to use the word 'cell' to describe the microscopic structures he saw in a cross-section of cork: 'these pores, or cells, were not very deep, but consisted of a great many little boxes'; he developed the universal joint still used in the driveshaft and steering assembly of the motor car, he suggested the use of the balance spring in watches, and invented the iris diaphragm still used in camera lenses. He used his improved barometer for weather forecasting, and was the first astronomer to discover the Great Red Spot on Jupiter, proving the rotation of the planet. He even anticipated Darwin and the theory of evolution by speculating that the presence of marine fossils in cliffs high above sea level was the result of species becoming extinct: 'There have been in former times of the World, divers Species of Creatures that are now quite lost . . . there may have been, by mixture of creatures, produced a sort of differing in Shape . . . from the true Created Shapes of both of them.'[4]

This was a radical suggestion, at a time when most people believed the biblical account in the Book of Genesis, according to which the world was only a few thousand years old and the species of animals and plants were unchanged since Creation.

Hooke was very jealous of his achievements, and this led him into a series of quarrels and disputes with other leading scientists, including Flamsteed, Huygens, Leibniz, Hevelius and, most notoriously, Isaac Newton. He accused Newton of plagiarizing his work on the composition of white light and the effects of gravity on planetary motion. Newton's famous letter to Hooke, ending with the apparently conciliatory phrase 'If I have seen further it is by

[4] Robert Hooke, 'Discourse
on Earthquakes', published
in *The Posthumous Works
of Robert Hooke* by Robert
Hooke & R. Waller, page 291

RISING FROM THE ASHES

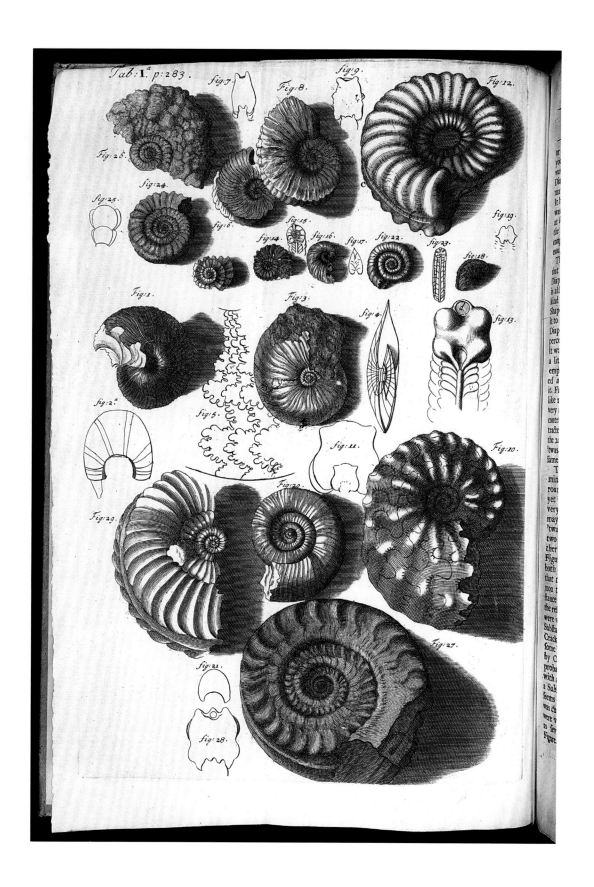

standing on the shoulders of Giants'[5] can be seen as a back-handed compliment – Hooke, suffering from curvature of the spine, was hardly a giant. Hooke's unprepossessing physical appearance was described by Waller:

> He was always very pale and lean, and laterly nothing but skin and Bone with a meagre Aspect, his Eyes grey and full, with a sharp ingenious Look . . . his Mouth meanly wide, and upper Lip thin; His Chin sharp . . . He wore his own Hair of a dark brown colour, very long and hanging neglected over his Face uncut and lank.'[6]

His friend John Aubrey was a little more flattering: 'of middling stature, something crooked, pale faced . . . He has a delicate head of Haire, browne and of an excellent moiste curle.[7]

No known image of Hooke survives, but his diary, which he kept intermittently, reveals him to be sociable and gregarious. He was also a committed hypochondriac: 'I took spirit of urine and laudanum with milk for three preceding night. Slept pretty well'.[8]

Other entries show that, although a bachelor (as required by his Professorship at Gresham), he was not celibate: 'Nell lay with me. ♓. Slept ill.'[9] Nell was his servant, who left him to get married.

Although his friend John Aubrey often visited him in his rooms at Gresham, most of Hooke's busy social life was conducted in the newly fashionable coffee houses, like Garaways and Jonathan's. There are frequent accounts of his meeting friends at these. On 27 August 1675 he was with 'Sir Chr Wren at Garaways'; 29 May 1674 was unusual enough for him to remark that he stayed away: 'It rained hard and I was not at Garaways.' But he's back on 2 November: 'To Garaways – Stayd all the morn for Sir Ch. Wren.' On 28 October 1677 he's mixing business with pleasure at the newly popular Jonathan's: 'Payd Jonathan 2½s. for chocolat kake . . . Ordered Crawley to fit tube for new micrometer.'

[5] 'Pigmaei gigantum humeris impositi plusquam ipsi gigantes vident'
[6] Hooke and Waller, *The Posthumous Works of Robert Hooke*, page xxvii
[7] Aubrey, *Brief Lives*, Section 411: Robert Hooke
[8] Hooke, *Diary*, 1 October 1672
[9] Hooke, *Diary*, 26 January 1673. Hooke uses the Pisces symbol ♓ as code for orgasm.

The Royal Declaration and the Rebuilding Acts

WITHIN DAYS OF THE FIRE, on 13 September, the King issued a 'Declaration to his City of London', which directed that 'the Lord Mayor and Court of Aldermen do . . . cause an exact Survey to be made and taken of the whole ruins occasioned by the late lamentable Fire.'[1]

The Declaration also provided for the appointment of Commissioners or Surveyors to undertake the survey and supervise the rebuilding. The King appointed the three men who had earlier advised on repairing St Paul's: Hugh May, Roger Pratt and Christopher Wren. The City authorities appointed Edward Jerman, Peter Mills and Robert Hooke. Jerman, or Jarman, was 'an experienced man in buildings', according to Pratt,[2] and Mills had been Bricklayer to the City of London.

Hooke, on the other hand, had no background in building or architecture. But his practical abilities, his skills as a mathematician and draughtsman, and his close friendship with Christopher Wren, must all have recommended him to the City authorities. So Wren and Hooke found themselves as joint Rebuilding Commissioners.[3]

The Rebuilding Act of February 1667, which followed the Royal Declaration, set the scene for London's resurrection from the ashes. It starts by declaring that it means business: for failing to comply with the 'Rules and Orders of Building' or failing to use 'materialls as are herein after perticularly appointed' the 'Offender shall be committed to the common Goale'. Parliament authorized 'The Lord Maior Aldermen and Common Council of the Said citty' to have the 'Breadth Length and Extent' of the 'Streets and Lanes [intended to be rebuilt] . . . to be marked or staked out'. Anyone caught moving the stakes faced a fine of £5, or if he was too poor to pay he was to be 'openly whipped . . . till his body be bloudy'.

The Act provided that there were to be 'onely fower sortes of Buildings and noe more', depending on whether they faced a 'By lane', a street or a 'high and pincipall Streete', or were the 'largest sort of Mansion house'. The numbers of storeys and the different heights of the rooms were all specified: 'The Houses of the second sort of building . . . shall consist of Three Stories high beside Cellars and Garrets . . . that the first Story containe full tenn foote in height from the Floore to the Sieling . . .'

The Act also dictated 'That all the outside of all Buildings . . . be henceforth made of Bricke or Stone' to avoid the danger of timber buildings catching fire. To enable the rebuilding to start quickly, the closed shop which restricted the building trades to Freemen of the City was suspended: 'all Carpenters Brickelayers Masons Plaisterers Joyners and other Artificers Workemen and

[1] Printed by John Bill and Christopher Barker Printers to the King's most Excellent Majesty, 1666
[2] H.M. Colvin, *A Biographical Dictionary of British Architects 1600–1840*
[3] The Royal Declaration also stated that 'any houses to be inhabited by Brewers, or Dyers or Sugar-Bakers which Trades by their continual Smokes contribute very much to the unhealthiness of the adjacent places' should be rebuilt away from the river, a clear echo of John Evelyn's complaints in his *Fumifugium*.

Labourers . . . who are not Freemen of the said Citty' were to 'have and enjoy such and the same liberty of workeing' as Freemen. The Act deals with the need for street widening: it lists the 'auntient Sreets and Passages . . . narrow and incommodious for Carriages and Passengers' which should be 'inlarged'.

The number of 'Parish Churches to be rebuilded . . . in lieu of those which were demolished by the late Fire' was limited to thirty-nine, and the proceeds of disposing of the others were to be used exclusively for rebuilding the Parish churches 'and for noe other use or purpose whatsoever'.

Clause XXXIV is in many ways the most important of all – it established a 'Custom upon Coals' to enable the City authorities 'to performe and accomplish the workes in this Act'. The Coal Tax, as it came to be known, was levied on all coal passing through the Port of London at the rate of twelve pence per 'chaldron or tun'. The proceeds were to pay compensation for 'such persons whose Grounds shall . . . be taken and imployed for the inlarging of the Streets and narrow passages', as well as compensation for those losing land to new riverside wharves and quays along the Thames and the Fleet River, and for building 'Prisons . . . for the safe Custody and Imprisonment of Felons and other Malefactors'.

A separate Act set up special courts, known as Fire Courts. These were to decide on compensation for land taken in street-widening schemes, and arbitrate in disputes about land ownership. They also ensured that the cost of rebuilding was shared between landlord and tenant: under the existing law the whole burden would normally have been borne by the tenant.

The visionary schemes for rebuilding the city on a new grid with elegant piazzas, as put forward by Wren, Evelyn and Hooke, had all been quietly dropped. The only element of Wren's plan to survive was the intention to build new quays along the Thames and the Fleet. *Parentalia* says: 'the only, &, as it happened, insurmountable Difficulty . . . was the obstinate Averseness of great Part of the Citizens to alter their old Properties, and to recede from building their houses again on their old Ground & Foundations.'

The reality was that there was no time to embark on such a radical reshaping of the City. If London wasn't rebuilt quickly, it was in danger of losing its position as a centre of commercial activity. On 27 and 28 September, less than three weeks after the Fire, Parliament debated the problem, and, as one MP wrote in his diary: 'It was the general opinion of the whole House that if some speedy way of rebuilding the City was not agreed upon that the City would be in danger never to be built', with the result that 'the merchants and wealthiest of the citizens would . . . remove themselves and estates into other countries and so the City would remain miserable for ever.[4]

There were also money worries, which were not helped by the war with the Dutch. In October 1666, within weeks of the Fire, Henry Oldenburgh wrote to

[4] *The Diary of John Milward, Esq.*, pages 8–9

Robert Boyle saying 'The great stresse will be how to raise money for carrying on the warre, and to rebuild ye Citty, at the same time.'[5]

The 1667 Act was followed by the Rebuilding Act of 1670, which trebled the Coal Tax and extended it for a further seventeen years, 'as it doth and will require farr greater summes of money' to accomplish the aims of the earlier Act. For the next seven years three-quarters of the money raised by the Coal Tax was to be used 'for the rebuilding of the respective Parish Churches by this Act appoynted to be rebuilt', and a quarter of that on rebuilding the cathedral.

The 1670 Act goes on to lay down how the original eighty-seven churches destroyed in the Fire are to be reduced to fifty-one. It explains that the figure of thirty-nine envisaged in the 1667 Act was impractical: 'It doth appeare that the Parishes . . . cannot conveniently by Union or otherwise be reduced to a lesse number then Fifty one.'

The Act then lists the parishes to be united, and those whose churches are to be rebuilt.

Surveying the City

THE ROYAL DECLARATION OF 1666 had instructed the City authorities to 'cause an exact survey to be made and taken of the whole ruins'. Surveying the ruins to determine the boundaries of each individual plot, and establish exactly who owned what, was a major undertaking and essential to the task of rebuilding the City. The King's Commissioners (Wren, May and Pratt) were less involved with this than the City Surveyors (Hooke, Jerman and Mills). Jerman – a reluctant nominee – died in 1668, to be replaced by John Oliver, whose name occurs frequently in connection with rebuilding the City churches and who was to become Wren's Assistant Surveyor at St Paul's. Mills was also ill and took little part, so at the beginning the task fell mostly to Hooke, already busy fulfilling the demands of the Royal Society. These included experiments on blood transfusion in dogs, as well as how best to make the bricks needed for rebuilding the City.

Before any surveys could be made, the land had to be cleared not only of rubble but also of any temporary buildings illegally put up by landowners. An important task facing the Surveyors was to stake out the streets, particularly those – such as Fleet Street and Thames Street – which were to be widened. When that had been done Hooke and his fellow Surveyors could start on staking out the individual building plots. One function of the Surveyors was to calculate compensation for those who lost land to street-widening schemes. Within four years they had measured and staked out almost two-thirds of the 13,200 properties destroyed in the Fire. Once a property had been surveyed it could

[5] Tinniswood, *By Permission of Heaven, the Story of the Great Fire of London,* quoting Hall and Hall (editors), *Correspondence of Henry Oldenburgh,* III, page 238

be returned to its original owner so that rebuilding could start. The Surveyors recorded their measurements in survey books, which would be referred to in case of later disputes. Hooke's survey books have been lost, which makes it difficult to know exactly how much of the work was done by him personally, but other evidence suggests that he was responsible for about 3,000 of the 8,394 surveys carried out. He was the only City Surveyor to work from 1667 to 1696, the year of the last recorded survey. Hooke's contribution has led to him being described as 'The man who measured London',[6] and one of 'The men who made modern London'.[7] Measuring London was a profitable business for the Surveyors, who received about ten shillings for each survey. Hooke's share for his 3,000 surveys would have been about £1,500, a substantial amount of money at the time.

Rebuilding the City Churches

As we have seen, the Rebuilding Act of 1667 originally provided for thirty-nine of the eighty-seven destroyed churches to be rebuilt, with forty-eight parishes disappearing. Protests from the threatened parishes led to this being changed in the 1670 Act, which listed fifty-one churches to be rebuilt and specified which parishes were to be combined, effectively sharing a rebuilt church.

The parishes were not only ecclesiastical bodies, they were also the local arm of civil government. They were responsible for parochial law and order, as well as cleaning and maintenance of the streets, which were all paid for by rates levied on their inhabitants. They also dealt with relief of the poor, including the important task of discouraging vagrants. The Churchwardens' Accounts[8] of the different parishes give us an insight into how cruelly this could work in practice. In 1679 St Swithun paid one shilling 'for clearing the Parish of a woman bigg with childe' and in 1702 two shillings for 'coach hire to carry a poor woman to prevent her dying in the parish'. In 1601 St Mary Woolchurch Haw made a payment of five shillings and four pence 'to Andrews for whipping the vagrants for one whole year'. The church building also served as the parish register office, legally the only place where parishioners could get married, and births and deaths could be registered. Foundlings were another charge on the parish, as the accounts for St Stephen Walbrook show: in 1640 there's a payment of three shillings and sixpence to the godparents 'at the Christening of Stephen Oylbut found in the Barge Yard upon an Oyl Butt'.

To oversee the rebuilding of the churches the 1670 Act appointed three Commissioners: the Lord Mayor, the Bishop of London and the Archbishop of Canterbury. (The Archbishop, Wren's former patron Gilbert Sheldon, was included because thirteen parishes, known as 'peculiars', were in his patronage.)

[6] Lisa Jardine, *The Curious Life of Robert Hooke: The Man who Measured London*
[7] Leo Hollis, *The Phoenix: The Men who Made Modern London*
[8] Gerald Cobb & Nicholas Redman, *London City Churches*, page 26

As a temporary measure a number of parishes built wooden chapels, known as 'tabernacles' after the portable places of worship used by the Jews during their forty years wandering in the Wilderness of Sinai. In 1670 the Commissioners agreed that Coal Tax money should be provided for ten parishes to build tabernacles on the sites of their burnt churches. They were to be made cheaply and 'of the least workmanship', and the majority were of timber on a brick base, with tiled roofs. A total of about thirty of these tabernacles were built, ranging in cost from £50 at St Pancras Soper Lane to £260 at St Mary Abchurch.

One of the first acts of the Commissioners was to appoint Wren to be in overall charge of the church rebuilding programme: '[We] . . . do hereby nominate constitute and appoint Dr Christopher Wren . . . to direct and order the dimensions, formes and Modells of the said Churches.' He was also given the task of organizing the contractors: 'to contract with . . . Artizans, builders and workmen as shall be employed', and finally he was authorized to handle the finances for the whole operation: 'to receive from the Chamber of London such . . . summes of Mony as we . . . shall appoint for the constant and speedy payment . . .'

Wren was well suited to the enormous task of being in charge of the church building programme. In addition to his architectural abilities, he also had great skill as a diplomat, and as a financier. His time as Bursar at All Souls probably stood him in good stead here. He was now responsible for handling very large sums of money and distributing them to the contractors. Copies of the accounts he provided for scrutiny by the public auditor survive, and are a useful source of information on how the churches were built.

Finance was crucial in another way: churches could only be rebuilt as money became available from the Coal Tax, so Wren and the Commissioners had to decide which parishes would get their churches rebuilt first. They devised a scheme to encourage local fundraising: the parish officers had to pay a deposit or loan of £500 to the City Corporation before work could start on their church, priority going to the parishes in the order in which they paid the deposit. The Corporation would in return provide funding of an additional £1500 from the Coal Tax. A list was drawn up of fifteen churches to be built in the first phase, including some of the best surviving examples: St Magnus the Martyr, St Mary-le-Bow and St Vedast-alias-Foster. A few parishes, including St Mary Aldermary, St Michael on Cornhill and St Dunstan-in-the-East did not wait for the Commission, but started rebuilding on their own account, using local funds or benefactions. The parishes had to make other contributions to the rebuilding cost: in particular the Coal Tax did not cover the internal furnishings, such as pews, pulpits and altarpieces.

Even Wren could not handle all this on his own, so in June 1670 the Commissioners appointed two deputies to assist him: 'Dr Christopher Wren,

Surveyor General of his Majesty's Works, Mr Robert Hooke and Mr Edward Woodroffe are hereby required to repair forthwith the aforesaid churches (the fifteen chosen for early rebuilding) and . . . prepare fit models and draughts to be presented for his Majesty's approbation.'

Edward Woodroffe had been Surveyor to Westminster Abbey since 1662, and later was Assistant Surveyor to St Paul's, where he received payments for assisting Wren with drawings and measuring masons' work. Other than that, not a lot is known about him. He had wide experience of the building trades, something which at this stage both Wren and Hooke lacked, so he may well have made a valuable contribution on the practical side of the rebuilding. The Commissioners' accounts from 1670 to 1675 (when Woodroffe died) show the payments made to the three men; Wren received almost £1,600, with Hooke and Woodroffe receiving about £800 each. This in itself suggests the scale and importance of Woodroffe's contribution. At his death he was replaced by John Oliver, who had previously replaced Jerman as one of the Surveyors appointed to survey the ruins after the Fire. Oliver also took over Woodroffe's position as Assistant Surveyor to St Paul's.

The churches rebuilt after the Fire are often referred to as 'Wren churches', as if Wren himself had designed them all. This impression is reinforced by the claim made by his son in *Parentalia*: 'Fifty-one parochial Churches of the City of London, erected according to the Designs and under the Care and Conduct, of Sir Christopher Wren, in lieu of those which were burnt and demolish'd by the great Fire.'

However, the only church Wren himself specifically claims to have designed is St James's Piccadilly, in Westminster, away from the City. During the years of church rebuilding Wren had many other duties. As Surveyor General to the King's Works, a post he retained until 1718, he was involved in several large royal projects, including Chelsea Hospital, Greenwich Hospital and Hampton Court. And from 1675 to 1710 he was also in charge of rebuilding St Paul's Cathedral. He was even briefly a Member of Parliament. All these activities suggest that the fifty-one City churches rebuilt after the Fire could not possibly all have been designed in detail by Wren himself. His office certainly approved the designs, but the undertaking was a collaboration between Wren and his assistants rather than a single-handed operation.

Like Wren, Robert Hooke makes no claim to have been the architect of any particular church, but he played a crucial part in the whole process. His diary entries for the years 1672–80 include many references to visiting various churches, particularly those in the north-eastern corner of the City, near his home at Gresham in Bishopsgate. On 21 August 1677 he 'Slept till 8. To Pauls. Met Sir Ch Wren . . . Viewd St Anns and Agnes, St Lawrence, All Hallows.'

Clear documentary proof is lacking, but Hooke is thought by many historians to have been the principal architect of several of the rebuilt churches, including St Benet Paul's Wharf, St Martin-within-Ludgate and St Edmund King and Martyr. Hooke and Wren enjoyed a long collaboration, free of the quarrels and recriminations which bedevilled Hooke's relations with many other colleagues. The accounts show that Hooke was paid a total of more than £2,800 by Wren 'on the city churches account'. These payments lasted from 1671 until 1696, and between 1666 and 1677 amounted to more than he received for his work as City Surveyor, suggesting the importance of his contribution to the whole rebuilding programme.

This was also the period when Hooke's own reputation as an architect was growing, and he built up a thriving architectural practice. In 1672 he started work on a new building for the Royal College of Physicians in London, whose theatre with its domed entrance porch was much admired. In 1675 he designed the new Bethlem Hospital for the insane. Bedlam, as it came to be known, was, according to John Evelyn, 'magnificently built, and most sweetly placed in Moorfields'. Between 1675 and 1679 he designed and built Montagu House, on the site now occupied by the British Museum.

Hooke's reputation as an architect has not been helped by the fact that all three of these major London projects have disappeared. Later generations may have forgotten Hooke's work, but there can be no doubt that he was one of the leading architects of his time, and well placed to help Wren with much of the work on the churches. Paul Jeffery, in his authoritative book *The City Churches of Sir Christopher Wren*, points out that:

> Wren's definite contribution to parish church design, as indicated by the documentary evidence (parish records, payments to him, patronage and so on) amounted to no more than about half a dozen churches . . . Evidence of some kind . . . exists to suggest that a few more may be by Wren. The rest may be by Hooke, but there also remains the possibility, or even probability, that some of these designs are the result of a collaboration between the two men.[9]

[9] Paul Jeffery, *The City Churches of Sir Christopher Wren*, page 93

The Monument to the Fire of London

The gilded urn at the top of the Monument, with strands of twisted copper representing flames.

THE CONSTRUCTION OF THE MONUMENT involved both Wren and Hooke; however the designs were mostly provided by Hooke, whose diary records frequent visits to the 'Fish Street Piller'.[1] The tallest free-standing stone column in the world, the Monument is central to the story of rebuilding London after the Fire. The 1670 Rebuilding Act provided 'That a Columne or Pillar of Brase or Stone be erected on as neere unto the place where the said Fire soe unhappily began'. The 202-foot tall fluted Doric column still stands close to Pudding Lane and, like the churches and St Paul's, was funded by the Coal Tax.

It was built with a cantilevered staircase around an empty core and the great hollow pillar was finished by 1675. Wren and Hooke hoped to use the central core as a telescope and for experiments on gravity, and they provided a large hinged opening at the top allowing for an unobstructed view of the heavens from the bottom of the staircase. Unfortunately, vibrations from local traffic made the Monument unsuitable as a scientific instrument.

There was much discussion as to what should be on the top of the Monument. Wren initially suggested a brass statue of a phoenix, an idea he subsequently rejected because 'the spread winges will carry in the winde'. He then proposed a statue of the King, or of a female figure brandishing a sword to represent London. The King opted for a 'large ball of metall guilt', and the City compromised on Hooke's design of a flaming urn, 'if the King liked it'. Hooke commissioned Robert Bird, a master brazier, to make the urn. His diary entry for 20 November says he was 'much disturbed in health and spirit' after he discovered that Bird had 'bungled' the urn, but by the following April the urn was ready to be installed: 'Piller at Fish Street Hill. At the top of it . . . directed about setting the Urne'. The gilded urn has very detailed work: around the lower section garlands hang from the mouths of horned beasts; higher up smaller and simpler garlands hang from more horned beasts. The top of the urn is covered in strands of twisted copper representing the flames that destroyed the City. My view, taken through a high-powered telescope, shows that there is also a modern weather station at the very top. So, more than three centuries after Wren and Hooke abandoned their scientific experiments here, the Monument is now being used for meteorological observations.

The square pedestal at the base of the Monument has Latin inscriptions on three sides. One gives the history the building of the Monument, saying it was started in 1671 and completed in 1677. Another tells of the destruction caused by the Fire. The phrase 'Popish frenzy, which wrought such horrors, is not yet quenched' was added in 1681 and left there until 1830.

[1] The Monument is usually seen as an example of the collaboration between Wren and Hooke. However, recent scholarship has concluded that Wren's involvement in the design of the Monument has been exaggerated. As the City, rather than the Crown, was responsible for the Monument, the designs were provided by the City's Surveyor, Robert Hooke. Wren's job, as the King's Surveyor-General, was to obtain the King's approval for Hooke's designs, rather than to provide the designs himself. In the words of Dr Walker, 'their roles in the designing of the column have been misunderstood . . . the final design can now be attributed to Hooke alone.' Dr Matthew F. Walker, *The Limits of Collaboration: Robert Hooke, Christopher Wren and the designing of the Monument to the Great Fire of London*, published in *Notes & Records of the Royal Society*, February 2011.

RIGHT At 202 feet, the Monument is the tallest free-standing stone column in the world.

OPPOSITE The cantilevered spiral staircase in the Monument creates an empty central core, but Wren's plans to use this as a giant zenith telescope had to be abandoned because of vibrations from traffic.

RISING FROM THE ASHES

The west side has a relief panel carved by Caius Gabriel Cibber, showing the destruction of the City in the Fire. On the left a woman, representing the City, feebly holds a sword (the City's emblem) as she sits forlornly among the ruins, with smoke and flames billowing from the buildings above, and the City's griffin looking up anxiously from below. She is supported by the winged figure of Time and by Industry, a bare-breasted female pointing a sceptre up to the clouds, on which sit two more female figures: Plenty (with a cornucopia) and Praise (with a branch of laurel leaves), holding out hope for a better future. A wicker beehive, symbolic of the busy bee, is at Industry's feet.

On the right-hand side King Charles, in a full wig and wearing a cape, stands at the top of a flight of steps, directing three women to go down the steps to the aid of the City. They represent Liberty (waving her hat in the air), Architecture (clutching compasses and plans), and Science (holding a small statue of the many-breasted Diana, or Artemis, of Ephesus representing Nature – and, by extension, natural Science). To the right of Charles stands his brother James, clutching a garland intended for the City. Behind him are two more allegorical figures: Justice, with a coronet, and Fortitude, waving a sword aloft as she controls the figure of the lion with a bridle in its mouth. Below this group the ugly figure of Envy eats her own heart as she tries to crawl out of an arched opening. On the top right-hand side London is being rebuilt, as masons work on a building covered in scaffolding poles tied together with cords.

When built, the Monument had an open balcony. As early as April 1676 it was used to commit suicide, as Hooke's diary reveals: 'A Pick pocket broke his neck from Fish Street Hill piller'. A spate of suicides led to the balcony being enclosed in a cage in 1842.

Caius Gabriel Cibber's carving on the west face of the Monument: on the left billowing flames consume the City of London; on the right masons rebuild the City using scaffolding poles lashed together.

Designing the Churches

FOR MOST PARISHES the urgent task was to get the main body of the church completed as fast as money from the Coal Tax would allow. As a result, many of the churches were originally built with a nave and perhaps a tower, but without a spire or steeple. The towers were boarded over to wait for Coal Tax money to be spared for steeple building – which means that in most cases the steeples are several years, or even decades, later than the churches they adorn.

These steeples, all crowded together within the square mile of the City, provided London with a famous skyline. In 1759 the Italian traveller Count Algarotti wrote that 'Londra è il paese de' bei campanili' ('London is the land of beautiful bell towers') and could think of only one Italian steeple in Mantua to compare with them. Engravings of London before the Fire show a skyline bristling with Gothic towers and steeples, dominated by the tower of old Saint Paul's. After the Fire the great contribution of Wren and his colleagues was to recreate this skyline using the forms of classical architecture, based on models from ancient Greece and Rome and the Italian Renaissance. But while a Roman

OPPOSITE Claes Visscher's view of pre-Fire London, 1616, with Old London Bridge, the spires of the City and St Paul's Cathedral.

BELOW *A Prospect of the City of London*, by Johannes Kip, engraved in 1724. The skyline bristles with the steeples of the rebuilt churches, dominated by the dome of St Paul's.

ABOVE LEFT The tower of Borromini's Sant' Ivo della Sapienza in Rome, with a crazy helter-skelter spire, built 1642–50.

ABOVE RIGHT Wren's tower of Christ Church Newgate Street, completed in 1704.

basilica could provide the model for the body of a church, there was no classical precedent for a bell-tower, especially one incorporated within the church itself, as was traditional in English churches. In Renaissance Italy the campanile tended to be a separate structure, as at Palladio's San Giorgio Maggiore in Venice.

One of the few examples of a church steeple in Roman Baroque architecture was Borromini's Sant' Ivo della Sapienza. Although the crazy helter-skelter spire of the top section was too bizarre to be much use as a model, the lower section, with pairs of columns breaking forward from the main body of the steeple, can be seen as the basis for a number of the London steeples.

The new classical churches Wren saw in Paris (the Sorbonne, Val-de-Grâce, Temple du Marais) didn't have steeples or bell-towers. There were more helpful examples in the Low Countries, including the recent Nieuwe Kerk in Haarlem and the Jesuit Church[1] in Antwerp, with a steeple attributed to Rubens, which showed how a Gothic form could be reinterpreted using the language of classical architecture. The spires and steeples of the London churches are very varied, ranging from plain towers topped by a balustrade (St Clement Eastcheap, St Andrew-by-the-Wardrobe), to square towers with obelisks or pinnacles at the corners (St Andrew Holborn, St Mary Somerset). St Benet Paul's Wharf has a lead lantern above a shallow dome, and St Peter Cornhill has a small spire above its dome. A handful (St Edmund the King, St Nicholas Cole Abbey), have trumpet-shaped spires. In a few cases, Wren produced Gothic designs (St Dunstan-in-the-East, St Mary Aldermary, St Alban Wood Street). The grandest steeples were multi-stage designs, as at St Bride's Fleet Street, with its diminishing octagonal stages, or Christ Church Newgate Street with its composition of three square stages ending in an elegant finial. St Magnus the Martyr, another multi-stage design, has a steeple clearly based on the Jesuit Church in Antwerp. The grandest of all is St Mary-le-Bow, a complex design rising from a square tower into a circular colonnade of free-standing Corinthian columns, all topped by a glorious dragon for its weathervane. There is another splendid weathervane in the shape of a fully rigged galleon at St Nicholas Cole Abbey (originally at St Mildred Poultry).

Hawksmoor, who replaced Hooke in the early 1690s, is thought to have had a hand in the designs for some of the best of the late steeples: St Vedast-alias-Foster, St James Garlickhythe and St Michael Paternoster Royal. The dramatic use of three-dimensional contrast between light and shade, projection and recession are features which drew on the lower stage of Borromini's Sant' Ivo, and would be prominent in Hawksmoor's own churches built in the early years of the eighteenth century.

Most of the City churches have a weathervane; the most common type is the simple arrow and pennant design as at St Magnus the Martyr.

[1] Now dedicated to Saint Charles Borromeo. See page 140.

CHURCH OF ST MARY ALDERMARY

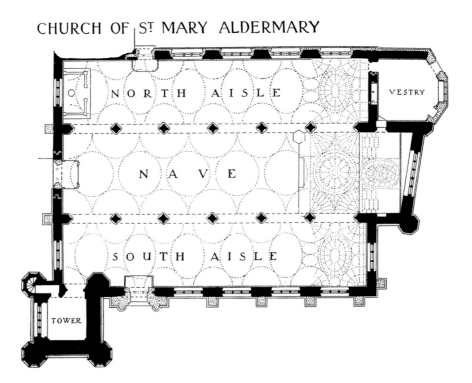

NORTH AISLE

VESTRY

NAVE

SOUTH AISLE

TOWER

RIGHT At St Mary Aldermary Wren reused the medieval foundations, and retained the skewed east end.

There is just as much variety within the ground plans. These were often dictated by the surviving foundations of the pre-Fire churches, which could be reused to save money. In these cases, the old plan's irregularity occasionally shows in the rebuilt church, as at St Mary Aldermary, where the east end is at an angle to the nave. Even if they didn't reuse the old foundations, the new churches were still restricted to the plots of the pre-Fire churches, and so most had to be built in cramped and enclosed positions, with other buildings crowding in on them. This led to some unusual ground plans: St Olave Old Jewry had a coffin-shaped plan, while St Benet Fink had a ten-sided oval design looking like a scent bottle on its side. Both churches were demolished in the nineteenth century.

Other plans fall into two basic types. One is the rectangular plan, based on the basilicas of ancient Rome and the early Christian Church, which have a long nave with or without aisles; the other is a squarish centralized plan with or without a dome. The rectangular basilica type is the most common, as at St Bride's Fleet Street and St Andrew Holborn, both of which have two aisles and a shallow chancel, with galleries over the aisles to provide extra space. Examples of longtitudinal plans with a single side aisle are St Lawrence Jewry and St Vedast alias Foster, while those at St Edmund King and Martyr and St Michael Paternoster Royal have no aisles at all. Centralized plans include St Martin-within-Ludgate and St Anne and St Agnes, both built on a square with a vault above.

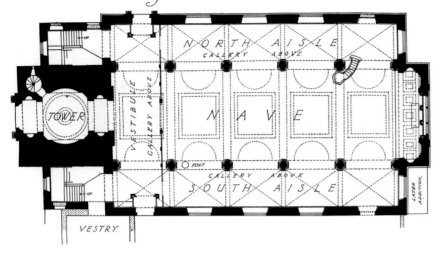

CHURCH *of* ST BRIDE, FLEET STREET.

CHURCH *of* ST ANDREW HOLBORN

LEFT TOP AND CENTRE
The rectangular basilica
plan, with aisles to north
and south, at St Bride's
Fleet Street and
St Andrew Holborn.

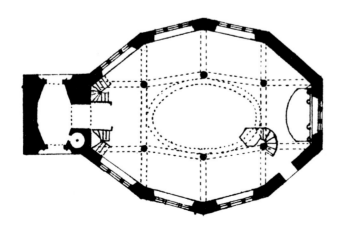

LEFT BELOW St Benet Fink
had a unique ten-sided
oval design.

CHURCH of S^T MARY ABCHURCH

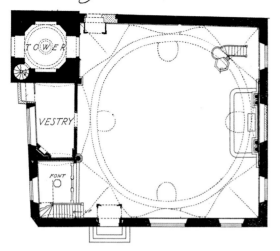

CHURCH of S^T MARTIN, LUDGATE

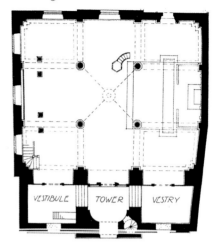

CHURCH of S^T MARY at HILL

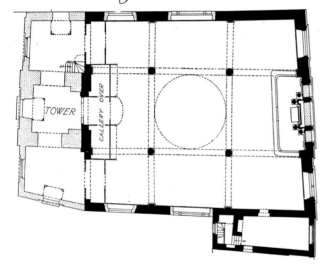

CHURCH of SS.ANNE & AGNES

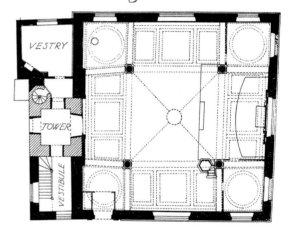

CHURCH of S^T STEPHEN WALBROOK.

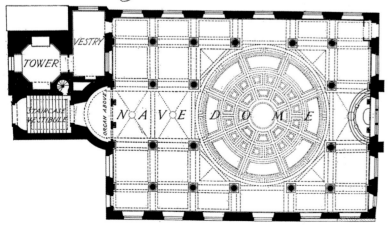

ABOVE Centrally planned 'cross-in-square' designs at St Martin Ludgate and St Anne and St Agnes. The ceilings are barrel-vaulted and where the vaults intersect they form a groin-vault.

LEFT TOP AND CENTRE Centrally planned churches with a dome: St Mary Abchurch and St Mary-at-Hill.

LEFT BELOW The rectangular basilica plan combined with a dome at St Stephen Walbrook.

CHURCH of Sᵗ LAWRENCE JEWRY

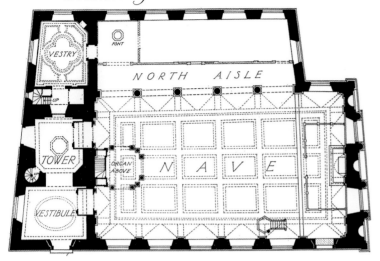

LEFT The rectangular basilica plan with a single aisle at St Lawrence Jewry and St Vedast-alias-Foster. The irregular medieval ground plans show clearly in these churches.

CHURCH of ST. VEDAST FOSTER LANE.

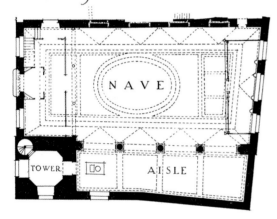

CHURCH of Sᵗ MICHAEL PATERNOSTER ROYAL

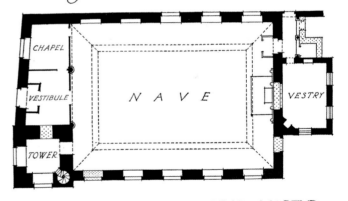

CHURCH of Sᵗ EDMUND THE KING & MARTYR

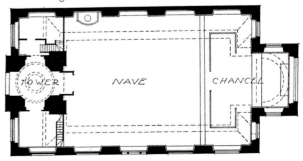

RIGHT The rectangular basilica plan without aisles at St Michael Paternoster Royal and St Edmund King and Martyr.

St Mary Abchurch is almost a square, but here a painted dome rises above the church floor. Other domes are at St Mary-at-Hill and St Stephen Walbrook. St Stephen, the most glorious of the Wren interiors, combines the rectangular basilica style with a dome.

In many cases the church exteriors were only visible on one or two sides, with the decorative elements reserved for these. But most of the churches had at least one front on display. St Lawrence Jewry's east front is a grand design, with a pediment carried on Corinthian columns connected by carved garlands of fruit and flowers. St Mary-le-Bow has two elaborate doorways featuring Tuscan columns in rusticated niches, with cherubs either side of an oval window.

At the end of his career, Wren set out his thoughts on how an ideal parish church should be built, stressing the importance of being able to hear and see the preacher in an Anglican service:

> In our reformed Religion, it should seem vain to make a Parish-Church larger, than that all who are present can both hear and see. The Romanists, indeed, may build larger Churches, it is enough if they hear the Murmur of the Mass, and see the Elevation of the Host, but ours are to be fitted for Auditories. I can hardly think it practicable to make a single Room so capacious, with Pews and Galleries, as to hold above 2000 Persons, and all to hear the Service, and both to hear distinctly, and see the Preacher.[2]

The position of the altar, or communion table, within a church was an important issue. The 1630s and 1640s, before and during the Civil War, had seen a conflict between the Puritans and the Royalists on this question. The Puritans wanted to avoid all priestly pomp, and make church services as simple as possible, with the preacher facing the congregation across the altar table. The Royalist followers of Archbishop Laud wanted to keep the altar behind altar rails at the east end of the church, in the chancel if one existed. Wren's uncle Matthew spent eighteen years in the Tower of London accused of 'causing the communion table to be placed altar-wise and to be railed in; and kneeling, and consecrating the bread and wine . . . with his back towards the people.'[3]

With the Restoration of the monarchy in 1660, the Royalist, or High Church, view of how to perform the liturgy prevailed, and many of the City churches went back to having an altar (or communion table) behind rails. Above this was an altarpiece or reredos, with the Ten Commandments, the Lord's Prayer and the Creed usually all written out in gold lettering, often framed by columns or pilasters and topped with a pediment and urns. These church furnishings, paid for by the parishioners rather than the Coal Tax, varied from the sumptuous to the plain. St Mary Abchurch has a wonderful reredos, decorated with exuberant

[2] *Parentalia*, pages 309–318
[3] *Parentalia*, pages 13–14
[4] All Hallows is not a Wren Church, as it survived the Fire and did not need to be rebuilt. And St James's, although very much a Wren church, lies outside the City.

garlands of fruit and flowers carved by Grinling Gibbons. Most of the churches would have had wainscot panelling round the walls, with the congregation sitting in box pews, so the overall effect was of dark wood in the lower part of the interior, with plain unpainted walls and clear windows above. The walls were usually articulated with pilasters or half-columns rising to the ceiling. Some churches with a large congregation carried the woodwork up into galleries supported on columns (St Bride's Fleet Street, St Andrew Holborn). Most of the original pews have gone, but good ones can be seen at St Martin-within-Ludgate. Some of the best-preserved pews used to be at St Mary-at-Hill, but although they survived a fire in 1988 they were removed and have not been reinstated. Other important features in the Anglican liturgy were the lectern and pulpit, which provided more opportunities for carvers to show off their skills. To help the preacher to project his voice, the pulpit also often had a tester, or sounding board, above. There is a lovely example at St Mary Abchurch.

Most of the churches had organs, usually installed in a gallery at the west end. The rival organ-makers Renatus Harris and Bernard 'Father' Smith are represented at St Clement Eastcheap with its Harris organ, and at St Peter upon Cornhill with its Smith instrument. The organ cases were often finely carved, as at St Magnus the Martyr where the instrument, the first swell organ in the country, is the work of the Jordan family.

All Hallows the Great had a very ornate screen dividing the nave from the chancel, unusual among the Wren churches, where a separate chancel carried suggestions of Roman Catholicism. When All Hallows was demolished in 1894 the screen was moved to St Margaret Lothbury, where it can still be seen.

Fonts and font covers offered more opportunities for fine carving. All Hallows by the Tower has a glorious font cover of 1682 by Grinling Gibbons, and at St James's Piccadilly there is another Grinling Gibbons font, this time in marble.[4]

Anglican churches usually displayed the Royal Coat of Arms as a symbol of their allegiance to the monarch as head of the Church of England. Some of these Coats of Arms, as at St Benet Paul's Wharf and St Edmund King and Martyr, are elaborately carved and show the English lion and the Scottish unicorn 'fighting for the Crown' – a reference to the Stuarts being monarchs of both Scotland and England.

Another unusual feature in some churches is the ornate sword rest, usually of painted wrought iron. These were made by a parish when one of its parishioners was elected Lord Mayor. During his year of office, the Lord Mayor visited a different church every Sunday, leaving his ceremonial sword on the sword rest during these state visits. Good examples are at St Sepulchre, St Martin-within-Ludgate and St Magnus the Martyr (which has three, as the parish provided more than one Lord Mayor).

OVERLEAF In the days before microphones, pulpits often had testers, or sounding-boards, to help the minister's voice carry to the faithful. One of the most lavishly carved is at St Margaret Lothbury; it comes from All Hallows the Great, demolished in the 1890s.

THE CHURCHES 1666-1711

The spire of St Martin-within-Ludgate framed between the lantern and the south-west tower of St Paul's Cathedral.

All Hallows by the Tower

ALL HALLOWS by the Tower, also known as All Hallows Barking, narrowly survived the Great Fire, as Pepys describes: 'it having only burned the dyall of Barking Church, and part of the porch, and was there quenched'. He climbed its tower to watch the progress of the blaze: 'I up to the top of Barking steeple, and there saw the saddest sight of desolation that I ever saw; every where great fires, oyle-cellars, and brimstone, and other things burning. I became afeard to stay there long, and therefore down again as fast as I could.'

All Hallows' survival meant the fabric of this church was not rebuilt by Wren and his office, but it is included here because it contains a masterpiece by Wren's greatest craftsman, Grinling Gibbons. In 1682 Mr James Foyle made the church a gift of this superb font cover, carved in limewood by Gibbons. It shows a dove with outstretched wings above garlands of fruit, fir cones, flowers and ears of wheat surrounded by three cherubs. Gibbons is at his brilliant best, the realism of the carving displaying his extraordinary technical ability to imitate fruit and flowers in wood. He received twelve pounds for his work.

OPPOSITE AND LEFT The font cover, carved in 1682 by Grinling Gibbons.

Wren's tower of All Hallows, which used to stand in Lombard Street in the heart of the City, was moved to Twickenham to provide the bell-tower for the new brick church built at the start of the Second World War.

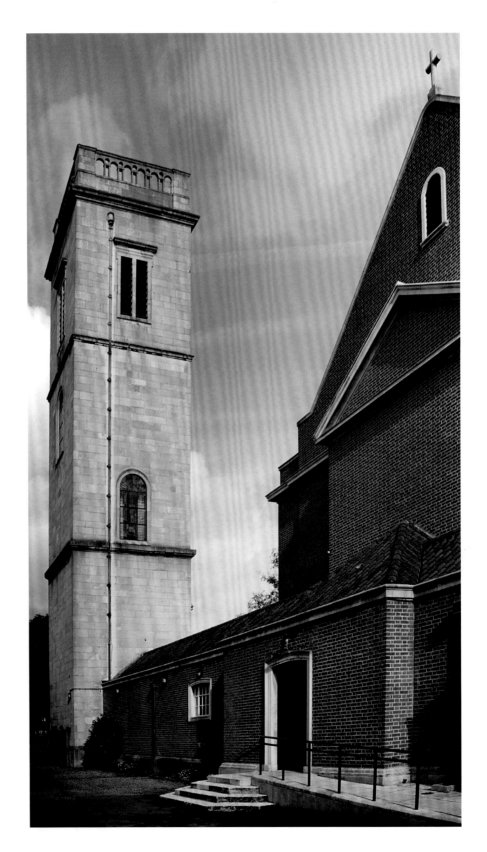

THE CHURCHES 1666–1711

All Hallows Twickenham

Formerly All Hallows Lombard Street

AN EYE-CATCHING white stone campanile stands on the Great Chertsey Road leading south-west out of London. This is the tower of Wren's City church of All Hallows Lombard Street, rebuilt here at the start of the Second World War. All Hallows Twickenham is now the Parish Church of the Rugby Football Union, whose famous stadium is nearby. The original Lombard Street church, first mentioned in 1053, was destroyed in the Great Fire and rebuilt by Wren's office. Work did not begin until 1686 and was finished by 1694, making it one of the last of the City churches to be completed. Wren's building survived the Union of Benefices Act of 1860, but in 1934 serious structural defects were discovered and All Hallows was declared a dangerous structure. In spite of opposition from many quarters, including the City Corporation, the Ecclesiastical Commissioners decided in 1938 to demolish the church, but agreed to move the tower and furnishings to a new site in Twickenham.

Despite the outbreak of war, the body of the new brick church was built between 1939 and 1940 to the designs of Robert Atkinson. A short cloister separates the new church from Wren's rebuilt tower, although in Wren's design the tower stood within the main building, at the south-west corner. Built of Portland stone, the tower is a simple design of three square sections topped with a cornice and parapet pierced by a balustrade, but without a spire or steeple. It houses ten bells, six of which came originally from St Dionis Backchurch. When St Dionis was demolished in the 1870s its bells were rehung at All Hallows, and eventually moved with the tower from Lombard Street to Twickenham, where they can now be heard ringing out for the Sunday morning services.

The old church had elegant woodwork, including the pulpit and a fine reredos, which have been incorporated into the new building. There is also a Renatus Harris organ.

The pulpit has marquetry panels surrounded by carved cherubs' heads and garlands of fruit and flowers, and a tester or sounding board decorated in the same style. John Wesley, one of the founders of Methodism, recalled preaching from this pulpit: 'In the year 1735, about forty years ago, I preached in this church . . . This was the first time that, having no notes about me, I preached extempore.'

The pulpit from which John Wesley once preached, decorated with cherubs' heads and garlands of fruit and flowers.

In 1870 the church underwent major repairs and restoration. The reredos was gilded, and the Lord's Prayer and the Ten Commandments replaced with Victorian painted panels showing scenes from the Passion of Christ. Above these a Pelican in her Piety feeds her young by piercing her breast, a symbol of Christian self-sacrifice. The reredos is more architectural in style than most: a complex composition of four Corinthian columns support broken segmental (or curved) pediments, capped by a large triangular pediment itself enclosing three smaller pediments, all lavishly decorated with fine Grinling Gibbons style carving. As usual, the church furnishings were paid for by the parish, and a panel in the church lists eighteen benefactors who paid £188 for the reredos.

Another survival from the old church is a cabinet with three 'bread shelves' where the more prosperous parishioners, when attending services, would donate loaves of bread for distribution among the poor of the parish.

RIGHT All Hallows has one of the few surviving examples of 'bread shelves', a feature once common in the City churches.

OPPOSITE In 1870 Victorian painted panels showing scenes from the Passion of Christ were added to the reredos.

THE CHURCHES 1666–1711

Christ Church Newgate Street

WREN'S CHURCH was built on the site of Greyfriars, a former Franciscan friary to the north of St Paul's, among whose buildings was a large church with a nave some 300 feet in length. Greyfriars had been closed in the Reformation and reopened in 1547 as a new church, Christ Church. The foundation included a school for orphaned children at Christ's Hospital (also known as the Blue Coat School, after the children's distinctive uniform).

The church and some of the Hospital buildings were destroyed in the Fire of 1666. Between 1677 and 1687 the main body of the church was rebuilt by Wren, probably with Hooke's assistance, with a much shorter nave of 113 feet. In spite of this reduction, Christ Church was still one of the longest of the City churches. The medieval foundations were reused, but reinforced by external buttresses on the west and east walls, the only example of these among Wren's churches. Internally there were large galleries to accommodate the pupils of Christ's Hospital.

Christ Church had fine furnishings, including a grand reredos and ornate plasterwork on the east wall, but these were lost when the church was destroyed on 29 December 1940, the worst night of the Blitz. Only the tower and some of the walls were left standing. In 1989 a garden was laid out on the site of the nave, with a series of square pergolas to mark the position of the columns of the bombed church. Today the west and north walls are still standing. Some of the east wall, complete with a round-headed window, also survived the bombing but this was shamefully removed in 1974 as part of a road-widening scheme.

The glorious steeple completed in 1704, seventeen years after the rest of the church, rises in diminishing square sections above the nave. The louvred bell stage is decorated with pilasters and supports curved segmental pediments and a balustrade. Above this an open square Ionic colonnade allows glimpses of sky through the columns, an effect repeated in the top stage with its four simple arches. Scrolls and buttresses, along with pineapples and flaming urns, are used for decorative effect.

OPPOSITE The site of Christ Church, which was badly damaged in the Blitz, has been laid out as a garden; the position of the columns in the nave is shown by pergolas with climbing roses. Wren's steeple survived the bombing, and, with its design based on a sequence of diminishing squares, is one of the best in the City. See page 50.

BELOW A flaming urn on the tower.

St Alban Wood Street

ST ALBAN, commemorated in the city bearing his name, was Britain's first Christian martyr, executed for his faith by the Romans in the late third century. Five centuries later, the Venerable Bede wrote that the executioner's eyes fell out of their sockets as he wielded the axe to behead the saint.

Wood Street is in the north of the City, and the earliest church on this site was possibly King Offa's private chapel, built in the eighth century and dedicated to St Alban. By the early seventeenth century St Alban's had grown to include several chapels and a tower. Rebuilt in the 1630s, the church was destroyed in the Fire, leaving a burnt-out shell.

After visiting the site in 1681 Wren wrote to the Commissioners that he thought 'it may be brought to a decent and useful Church' and St Alban's was rebuilt between 1682 and 1687 in Wren's version of the Perpendicular Gothic, a choice possibly dictated by the opportunity to reuse some of the surviving fabric. The plan shows Wren's plaster Gothic lierne vaulting in the nave, with aisles to the north and south, and a tower in the north-west corner. In the 1850s George Gilbert Scott added a chancel at the east end, complete with radiating buttresses.

Corbel with grotesque mask, carved by Samuel Fulkes.

The tower was boarded over in 1687, at a height just above the corbels which were level with the roof of the main church. On three sides these corbels, carved by Samuel Fulkes, take the form of grotesque masks. Work resumed in 1696, and was completed two years later. Above the corbels the tower rises through two new stages to the top balustrade with its crocketed pinnacles. Each side has three flat buttresses between which are pairs of Gothic windows complete with cusped tracery.

The Barber Surgeons Company, whose Hall is round the corner in Monkwell Square, used the churchyard of St Alban's as a burial place for hanged felons who had been publicly dissected before the Surgeon Members, a scene gruesomely depicted in Hogarth's *Four Stages of Cruelty*.

This is one of the Wren churches where only the tower survived the Blitz. The ruins of the rest of the church were removed in the 1950s, leaving the tower isolated in the middle of Wood Street. The door shown in the photograph originally provided access from the nave: the large recessed arch with the door faced south into the church. The tower has since been converted to secular use.

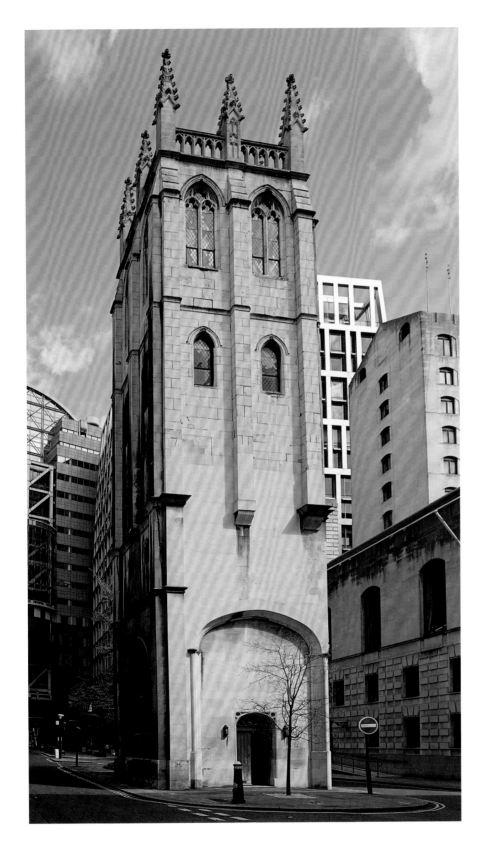

Wren rebuilt St Alban's
in his version of the
Perpendicular Gothic.
Other examples of
Wren churches in
the Gothic style are
St Mary Aldermary and
St Dunstan-in-the-East.

St Andrew Holborn

Although St Andrew's escaped the Great Fire, Wren rebuilt it anyway as it was in a poor state of repair. At the east end is a double-storeyed Venetian window, with a small domed vestibule either side of the shallow chancel.

THIS IS ONE OF THE LARGEST of Wren's City churches, measuring 100 feet in length with seven bays. Excavations have uncovered Roman pottery in the crypt, suggesting this was originally a Roman site, although outside the City walls. The earliest written record comes in the late tenth century and refers to a wooden church of St Andrew, the Apostle and patron saint of Scotland (as well as of the Ukraine and Barbados, among other countries). By the mid-fifteenth century this had been replaced by a stone church, and this large parish included some of the nearby legal institutions knows as the Inns of Chancery. More than three thousand parishioners perished in the Plague of 1665. In 1666 St Andrew's escaped the Great Fire when the wind direction changed at the last minute, but being in a bad state of repair it was rebuilt anyway between 1684 and 1686. The need to rebuild may also have been the result of an increased population, as some inhabitants who fled the City in the aftermath of the Fire settled in this area, rather than returning to their burnt-out homes.

The rebuilding was paid for by the parish, as St Andrew's was not eligible for Coal Tax money. Externally, Wren's church is double-storeyed: the five central bays have large round-headed windows above shorter, curve-headed windows, suggesting an interior arrangement of galleries above side aisles. At the east end are two small domed vestibules either side of the shallow chancel.

In 1703–4, some twenty years after the main rebuilding, Wren remodelled the fifteenth-century tower in stone to match the body of the church, retaining its Gothic buttresses and pointed windows on the lower storeys. The upper section was increased in height and given a bell loft and an elegant balustrade. By 1703 Hawksmoor was working for Wren, and he may have been involved in the design of the tower: on the louvred bell stage there are elements typical of him, such as the lion's mask keystones on the round-headed arches, within which are oval cartouches and shallower arches supported by double pilasters. Hawksmoor's hand can also be seen in the unusual finials on the corners above the balustrade which Mervyn Blatch, writing in 1978, describes as 'clumsy pinnacles looking like Roman altars with pineapples on top' which 'give the steeple a top-heavy appearance'.[1] The four weathervanes on the pinnacles have only just been reinstated in 2015; they were lost when St Andrew's was destroyed by bombing in April 1941 (when only the fabric of the exterior walls and the tower were left) and not replaced in the post-war rebuilding. It is particularly good to see them back, as St Andrew's is the only surviving Wren church with four weathervanes.

The interior, which had been drastically altered by S.S. Teulon in the 1870s, was also gutted in the bombing. It was rebuilt to Wren's original designs by

[1] Mervyn Blatch, *A Guide to London's Churches*

BELOW 'Charity children' clutching bibles and wearing their blue coats.

OPPOSITE On the arches of the tower are lion's mask keystones, typical Hawksmoor details. His hand can also be seen in the unusual finials above the balustrade. The four weathervanes were only reinstated in 2015.

Seeley and Paget and reopened in 1961. The plan is similar to Wren's St James's Piccadilly (likewise built for a large population), a simple rectangle with aisles and galleries lit by the two tiers of windows visible on the outside. Rising from the galleries, Corinthian columns carry an arcade supporting the barrel-vaulted roof, all decorated with elaborate plasterwork. The east end has a two-storeyed Venetian window, again following the pattern of St James's. The organ case, pulpit and font all come from the old chapel of the nearby Foundling Hospital, founded by Thomas Coram, who is buried in the church.

In 2005 a large hanging crucifix was installed at the east end; made in Vallechiara, in Tuscany, it is based on the crucifix by Cimabue in the church of Santa Croce in Florence. On the exterior west wall are two figures of 'charity children' with their distinctive blue coats. These were formerly on the wall of the local parish school in Hatton Garden, founded in 1696 (as shown in Roman numerals on the plaque carried by the girl).

St Andrew's was rebuilt
to Wren's original designs
after the war. The large
hanging crucifix at the
east end is based on the
one by Cimabue that
hangs in the church of
Santa Croce in Florence.

St Andrew-by-the-Wardrobe

THIS CHURCH'S SURPRISING NAME comes from the neighbouring Royal Wardrobe, established by Edward III as a store for his personal clothes, armour and treasure. First mentioned in the mid-thirteenth century as Saint Andre de Castello, from nearby Baynard's Castle, this earlier church burnt down, along with the Royal Wardrobe, in the Great Fire. The present church was one of the last churches to be rebuilt by Wren, between 1685 and 1694. Its imposing south front stands above Queen Victoria Street, but the other fronts are hemmed in among narrow alleyways. The churchyard wall, with

The south front and tower of St Andrew-by-the-Wardrobe, of warm red brick contrasting with stone quoins and window surrounds.

classical urns and gateway leading up to the south door, was built in 1901 as a memorial to the great architectural historian Sir Banister Fletcher. St Andrew's shares several features with St James's Piccadilly, built about the same time – an economical red brick exterior with stone dressings, and five bays of round-headed windows above smaller segmental, or curved, windows suggesting an interior arrangement of galleries (lit by the upper windows) above aisles (lit by the lower ones). The tower is on the south-west corner – unlike that of St James's. It has four stages ending in a simple balustrade. The galleries on the interior have square piers, instead of columns as at St James's, supporting the barrel-vaulted roof over the nave and cross vaults

The interior was remodelled after being gutted in the Blitz: the space of the nave was reduced by introducing wooden panels to close off the aisles. The galleries remain, and are now used for bookcases.

over the galleries. The nave ceiling is decorated with panels of moulded plaster enclosing circular wreaths.

St Andrew's was one of the churches gutted by bombs in 1940. Marshall Sisson rebuilt it in 1959–61, and reduced the space of the nave by installing wooden panels to close off the aisles, converting them to a chapel, a vestry and office space. The galleries above are still open, and now used for bookcases. The result is that the nave feels strangely boxed-in. The ornate plasterwork ceiling was faithfully restored at the same time. After the Fire the parish was too poor to afford church furnishings, so, very unusually, the Coal Tax provided the funds for these. Most were destroyed in the bombing, but the pulpit and font come from St Matthew Friday Street, itself demolished in 1886. Both were the work of Edward Pierce or Pearce (who carved Wren's bust in the Ashmolean Museum in Oxford, as well as the wooden model of the dragon weathervane at St Mary-le-Bow). The pulpit is particularly fine, with panels of marquetry set between pendants of flowers, with cherubs' heads above. The sounding board and back piece are missing, and the base stem and stairs have been replaced. The early eighteenth-century chandeliers are made of latten, a brass-like compound.

St Andrew's most famous parishioner was William Shakespeare, who in 1613 bought a house in Ireland Yard round the corner from the church.

OPPOSITE The ornate plasterwork ceiling was faithfully restored after the war.

LEFT The original pulpit was destroyed in the Blitz. This elegant replacement from St Matthew Friday Street (demolished in 1886) was the work of Edward Pierce, who also carved the wooden model of the dragon for St Mary-le-Bow's weathervane.

St Anne and St Agnes

THIS SMALL CHURCH on Gresham Street, built between 1677 and 1687, is the only City church dedicated to two saints. Saint Anne was the mother of the Virgin Mary, and Saint Agnes was a Roman girl martyred for her refusal to marry, as she had promised to be the bride of Christ. The church has a red brick exterior; on three sides there is a pedimented gable above a large round-headed window. In the 1820s the brick was covered with stucco, which survives on

RIGHT ABOVE Winged cherub on the keystone of the south door.

RIGHT BELOW The weathervane: a beaked creature below the letter A, the initial of the two dedicatee saints. This is the work of Robert Bird, who also made the flaming urn for the Monument, as well as the copper dragon on the weathervane of St Mary-le-Bow.

OPPOSITE View from the south, showing the large central window and the simple tower with plain weatherboarded lantern.

the north side. The fourth side, the west, has a small stone tower and a simple weatherboarded lantern, which Bradley and Pevsner say 'looks more like an artisan's design than anything from the Wren office'.[1] The symmetrical south and east sides show the church is built on a centralized plan, and this is even more apparent on the interior, which is almost square. This arrangement is known as a quincunx, or cross-in-square, plan, like that of St Martin-within-Ludgate and St Mary-at-Hill. The central square is groin-vaulted, and rises from four wooden Corinthian columns. Gilded corbels connect the walls to

[1] Simon Bradley and Nikolaus Pevsner, *The Buildings of England: London, The City Churches*

THE CHURCHES 1666–1711

the small lower corner sections. These are decorated with circular panels with plasterwork garlands and cherubs. The church was badly damaged by bombing in the war, when most of the roof fell into the nave. After restoration in the early 1960s, by Henry Braddock and Martin Smith, it was rededicated as the Lutheran Church, serving the exiled Estonian and Latvian communities in London. In 2014 St Anne and St Agnes ceased to function as a church when it became the home of the Gresham Centre, an educational charity supporting vocal music.

Above the west door to the tower there is a charming small figure of Father Time with gilded scythe and hourglass, which came from the church of St Mildred Bread Street, destroyed in the war and not rebuilt. Also from St Mildred is the bell-shaped font cover, beautifully decorated with scrolls and roses, carved by William Cleere in 1682. The wainscoting is original to the church, as is the weathervane showing a beaked creature below the letter A. This was the work of Robert Bird, who also made the flaming urn for the Monument, and the dragon weathervane for St Mary-le-Bow.

OPPOSITE The plan of St Anne and St Agnes is a centralized, cross-in-square, design. The central square is groin-vaulted, and rises from four Corinthian columns.

BELOW Two pieces of sculpture originally from St Mildred Bread Street, destroyed in the Blitz: an unusual small figure of Father Time with gilded scythe and hourglass; and a bell-shaped font cover carved by William Cleere in 1682.

St Augustine Watling Street

BELOW LEFT One of the obelisk pinnacles with faces looking out from all four sides, a favourite device of Hawksmoor's.

BELOW RIGHT The elegant weathervane, an example of the arrow and pennant type.

OPPOSITE The slender spire of St Augustine's acts as a counterfoil to the very large dome of St Paul's, standing nearby.

ST AUGUSTINE'S was bombed in 1940, and only the tower of this small church survives. First mentioned in the twelfth century, the church was destroyed in the Fire and rebuilt by Wren in 1680–84. St Augustine's stands very close to St Paul's, just to the south-east of the cathedral. The tower was completed in 1695, several years after Hawksmoor had joined Wren's office, and the younger architect's influence can be seen in the four obelisk pinnacles each with four faces looking out, a device he used on a number of steeples. The obelisks sit on an intricate pierced Baroque balustrade, and above them is a lead-covered section, rising through square stages supported by curved brackets to a slightly bulbous tapering spire, a bit like an elongated shallot, topped with an elegant weathervane. Wren and Hawksmoor's spire had been repaired and altered in the nineteenth century, but was destroyed in the bombing. In 1966 the original design was reinstated, this time in fibreglass, by Paul Paget. St Paul's Choir School was built on the site of the church.

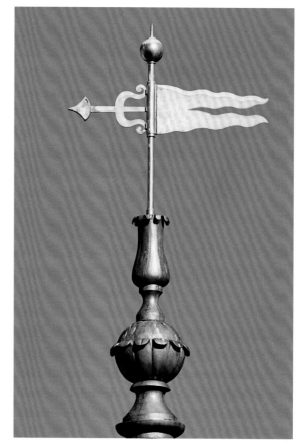

St Benet Paul's Wharf

THE NAME BENET is a shortening of Benedict, the saint and founder of the great monastic order to whom the church is dedicated. It is close to the river and the wharf belonging to St Paul's, where stone for the cathedral was unloaded. Its first mention, as Sancti Benedicti super Tamisiam, was in 1111. The earlier church was destroyed in the Great Fire, and the present building was completed by 1684. Its Dutch appearance has led to Robert Hooke being credited with the design. The exterior is a chequerwork of dark red and blue brickwork, which contrasts with the Portland stone dressings on the corners and on the tower. Stone is also used for the distinctive swags or festoons of flowers above the round-headed windows on the north and south fronts. On the east front the central festoon, above a blank rectangular window, has a delightful cherub's head at its centre. A modillion cornice runs round the body of the church, and is repeated at the top of the tower, a simple design of three stages divided by bands of stonework. The top storey is a louvred belfry. Above this a leaded dome, pierced by eight oval dormer windows, rises to an open lantern and a short curving spire, topped with a gold ball and weathervane in the form of a pennant. Although the church escaped damage in the war, in the 1970s it

OPPOSITE The stone quoins on the corners of St Benet's are unusual in the way they alternate with brick to produce a distinctive banded appearance – compare the more usual treatment at St Andrew-by-the-Wardrobe (page 78), St James's Piccadilly (page 124) and St Mary Abchurch (page 160), which use alternating long and short stone quoins.

LEFT Festoon and cherub's head, beneath the modillion cornice running round the body of the church.

BELOW LEFT The
Communion table is
supported on figures
of winged angels at the
corners and the Madonna
and child at the centre.
The carving is in the style
of the woodwork at the
Jesuit Church of Antwerp,
typical of the Catholic
churches of Flanders.

BELOW RIGHT The coat of
arms of the House of Stuart,
with the lion of England and
the unicorn of Scotland.

OPPOSITE Welsh flags hang
from the gallery on the
north side of the church,
reflecting St Benet's
association with the Welsh
Episcopalian Church.

suffered from a road-widening scheme which included building a flyover next to the church; this has left St Benet's feeling marooned. To reach the entrance from Queen Victoria Street you have to go down a flight of steps.

The interior is almost square. On the north side there is an aisle with a gallery above, and Corinthian columns rising to the flat ceiling, with Corinthian pilasters on the other walls. The church has kept its pews, and there is a fine reredos, with gilded frames containing the Ten Commandments, in the two central panels (shaped as usual like the tablets of stone Moses brought down from Mount Sinai), flanked by the Lord's Prayer on the left and the Creed on the right. Below the reredos is a delightfully ornate Communion table, probably Flemish, decorated with figures of winged angels at the corners and the Madonna and child at the centre. A colourful Royal coat of arms is over the door in the north-west corner, next to the gallery.

In 1877, under the Union of Benefices Act, St Benet's was proposed as one of nineteen City of London churches to be demolished. Luckily it was instead taken over by the Welsh Episcopalian Church in 1879, and services are still conducted in the Welsh language, while Welsh flags hang from the gallery. There is an earlier Welsh connection: the architect Inigo Jones, the son of a Welsh clothworker, was buried in the chancel of the old church of St Benet's.

St Bride's Fleet Street

St Bride's takes its name from the popular Irish saint Bridget of Kildare, born in the mid-fifth century. She is credited with miraculously turning water into beer, and churches dedicated to her are often found near wells. St Bride's had its own well, reflected in the name of the nearby Bridewell Palace, which included Bridewell Prison, notorious for its public floggings of prisoners. Following the church's destruction in the Blitz, excavations in the crypt revealed the remains of a large Roman house, as well as the foundations of a succession of churches, of which the earliest is Saxon, possibly built for an Irish community. The church destroyed in the Fire had been built in the fifteenth century, when the long association of St Bride's with printing and journalism began. William Caxton's apprentice, the aptly named Wynkyn de Worde, set up a printing press in Fleet Street. Other literary parishioners over the centuries have included the poets John Dryden and John Milton, and the diarist John Evelyn. Samuel Pepys and his eight brothers were all christened here. Its connections with the press and its situation on Fleet Street, the traditional home of London newspapers, have made St Bride's 'The Journalists' Church'.

RIGHT On the corners of the tower are pairs of flaming urns each decorated with four faces, now sadly weatherworn. This is a device associated with Hawksmoor (compare St Augustine Watling Street, page 86).

OPPOSITE St Bride's steeple, the tallest of all the City churches, is a simple and elegant design of diminishing octagonal stages which look as if they could collapse down into each other, like a telescope.

THE CHURCHES 1666–1711

Woodcut of the Tower
of the Winds in Athens,
published by Cesariano
in 1521.

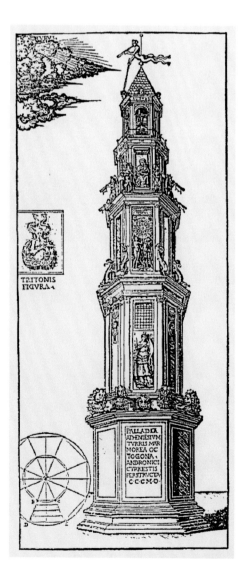

After the Fire the vestry soon raised the £500 deposit needed to get the City to authorize rebuilding, and Wren started work on the new church in 1672. It was opened for worship in 1675. The steeple had to wait until October 1701 for the first stone to be laid, but it was finished within three or four years. The tallest of all the City church steeples, it was originally 234 feet tall but was reduced to 226 feet after being struck by lightning in 1764. It is a simple and elegant design of three diminishing octagonal arcades, above which is another octagonal stage with rectangular openings, below a spire. This takes the form of an obelisk on a pedestal, also octagonal. All these stages look as if they could collapse down into each other, like a telescope.

The design is similar to Wren's own Warrant Design for St Paul's, made almost thirty years earlier (see page 249); both have similarities to the Chinese pagodas which had recently been illustrated in Johan Nieuhof's accounts of his travels in China, published in English in 1669. Another source for the design is a woodcut showing the five diminishing octagonal stages of the Tower of the Winds in Athens, included in Cesariano's 1521 translation of Vitruvius's *De Architectura*.

The association with multi-tiered weddings cakes goes back to the early eighteenth century, when a local pastry chef, Thomas Rich, is said to have modelled his own wedding cake on St Bride's steeple.

At the top of the tower, below the octagonal stages, are four pairs of flaming urns each decorated with four faces (sadly weatherworn), a device associated with Hawksmoor, who had been Wren's assistant since the late 1680s and worked with him on a number of steeples for the City churches.

Wren's church has five bays, reflected internally in the five panels of the barrel-vaulted ceiling, with light provided by oval clerestory windows. It originally had aisles and galleries, divided from the nave by a series of double Doric columns in the manner of a classical basilica, but the interior was gutted by incendiary bombs on 29 December 1940. It was rebuilt by Godfrey Allen and the church was reopened in 1957. Allen rearranged the interior, eliminating the galleries and setting up wooden screens to divide the nave from the aisles. While the original seating had faced the altar, pews now face each other across the nave.

Wren's reredos was at the east end in a shallow chancel. In the rebuilding, the east wall of the chancel was decorated

St Bride's is hemmed in by buildings on all sides. St Bride's Passage, to the south of the church, provides the clearest view of the exterior.

with illusionist painting by Glyn Jones. The modern free-standing reredos by Godfrey Allen, which has been brought forward by several feet, contains an oval stained glass window showing Christ in Majesty. Bradley and Pevsner are dismissive of the new east end arrangements: 'a juxtaposition so unsympathetic it is a surprise to learn it was designed as an ensemble'.[1] The side aisles have more pews facing inwards, many sponsored by media moguls and newspapers. In the north aisle is the Journalists' Altar, dedicated to journalists who are missing or have died while reporting from troubled areas of the world.

[1] Simon Bradley and Nikolaus Pevsner, *The Buildings of England: London, The City Churches*

THE CHURCHES 1666–1711

OPPOSITE In the post-war remodelling of the interior, the galleries have gone, screens divide the nave from the aisles, and pews face each other across the nave. At the east end is a free-standing reredos with an oval stained glass window.

ABOVE The Journalists' Altar at the east end of the north aisle.

OVERLEAF The barrel-vaulted ceiling, lit by oval clerestory windows.

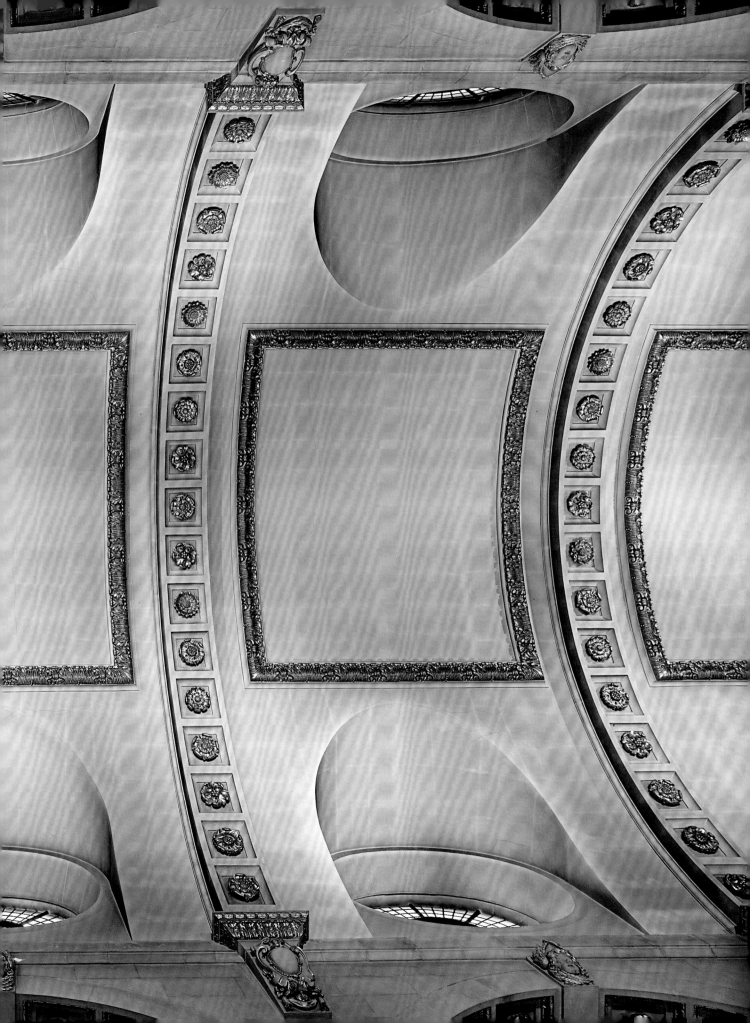

St Clement Danes

THERE ARE TWO LONDON CHURCHES dedicated to St Clement, and both claim to feature in the rhyme 'Oranges and lemons, Say the bells of St Clement's'. Where St Clement Eastcheap is tucked away in a small alleyway in the City, St Clement Danes lies just outside the City, occupying a prominent position on an island in the middle of the Strand, with traffic flowing on all sides. The name is thought to refer to Danes who were allowed to settle here by Alfred the Great after they had taken English wives.

By 1022 a stone church had been built on the site, replacing earlier timber structures. St Clement's escaped the Great Fire, which didn't get this far west, but by 1679 the fabric was unsafe and Wren designed a completely new church. The nave and tower were finished by 1682; above the square belfry is the elegant spire, added by James Gibbs in 1719. The bottom section is an octagon with four openings; above this another octagonal stage has each section curving inwards to create a dynamically Baroque outline for the entablature.

BELOW LEFT Flaming urns on the corners of the spire.

BELOW RIGHT St Clement was martyred by being thrown into the sea tied to an anchor, as shown on the weathervane.

OPPOSITE Wren's church is crowned by Gibbs's elegant spire, added in 1719.

Garlands of flowers hang between pilasters above round-headed openings, and there are urns on the corners of all these stages. The top section reverts to a regular octagon with tall thin openings, capped by a shallow dome and lantern. The whole effect is a worthy complement to Gibbs's other steeple at St Mary-le-Strand, a few minutes' walk to the west. The weathervane has an anchor-shaped cut-out, referring to St Clement's martyrdom: he was a first-century pope who suffered martyrdom by being thrown into the sea tied to an anchor, on the orders of the Roman Emperor Trajan. St Clement is now the patron saint of mariners.

Wren's interior was destroyed in an air raid in 1941 and rebuilt by Anthony Lloyd in the 1950s, preserving the original arrangement of galleries and pews, all recreated in dark oak. White columns with gilt Corinthian capitals rise to support the barrel-vaulted ceiling, decorated with elaborate plasterwork. The east end narrows to a semicircular apse with gilded coffering, with the aisles and galleries curving round to form an ambulatory, unique in Wren's church architecture. The new benches in the nave have an ingenious telescopic mechanism: they can be extended sideways into the nave to increase seating capacity when the church is full. (In 1712, when the Act for Building Fifty New Churches had recently been passed, the Commissioners aspired to a similar telescopic arrangement stipulating that: 'Movable Forms or Seats be so contrived in the middle Isles, as to run under the seats of the pewes, and draw out into the said Isles.')

The large Royal coat of arms has a panel with a Latin inscription including the words: 'DIRUERENT AERII BELLI FULMINA AD MCMXLI', which translates as: 'DESTROYED BY THUNDERBOLTS OF AERIAL WARFARE IN 1941', and goes on to say that it was restored by the Royal Air Force in 1958. St Clement's is now the Central Church of the RAF, and the connection is evident throughout the building: there are over seven hundred badges of RAF squadrons set into the floor, RAF flags are displayed in the galleries, and the entrance has a memorial to the air forces of the nations of the Commonwealth who fought in the war. Books of Remembrance are displayed in cases under the windows, including one for the 1900 US airmen based in Britain who were killed in action.

Over the centuries St Clement Danes has had connections with many distinguished men and women. Robert Cecil, the first Earl of Salisbury and trusted adviser to Elizabeth I and James I, was baptised here in 1563. Ann Donne was buried here: the wife of John Donne, the poet and Dean of St Paul's, she died giving birth to their twelfth child in 1617. In the 1770s and 1780s Doctor Samuel Johnson regularly attended divine service at St Clement's, occupying seat number 18 in the north gallery, near enough to the pulpit to hear the sermons. And in the 1840s and 1850s the rector was William Webb-Ellis, who, as a pupil at Rugby School, according to legend picked up the ball and ran with it, so creating the game of rugby football.

OPPOSITE The steeple of St Clement Danes towers over the Gladstone Memorial of 1905, with a bronze statue of the Liberal leader by Sir William Hamo Thorneycroft.

OVERLEAF The interior was destroyed in the Blitz, and restored by the Royal Air Force in 1958. St Clement's is now the Central Church of the RAF, and has over seven hundred badges of RAF squadrons set into the floor.

St Clement Eastcheap

ST CLEMENT EASTCHEAP, like St Clement Danes, claims ownership of the 'Oranges and lemons' of the nursery rhyme, asserting that it refers to the citrus fruit unloaded on the nearby wharves on the Thames.

Despite its name, St Clement's no longer stands on Eastcheap, a road shortened in the 1830s with the building of the new London Bridge. Situated in a narrow winding lane, this is one of the smaller City churches. It was first recorded in the eleventh century, and rebuilding after the Fire did not begin until the early 1680s. The plain tower was completed in 1687, when the parishioners showed their gratitude by sending Wren a third of a hogshead of wine. Now stuccoed, it was originally brick with stone quoins. It is topped by a simple balustrade.

In the late 1680s Jonathan Maine was paid by the parish for carving the woodwork of the interior, including the delightful cherubs dancing round the tester, or sounding board, of the pulpit. The organ is by the great organ builder Renatus Harris, and dated 1696. When the vestry dispensed with Harris's services and instead entrusted the organ to Christian Smith (nephew of Harris's hated rival, 'Father Smith'), they found that Harris had put a 'cheat into the organ to put the organ out of order'.[1] They had to pay Smith five shillings to undo the sabotage.

The interior is a simple rectangular nave with a small south aisle. In the 1870s, William Butterfield made major alterations to the church to bring it more into keeping with Victorian High Church taste, including the destruction of the galleries, and moving the organ to the south aisle where it was 'shorn of its topmost embellishments'.

Butterfield also installed stained glass, as well as dividing the reredos into three separate panels. In 1933 Sir Ninian Comper reversed much of Butterfield's work, moving the organ back to the west wall of the nave, and reuniting the altarpiece panels. In the process he painted them blue and gold, and replaced the Ten Commandments with figures of St Clement and St Martin in the central panels. The colour scheme is repeated in the decoration of the panels of the flat ceiling.

St Clement's has recently been converted to serve as the headquarters of the Amos Trust, a Christian charity promoting reconciliation and human rights in troubled areas of the world. Their office is in the nave.

[1] James Boeringer, *Organa Britannica 1660-1860*

St Clement Eastcheap is tucked away on Clements Lane.

OPPOSITE In 1933 Sir Ninian Comper painted the altarpiece panels blue and gold, and replaced the Ten Commandments with figures of St Clement and St Martin in the central panels.

LEFT ABOVE Cherubs dancing round the tester, or sounding board, of the pulpit are the work of Jonathan Maine, who worked at St Clement's in the 1680s.

LEFT BELOW The organ of 1696 is by the great organ builder Renatus Harris; in the 1870s it was 'shorn of its topmost embellishments'.

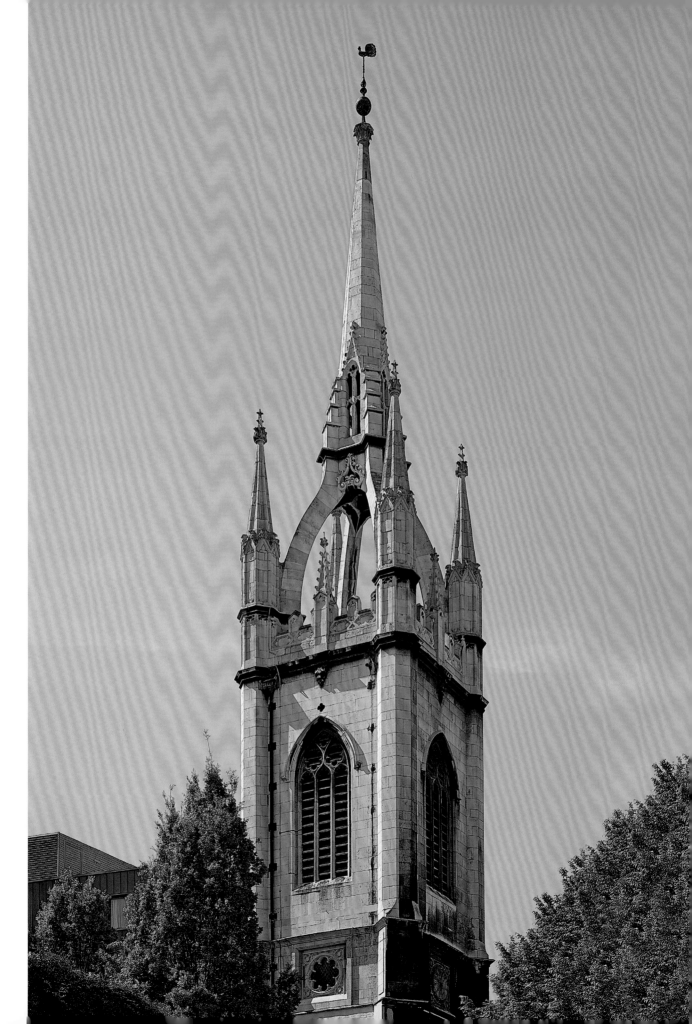

St Dunstan-in-the-East

St Dunstan-in-the-East was destroyed in the Blitz, leaving only the tower and some of the church walls standing. Although St Dunstan was the Saxon Archbishop of Canterbury, the first mention of a church here is in the late thirteenth century. The Gothic building survived the Great Fire better than most, as it had been repaired with Portland stone in the 1630s. After the Fire the church received a private donation of £4000 towards rebuilding, and it proceeded promptly with repairs on its own account. But by 1693 these early repairs proved inadequate and the City Churches Commissioners approved the rebuilding of the steeple, which had become unstable. The new tower and steeple were built between 1695 and 1701. Although Wren preferred the Classical style for a new building, he was prepared to use Gothic designs when working with an existing Gothic structure.[1] The belfry stage of St Dunstan has pointed Gothic windows complete with tracery. Above this four curved flying arches, held in place by the weight of large pinnacles, rise from the corners of the tower to support the long tapering needle spire. Seeing the sky through the open space between the arches gives a feeling of lightness and delicacy, as the spire appears to be floating almost weightlessly. The pre-Fire steeple at St Mary-le-Bow had a similar arrangement of the spire being carried on flying arches. The weathervane is a splendid cockerel, the only example of a weathercock on a Wren City church.

By 1810 the main body of the church had became structurally unsound, and it was demolished and rebuilt by David Laing, also in the Gothic style. This church was destroyed by bombing in 1941, and in the 1970s a charming garden was built in the ruins, with a fountain in the middle of the former nave.

OPPOSITE Wren's tower and steeple continued the Gothic style, complete with tracery windows and a needle spire supported by flying arches.

BELOW The weathervane is a splendid cockerel, the only weathercock on a Wren City church.

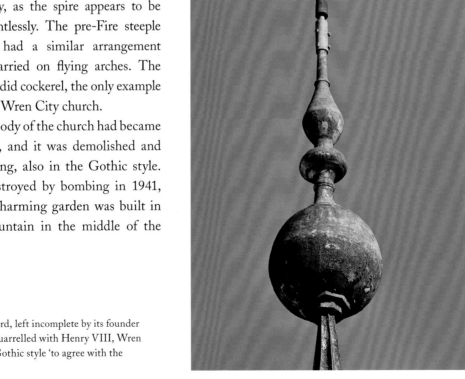

[1] At Christ Church in Oxford, left incomplete by its founder Thomas Wolsey when he quarrelled with Henry VIII, Wren built Tom Tower in a late Gothic style 'to agree with the Founder's worke'.

St Edmund King and Martyr

ST EDMUND was King of East Anglia, martyred in 869 by the Danes for his refusal to renounce Christianity. The legend is that he was executed, on the orders of Ivar the Boneless, by being tied to a tree and shot with arrows. His grave in Suffolk became a place of pilgrimage, leading to the founding of the great Abbey of Bury St Edmunds. After Charles I was beheaded in 1649, his supporters indentified him with Edmund as a royal predecessor who had suffered execution and martyrdom. The royal connection is shown in the crown on top of the elegant weathervane.

The first mention of a church here is in the second half of the twelfth century, but little is known about the medieval church destroyed in the Great Fire. Work started quickly after the Fire, and there is a drawing by Robert Hooke for the west front, which has Wren's initials in the central pediment and the words 'With his M(ajes)ties Approbation', showing that the design was approved by both Wren and King Charles II. The church was built between 1670 and 1674, and the west front faces south on to Lombard Street. Above the doorway leading into the church are three round-headed windows, with cherubs in the keystone masks underneath straight lintels. Over the middle

BELOW LEFT After the execution of Charles I in 1649, his supporters identified him with St Edmund as a royal predecessor who had also suffered execution and martyrdom. The connection with the 'King and Martyr' is shown in the crown on top of the elegant weathervane.

BELOW RIGHT Lemercier's Sorbonne Chapel has curved side buttresses decorated with garlands of flowers.

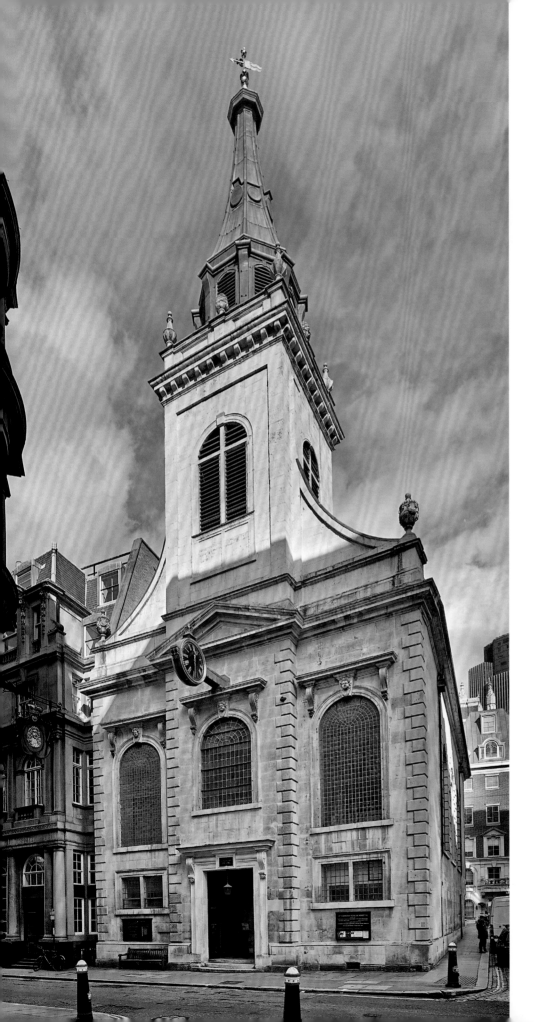

Hooke's design for
St Edmund's included
garlands of flowers
running down the sides of
the buttresses, following
the example of the
Sorbonne Chapel. These
garlands were originally
installed in the 1670s,
but removed from
St Edmund's in 1707.

OPPOSITE ABOVE St Edmund's
contains much fine
woodwork of the late
seventeenth century. The
pews have elaborate urns
decorated with garlands,
and either side of the
chancel are doorcases with
curved broken pediments.

OPPOSITE BELOW LEFT Gilded
statues of four Apostles on
the font cover.

OPPOSITE BELOW RIGHT The
Stuart coat of arms on the
organ case.

window a large clock projects into Lombard Street. The tower rises from a shallow parapet running the full width of the church, with large urns on the corners, and curved side pieces swooping up to the tower, halfway up the belfry. These curving side pieces were a feature of many Italian churches and had been illustrated by Sebastiano Serlio in 1537. In Hooke's original drawing they are edged with garlands of flowers running down their sides. This arrangement follows the precedent of Lemercier's Chapel of the Sorbonne, which Wren would have seen on his visit to Paris in 1665. These garlands, installed in the 1670s, were removed from St Edmund's in 1707. The buttresses lead the eye up to the octagonal lead-covered lantern with a trumpet-shaped spire – this used to have eight flaming urns on little platforms over the pilasters, and four more on the oval windows above, but these were all removed around 1900. The stone tower has kept its urns and pine cones on the top parapet. As was often the case, the spire was built decades after the rest of the church: it was finished by 1707. This was about twelve years after Hawksmoor had taken over from Hooke in Wren's office, and a drawing by the younger architect suggests that he was involved in replacing the simple octagonal domed lantern of Hooke's design. As Bradley and Pevsner say: 'So here, it seems, is a "Wren" church designed by two other architects, albeit under his supervision.'[1]

St Edmund's is unusual in having the altar facing north instead of the liturgically correct orientation to the east. The interior is a plain rectangle, apart from the chancel on the north. There is much original woodwork surviving in the church, with panelling running round most of the walls. Next to the chancel are two fine doorcases with broken curved pediments, and in the chancel the reredos has six panels. The central pair, in the traditional tombstone shape of the stone tablets Moses brought down from Mount Sinai, contain the Ten Commandments. These are flanked by early nineteenth century paintings of Moses and Aaron, and the outside panels show the Creed and the Lord's Prayer. The font cover, in the southwestern corner, has gilded statues of four of the Apostles. Below the organ is a fine royal coat of arms.

Although St Edmund's escaped the worst of the Blitz, it was the City church most damaged by bombing in the First World War. In July 1917 it received a direct hit in the first attack by German Gotha bombers that replaced the unwieldy Zeppelins. The roof was destroyed and had to be rebuilt, and remnants of the bomb are on display in the church, which is now the home of the London Spirituality Centre.

[1] Simon Bradley and
Nikolaus Pevsner,
*The Buildings of England:
London, The City Churches*

St James Garlickhythe

HYTHE is Old English for a harbour or landing place, so Garlickhythe means the place where garlic was landed, as confirmed by Stow's 1598 *Survey of London*: 'of old time, on the bank of the river of Thames, near to this church, garlick was usually sold.' Garlic was an important commodity in seventeenth century London. Gerard's *Herball* of 1636 praises the 'vertues' of garlic as a medicine, claiming: 'being eaten, it heateth the body extremely . . . it openeth obstructions . . . it helpeth an old cold; it killeth wormes in the body.'

The church of St James Garlickhythe is first mentioned around 1170; it was rebuilt in 1320 and destroyed in the Great Fire. The dedication is to St James the Apostle, whose tomb at Santiago de Compostela in Spain has been one of the great pilgrimage sites of Christendom since the ninth century. There is a small statue of James above the clock over the west door; the inscription on the clock gives a date of 1682, although the one we see today is a copy made in 1988 after the original was destroyed in the Blitz. Below the clock is a scallop shell, the emblem of St James. Scallop shells were once abundant on the shores of Galicia, near Santiago, and the fan-like grooves radiating from the hinge of the shell were seen as representing the different pilgrimage routes converging on the shrine; for centuries those who had completed the journey to Santiago carried a scallop shell as a symbol of their pilgrimage.

For many years the church had a petrified mummy on display in a glass case; Jimmy Garlick, as he became known, was discovered in the vaults in 1855, and thought to be the body of an adolescent, although recent investigations have shown that he was old enough to be balding and suffering from osteoarthritis. He has been reburied close to the tower.

The foundation stone for Wren's new building was laid in 1676, and the church (except for the spire) was finished in the 1684. It is unusual in having a separate chancel at the east end, where Corinthian half-columns, with capitals and fluting picked out in gold, divide the reredos into the usual sections: the Ten Commandments in the centre, flanked by the Lord's Prayer and the Creed.

ABOVE The clock over the west door.

OPPOSITE In Wren's time other buildings were up against the south wall, accounting for the blank windows. At street level the wall is flat and without transepts; higher up, the brick clerestory level is set back, except for the middle bay, which projects forward to create the effect of a transept.

OPPOSITE ABOVE LEFT
The organ is decorated
with a large scallop shell
and trumpeting angels.

OPPOSITE ABOVE RIGHT
A dove nestling on the
base of the Communion
table.

OPPOSITE BELOW The pulpit
comes from St Michael
Queenhithe, demolished
in 1876.

There was originally a large window above the reredos, but this was removed in 1815 because of structural problems. The space was filled by a painting of Christ's Ascension by the Scottish painter Andrew Geddes, grandfather of the novelist Wilkie Collins.

In the nave, Ionic columns carried on octagonal plinths create aisles to the north and south. But the spacing of the columns is wider in the middle bays, where the entablature returns to the outer walls, creating the effect of transepts. Real transepts would project beyond the side walls, but looking at the exterior from the southwest, at street level we see the south wall is flat and transept-less. Higher up, where stone gives way to brick, the clerestory level is set back, except for the middle bay which projects forward to the plane of the outer wall, as in a real transept. In placing these pseudo-transepts in the middle bay of the nave, Wren displays his spatial ingenuity: he introduces an element of Baroque central planning in what is otherwise a straightforward rectangular basilica. In Wren's original church the central north-south axis used to be more apparent: there was a ceremonial doorway on the north side, but this was removed in the nineteenth century, when circular rose windows were installed in the 'transepts' in place of Wren's longer round-headed windows. The blank windows on the south wall are explained by the fact that in Wren's time the south front was up against other buildings, although today we have a clear view thanks to the widening of Upper Thames Street in the late 1960s.

In spite of the windowless south wall light from the clerestory and north aisle windows fills the church, which is known as 'Wren's lantern'. The effect would have been less when the aisle windows were filled with Victorian stained glass. During the Blitz a 500 pound bomb hit the south east corner – luckily it didn't explode, but in the impact the Victorian glass was lost. The interior is light and airy with a flat ceiling, at forty feet the highest of the Wren churches. It is divided into three sections, which were painted with clouds in the 1920s. In 1991 a crane working on a nearby building site collapsed on to the church, damaging the ceiling and the south window, as well as the glass chandelier which had been given to the church by the Glass Sellers Company in 1963. The chandelier was restored by the Company using the original designs. Other interesting furnishings include a fine organ, probably built by 'Father Smith', installed in a gallery added to the west end in about 1714. It is decorated with a large scallop shell and trumpeting angels. A staircase of twisted balusters leads to the pulpit with elegantly carved cherubs between garlands of fruit and flowers; the pulpit comes from St Michael Queenhithe, as do the choir stalls nearby. There is more fine carving in the Communion Table, with doves nestling on the feet. There are two good ironwork sword-rests, each with lion and unicorn supporters, and capped with a crown.

Ionic columns on octagonal plinths create aisles to the north and south of the nave. But the spacing of the columns is wider in the middle bays, where the entablature returns to the outer walls, creating the effect of transepts. St James's is unusual in having a separate chancel at the east end. The painting of Christ's Ascension replaced a large window above the reredos which was removed in 1815 because of structural problems.

121

The church accounts for July 1682, when the church was reopened, record that the 'Churchwarden was to pay Sir C Wren's two clerks 40*s* [shillings] apiece for their care and kindness in hastening the building of the church, and to induce them to do the like for the more speedy finishing of the steeple.' But this had little effect, as the steeple had to wait more than thirty years before it was completed in 1717. The design, with similarities to the nearby churches of St Michael Paternoster Royal and St Stephen Walbrook, probably dates from about 1700. It has elements typical of Nicholas Hawksmoor (who was at that time working for Wren in the City Churches office), including the dynamic silhouette created by pairs of small columns, topped by ornate square urns, projecting diagonally from the square central core. This core has a louvred opening, as does the stage above, which is much shorter, and is supported by strangely squashed scrolled buttresses. Above this much taller square urns surround a slender concave section, pierced by deeply recessed elongated openings which provide shadows in the white stonework. The distinctive shape of this opening is used again by Hawksmoor at St George-in-the-East.[1] An elegant gilt weathervane completes the exuberant Baroque design.

[1] As well as at St Anne's Limehouse and St Mary Woolnoth – in these late churches the device is used in groups of three.

OPPOSITE The steeple, dating from about 1700, was probably the work of Nicholas Hawksmoor. The dynamic silhouette, with pairs of columns breaking forward diagonally from the central core, is typical of him, and can be traced back to Borromini's Sant'Ivo della Sapienza (see page 50).

RIGHT The simple weathervane is an example of the arrow and pennant design, a pattern to be found on many City churches including Christ Church Newgate Street, St Stephen Walbrook and St Vedast-alias-Foster.

St James's Piccadilly

The south side of
St James's. The
interior arrangement
of aisles and galleries
is expressed in the
two tiers of windows:
the aisles are lit by the
smaller lower windows,
the galleries by the
larger ones above.

'I think it may be found beautiful and convenient and as such, the cheapest of any Form I could invent,' Wren claimed of his design for St James's Piccadilly. Two miles outside the City of London, it was built as a new church on a new plot, as part of a development carried out by Wren's friend and patron Henry Jermyn, Earl of St Alban's (they had met in Paris in 1665). In this respect it is unlike the City churches, where Wren had to rebuild on the site of a former church destroyed in the Great Fire. It is also the only parish church he specifically claims as his design. As one of the Commissioners for the Fifty New Churches Wren set out his thoughts on the ideal form of the parish church.

Unlike Catholics, who are happy to 'hear the Murmur of the Mass, and see the Elevation of the Host', Protestants need to be able 'both to hear distinctly, and see the Preacher'. This would be impossible in a 'single Room . . . with Pews and Galleries' with a capacity of more than 2000.

He gives St James's as the model: 'I endeavoured to effect this, in building the Parish Church of St. James's, Westminster, which, I presume, is the most capacious, with these Qualifications, that hath yet been built; and yet at a solemn Time, when the Church was much crowded, I could not discern from a Gallery that 2,000 were present.'

St James's was built between 1676 and 1699, with the spire added fifteen years later. It soon became a fashionable tourist attraction, with visitors being charged for entry; John Macky writing in 1714, complained 'a Stranger cannot have a convenient Seat without paying . . . it costs one almost as dear as to see a Play. It is pity that the Worship of God should be put to Sale.' But he admitted that 'St James's church is worth seeing . . . when the fine assembly of beauties and quality come.' In October 1940 the church was severely damaged by enemy bombing, and much of the roof collapsed. It was beautifully restored by Sir Albert Richardson in the 1950s.

The exterior is of plain brick with Portland stone dressings. The east end has a large Venetian or Serlian window above a rectangular window (as it faces a narrow lane, this is easier to see from the inside). The nave has five regular bays with two tiers of windows: round-headed windows above, and smaller segmental (with a shallower curve) windows below. At the west end the tower projects beyond the nave: it has four stages and is topped by a stone balustrade. Above this is a simple but elegant spire. In April 1699 Edward Wilcox, one of Wren's carpenters, was asked by the parish to 'Prepare some pretty design' for a new spire, but it is not clear whether the spire as built was designed by Wren or Wilcox. The spire was damaged in the war and, like St Lawrence Jewry's, the modern spire is of fibreglass.

The interior is wide and spacious, with a rectangular plan of the basilica type. Square piers

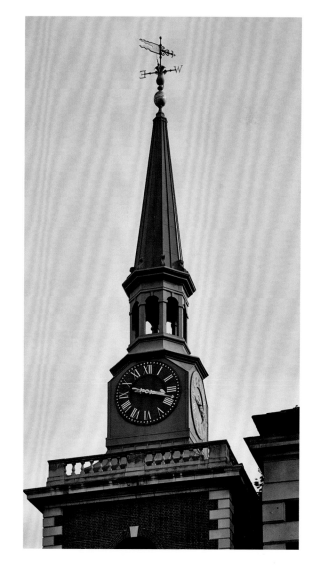

The spire was damaged in the Blitz and replaced in the 1960s by this fibreglass replica.

ABOVE Centrepiece of
the reredos by Grinling
Gibbons: the Pelican in
her Piety, feeding her
young on her own blood,
is a symbol of Christ's
Passion.

RIGHT Scallops shells, the
emblem of St James, on
the reredos.

cased in oak divide the nave from aisles on the north and south. The aisles are lit by the smaller segmental windows described above, while the larger rounded headed windows light the galleries which are supported on the piers. From these galleries rise Corinthian columns supporting the barrel-vaulted roof of the nave, and the transverse aisle vaults running north and south. The vaulting of the nave is divided into panels and is elegantly decorated with gilded plaster mouldings. The post-war restoration of these is particularly successful.

St James's has a glorious collection of carvings by Grinling Gibbons, the man who, in Horace Walpole's words, 'gave wood the loose and airy lightness of flowers'. The limewood reredos is a wonderful example of his skill. Clusters of fruit and flowers hang in pendants beside a Pelican in her Piety, a symbol of Christ's Passion as she plucks her breast to feed her young on her own blood. Above her is a virtuoso display of interlaced scrolls of leaves and branches, while doves fly by with twigs in their beaks. Swags of sea-shells include scallops, the emblem of St James the Apostle, which were worn by pilgrims who had visited his shrine at Santiago de Compostela. Gibbons also carved the organ case originally built for James II's Catholic chapel at Whitehall Palace, as well as the marble font whose base shows Adam and Eve being tempted by the Serpent in the Garden of Eden. The visionary poet and artist William Blake was baptized in this font.

BELOW LEFT One of the winged cherubs on the arches of the nave.

BELOW RIGHT Adam and Eve in the Garden of Eden, on the base of the marble font by Grinling Gibbons.

OVERLEAF In October 1940 the church was severely damaged by enemy bombing, and much of the roof collapsed. It was beautifully restored by Sir Albert Richardson in the 1950s.

St Lawrence Jewry

THERE HAS BEEN A CHURCH on this site since the twelfth century. The area, known as Jewry or Old Jewry, was a ghetto for the Jewish community until they were expelled by Edward I in 1290. St Lawrence was treasurer of the early Christian church in Rome, and in AD 258 he was martyred by being burnt alive on a gridiron. The gridiron became the saint's symbol, as shown on the weathervane which also has flames licking round the topmost finial.

The original church was destroyed in the Great Fire, and the churchwardens were among the first to make deposits with the Chamber of London to ensure St Lawrence's was high on the list for rebuilding. Their first deposit is recorded on 21 October 1670, and work started soon afterwards. A carpenter, John Longland, was paid to drive thirty piles into the ground to overcome initial problems with the stability of the foundations. But by 1676 the shell of the church was more or less complete. The south front is seven bays long: the inner five bays have tall round-headed windows, and the outer bays have circular windows above doorcases decorated with cherub heads. There are clerestory windows in the attic above. The east front is grander still. Above a high podium Wren created a composition of five bays between Corinthian pilasters and attached

BELOW LEFT The weather-vane takes the form of a gridiron, symbol of the martyrdom of St Lawrence.

BELOW RIGHT A cherub keystone over the south-west door.

OPPOSITE Wren provided St Lawrence's with grand fronts on the south and east, which formed part of the ceremonial route to the Guildhall.

ST LAWRENCE JEWRY

columns, with lavish garlands of fruit and flowers draped between the capitals. Above the middle three bays a pediment breaks into the attic storey. Wren provided these grand fronts on the south and east as part of the ceremonial route to the Guildhall, just to the north.

At the west end the plain stone tower rises to a balustrade and four corner obelisks, supporting a steeple that starts off square with four pedimented fronts, rising to an octagonal spire. The steeple, apparently made of lead-covered timber, is a fibreglass replica of the original destroyed in the war. As the ground plan shows, the western wall is at about 80 degrees to the rest of the church, or 10 degrees less than a true right angle. As a result when seen from the west there is a distinct mismatch between the stone tower which follows the west wall and the fibreglass steeple which is aligned with the main body of the church. From the south and east there is no mismatch. This is typical of Wren's pragmatism – the church was not then open to the west, and he expected that it would be seen mainly from the south and east.

The church was severely damaged by incendiary bombs in December 1940, and rebuilt by Cecil Brown in the late 1950s. The restoration is faithful to the old building, with chandeliers and woodwork designed by Brown in the spirit of the seventeenth century. In spite of the irregularity of the site the interior

BELOW The ground plan shows the skewed angle between the west wall and the rest of the church.

OPPOSITE The stone balustrade of the tower is at an angle compared to the horizontal lines of the steeple above, reflecting the skewed angle of the west wall.

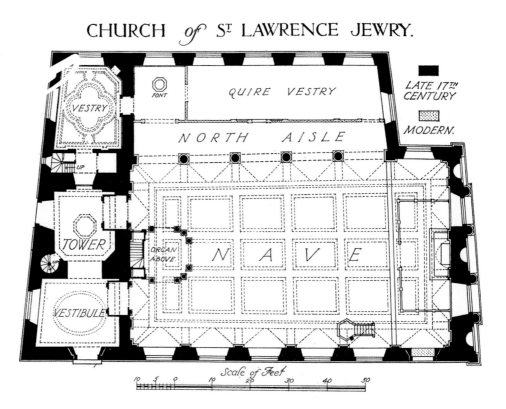

CHURCH *of* S^T LAWRENCE JEWRY.

THE CHURCHES 1666–1711

ABOVE The double organ, one of the largest in the City churches.

OPPOSITE The church suffered severe damage in the Blitz, and was rebuilt by Cecil Brown in the late 1950s. The restoration is faithful to the old building, with chandeliers and woodwork designed by Brown in the spirit of the seventeenth century. Wren's gallery over the north aisle had been removed in the 1860s; Brown installed a wooden screen to separate the aisle from the nave.

is a plain rectangle, except for a single aisle on the north, divided from the nave by four giant Corinthian columns with gilded capitals. The Corinthian order is carried round the rest of the church by pilasters. Wren's original gallery in the north aisle was removed by Blomfield in the 1860s. In Brown's rebuilding the gallery was not replaced; instead the spaces between the columns are filled by a carved screen of smaller Corinthian columns of dark oak, above which angels raise their outstretched wings (similar to the eagle's wings on the pulpit at St Margaret Lothbury, originally from All Hallows the Great, see pages 146–7). The clerestory windows light a large flat ceiling, divided into recessed panels. At the west end is an impressive double organ, befitting St Lawrence's status as the official church of the Corporation of London. The organ was made in 2001 by the German firm of Johannes Klais Orgelbau, and installed in a case made in 1957, following the style of the seventeenth century original by Renatus Harris. Also from the 1950s is the complete sequence of windows by Christopher Webb, whose designs have central panels depicting saints, surrounded by large areas of plain glass allowing natural light to fill the church. One shows St Lawrence with a bag of money (symbolizing his position as Treasurer of the early church) hanging from his left hand, while his right hand rests on his gridiron. The two windows at the east end show St Catherine on the south, and St Paul (the City's patron saint) on the north: he is leaning on a sword, the symbol of the City of London. Beneath him an angel holds the bombed out church, with its steeple missing. The angel below St Catherine is holding the restored church with the steeple back in place. Both these windows are set off-centre within their bays, another result of the site's irregularity; like the west wall, the east wall is not set perfectly square. As a result the outside wall containing the windows is not parallel to the interior wall – the off-centre placing helps to disguise this, while a the same time having the optical effect of making the end wall seem much thicker than it really is.

RIGHT 1950s window by Christopher Webb shows St Lawrence with a purse hanging from one hand, while the other rests on a gridiron, the emblem of his martyrdom.

RIGHT 1950s window by Christopher Webb shows St Lawrence with a purse hanging from one hand, while the other rests on a gridiron, the emblem of his martyrdom.

OPPOSITE 1950s window by Christopher Webb shows St Paul leaning on a sword, symbol of the City of London. Below him an angel holds the bombed-out church, missing its steeple. The window is off-centre within the opening, with the optical effect of making the end wall seem much thicker than it really is.

St Magnus the Martyr

The small pedimented doorway was once in the centre of the north front, which has been unbalanced by losing two bays on the right hand side, where a tree now stands.

THE MAGNUS OF THE DEDICATION is probably the saintly Magnus Earl of Orkney, who was murdered by his cousin Haakon on the island of Egilsay in 1116 and canonized in 1135. There has been a church here since the mid-twelfth century, and its various names 'St Magnus towards London Bridge' and 'Sanctus Magnus ad Pontem' refer to its position at the northern bridgehead of Old London Bridge, until the mid-eighteenth century the only bridge over the Thames in London. In the 1620s, according to Seymour's *Survey* of 1733, 'The old Church of St Magnus had 500 pounds laid out in the Repairs thereof . . . and was richly beautified.' It was one of the first churches to be destroyed in the Great Fire, which started in nearby Pudding Lane. The parish quickly started rebuilding the church on their own account. In 1670 the Rebuilding Act allowed the Commissioners to take over the work; this now became the responsibility of Christopher Wren's office, although it is not clear who provided the plans. The design seems to have reused the original south wall, and possibly the foundations of the original columns or piers in the nave. The north front facing Lower Thames Street has been substantially altered: it was originally nine bays long with the three central bays, marked by stone quoins, breaking forward to frame a large doorway under a three-bay pediment. The north doorway has since been closed, the pediment has gone, and the round-headed windows have been replaced by circular ones. The two western bays were demolished in 1762 when London Bridge was widened, and a passageway for pedestrians was cut through the base of the tower. The result leaves the north front unbalanced as the three bays which were once central are no longer so: to the east there are three more bays, while to the west there is only one.

Work on the main body of the church, and the tower up to a height of about 60 feet, was complete by 1678. As usual, work on the upper stages of the tower was delayed, and in 1697 the parish pressed Wren and the Commission to complete the work. Parish records in the Guildhall Library show a shady payment of forty guineas 'properly disposed of for Secrett Services for the benefitt of the Parish, & in procuring the steeple to be finished'. Another nine years passed before it was completed in 1706. A large clock dating from about this time projects out from the west face of the tower; above this are two more stages, the first plain, the second with coupled pilasters and louvred bell-openings, capped by a parapet with a balustrade and flaming urns. The steeple is an octagonal lantern, with an arcade running between Corinthian pilasters; above this is a leaded octagonal dome with dormer windows set into the cardinal faces, topped by another open arcade and a tapering spirelet. The design is similar to the

ABOVE The tower of the Jesuit church in Antwerp, now dedicated to St Charles Borromeo.

OPPOSITE Modelled on Antwerp's Jesuit church, St Magnus has a square tower rising to an octagonal section with round-headed openings; above this a domed section leads to a spire.

tower of the Jesuit church of St Charles Borromeo in Antwerp, built between 1615 and 1624. Peter Paul Rubens was closely involved in the building of St Charles Borromeo, and may have helped design the tower. In 1622 Rubens wrote in praise of the new style of classical architecture as adding to 'the great splendour and beautification of our country; as may be seen in the famous temples recently erected by the venerable Society of Jesus in the cities of Brussels and Antwerp'. A drawing of the Antwerp tower was in Wren's office, and St Magnus's tower is probably the work of Robert Hooke.

The interior has aisles on the north and south, divided from the nave by tall fluted Ionic columns on high hexagonal bases. The nave has a semicircular barrel vault lit by oval clerestory windows. Early drawings by Wren show these windows as either square or with curved tops, so the oval windows are 'almost certainly a later introduction'.[1] St Magnus has many fine furnishings which survived the war, including a large two-storey reredos with paintings of Moses and Aaron on the lower section, and in the upper stage a circular painting of winged cherubs below the Holy Ghost in the form of a dove. At the west end is a gallery with an organ made by the Jordan family in about 1712; the organ case is lavishly decorated with musical instruments. The candlesticks on the gallery have brass crowns above Queen Anne's cypher, AR, for Anna Regina. St Magnus escaped serious damage during the Blitz, although in 1940 a bomb blew out all the windows. These were repaired in the 1950s, when the circular windows of the north wall were filled with stained glass by Alfred Wilkinson. St Magnus is the Guild Church of the nearby Fishmongers' Company, and one of Wilkinson's windows shows their coat of arms, which includes a merman carrying a sword, and a bare-breasted mermaid holding a mirror.

[1] Simon Bradley and Nikolaus Pevsner, *The Buildings of England: London, The City Churches*

THE CHURCHES 1666–1711

OPPOSITE The interior has aisles on the north and south, divided from the nave by tall fluted Ionic columns on high hexagonal plinths. The barrel-vaulted ceiling is lit by oval clerestory windows.

ABOVE LEFT A candlestick with Queen Anne's cypher, AR, for Anna Regina.

ABOVE RIGHT The organ case, lavishly decorated with musical instruments, was made in about 1712.

LEFT The Fishmongers' coat of arms: three crowned dolphins and two pairs of stockfish on a shield, between a merman carrying a sword and a bare-breasted mermaid holding a mirror.

St Margaret Lothbury

THE DEDICATION HERE is to Saint Margaret of Antioch, who was martyred in AD 304. The Roman governor of the city wanted to marry her, but she refused to break her vow of virginity and was cruelly put to death, having survived an encounter with Satan in the form of a dragon. Rather surprisingly she is regarded by some as the patron saint of pregnancy, and although her historical existence has been questioned there are over 250 churches dedicated to her in England.

St Margaret's stands in Lothbury, close to the Bank of England. The first mention of a church here is in the late twelfth century; this was enlarged and rebuilt in the fifteenth century, and again in the early seventeenth century, but destroyed in the Great Fire. Rebuilding started in the 1680s, but the body of the church was not completed until 1692. The tower and steeple were finished in 1700. The entrance is on the south side through a fine doorway with a pediment above free-standing columns. The plain tower rises through three more stages to a lead-covered spire consisting of a square dome supporting a simple panelled obelisk. Paul Jeffery attributes the design to Hooke: 'there is no difficulty in recognising his hand in the designs for St Margaret.'[1]

The interior has Corinthian pilasters running round the walls, with two Corinthian columns between the nave and the single south aisle. Round clerestory windows pierce the coving to light the flat ceiling with three circular plasterwork panels. St Margaret's has some of the finest furnishings of any of the City churches. There is a beautifully ornate screen, originally from All Hallows the Great (demolished in 1894); this is an unusual feature in a Wren church, the only other example being the plainer screen at St Peter upon Cornhill. Presumably in these cases the parish wanted a screen: liturgically Wren would have preferred not to make a division between the nave and the chancel, concerned as he was for 'all to hear the Service, and both to hear distinctly, and see the Preacher' (see page 125). The All Hallows screen is divided into nine sections by tapering columns, formed by interlocking barley-sugar balusters which allow us to see through the openwork. The central section has more openwork carvings of foliage and flowers on the pierced pilasters, these support the lion and the unicorn of the royal arms in a broken pediment above an eagle. Also from All Hallows is the equally exuberant tester above the pulpit, with cherubs frolicking round the canopy between garlands of fruit and flowers and an eagle with outstretched wings.

The original fittings of St Margaret's include the openwork interlocking balusters in the Communion Rails and the reredos. This has four Corinthian columns dividing it into three sections; the two outer sections are topped by curved segmental pediments and flaming urns, with scrolly brackets on the sides.

[1] Paul Jeffery:
*The City Churches of
Sir Christopher Wren*

LEFT A delicate lead-covered spire has a tapering obelisk above a square dome. At the base of the tower a fine pedimented doorway provides the entrance from Lothbury. It was characteristic of London's pre-Fire churches for the main entrance to be through the tower rather than a distinct porch, a tradition surviving here at St Margaret and also at St Martin-within-Ludgate.

OVERLEAF St Margaret's has some of the finest furnishings of any of the City churches. There is an exuberant tester with dancing cherubs and a beautifully ornate screen, both originally from All Hallows the Great (demolished in 1894).

As usual, the outer sections contain the Lord's Prayer and the Creed, while the inner section has the Ten Commandments. Either side of the reredos are large paintings of Moses and Aaron, originally from the nearby Christopher-le-Stocks, the first of the Wren churches to be demolished. It was removed in 1782 to make way for an extension to the Bank of England, and to deny rioters a platform from which they could attack the Bank, as happened in the Gordon Riots of 1780.

The marble font comes from St Olave Old Jewry. Although there is no documentary evidence for his involvement, the style is similar to that of the font by Grinling Gibbons at St James's Piccadilly. It has exquisite carving, with cherubs' heads between low-relief panels depicting biblical scenes, including the Baptism of the Eunuch, showing an elaborate chariot being pulled by two horses, while St Philip baptizes the Eunuch in a shallow pond.

The reredos has curved broken pediments capped with flaming urns; on either side are large paintings of Moses and Aaron.

ABOVE LEFT A door frame decorated with a garland of flowers and fruit.

ABOVE RIGHT Above the ornate screen is a finely carved coat of arms of the Stuart dynasty. The screen, which comes from All Hallows the Great, was carved in the Flemish style by Woodruffe and Thornton.

LEFT The marble font, in the style of Grinling Gibbons, shows the Baptism of the Eunuch.

St Margaret Pattens

LIKE ITS NAMESAKE in Lothbury, this church is dedicated to Saint Margaret of Antioch. According to Stow's *Survey*, the name St Margaret Pattens refers to the pattens made locally; these were wooden overshoes which helped to keep the wearer above the mud and filth of medieval streets. The church has long been associated with the Worshipful Company of Pattenmakers, whose charitable activities today include the provision of orthopaedic shoes for servicemen injured in the line of duty.

In 1067 there was a small wooden church here; in 1538 this was replaced by a stone building which was destroyed in the Great Fire. In spite of repeated requests to Wren from the churchwardens 'to put him in mind of building the church', rebuilding did not start until 1684. On the outside of the north wall are two lead rainwater hoppers bearing the date 1685. The main body of the church was finished in 1688, but a further ten years passed before work on the tower and spire was resumed in 1698, and finished in 1702.

The steeple is very striking: a lead-covered octagonal spire rises like a needle to an elegant pennant weathervane at a height of about 200 feet. Each of the cardinal faces has three small louvred openings: an oval, a circle and a pedimented rectangle. Above the middle circular openings are brackets that used to support small urns, now sadly gone. Hawksmoor seems to have been involved in building the spire, as the churchwardens' accounts record several payments to 'Sir Christopher Wren's clerk', the position he held at the time. The needle-like profile soaring into the sky is echoed in the four stone obelisks at the base of the spire; together they form a dramatic silhouette typical of Hawksmoor and more than a match for the tall modern buildings surrounding it. Hawksmoor may have had in mind the pyramids on the tomb of Lars Porsenna, one of the lost buildings of antiquity which also interested Hooke and Wren. Hooke's diary of 1677 says he 'discoursed with him [Wren] long of Porsenna's tomb'. Wren discusses it in one of his *Tracts on Architecture*, calling it a 'Stupendous Fabrick' and he uses it as a model for a funeral monument to Queen Mary. In 1646 John Greaves illustrated his interpretation of Porsenna's tomb in his book *Pyramidographia: or a description of the pyramids in Egypt*, and quotes the account of it 'in M. Varro's own words' as 'a monument of square stone . . . upon this square there stand five Pyramids, four in the angles, and one in the middle.'[1] This is a good description of the spire of St Margaret's, allowing for the difference in height between the main spire and the corner obelisks.

[1] Greaves says Varro's account comes down to us through Pliny the Elder: 'Supra id quadratum pyramides stant quinque, quatuor in angulis, & in medio una.'

OPPOSITE Porsenna's
tomb, from Greaves's
Pyramidographia. The
five obelisks, one in the
middle and the others
on the corners, may
have been the source for
Hawksmoor's design for
St Margaret's steeple.

LEFT The needle-like
spire rises to some 200
feet, and is echoed in
the four obelisks at its
base. The accounts show
several payments to
Hawksmoor, suggesting
he was responsible for
the design.

ABOVE The interior is a plain rectangle, except for a shallow chancel at the east end and an aisle and gallery on the north side.

RIGHT The gallery on the north side was enclosed and glazed over in the 1950s to provide office space.

The interior is a plain rectangle, except for a shallow chancel at the east end, and an aisle and gallery on the north side. These are separated from the nave by Corinthian columns, with matching Corinthian pilasters elsewhere. A staircase cuts across the aisle to provide access to the gallery. There is also a gallery beneath the organ at the west end. Circular clerestory windows pierce the coving to light the large flat ceiling, while artificial light is provided by the modern but traditional chandeliers recently donated by the Pattenmakers and Basketmakers Companies. The finely carved reredos set into the shallow chancel has fluted Corinthian columns and gilded reliefs of plants and flowers. Between the columns is a painting by the Italian Baroque artist Carlo Maratta, showing Christ with ministering angels in Gethsemane. There is much fine woodwork in the church, including the churchwardens' pews at the west end, one inscribed with the date 1686. The canopies are carried on slender brass columns, and below these are elegantly carved openwork friezes.

A churchwardens' pew at the west end. Once a regular feature of the City churches, these special pews only survive at St Margaret's. They were reserved for the use of churchwardens, lay officials of the parish vestry.

St Martin's faces on to Ludgate, with three doors at street level, beneath three tall round-headed windows. Above the outer windows are large scrolly buttresses, derived from Italian and French models.

St Martin-within-Ludgate

St Martin-within-Ludgate is dedicated to St Martin of Tours, a soldier in the Roman army who cut his cloak in two with his sword to share it with a freezing beggar. He became a patron saint of travellers, and churches near city gates are often dedicated to him. As the name implies, this church stood close to Ludgate, the westernmost gate in London Wall. Writing in the twelfth century, the unreliable Geoffrey of Monmouth says the gate was named after King Lud, a king of Britain who fortified London in pre-Roman times and was buried here. A more likely explanation is that the name derives either from 'floodgate', or from 'hlid-geat', the Old English name for a swing gate. Ludgate was rebuilt at various times before being removed, along with the other City gates, in 1760.

There has been a church here since at least 1174; rebuilt in 1437 the medieval church was destroyed in the Great Fire of 1666. The ruins were not removed for seven years, and it was another four years before rebuilding began in 1677, taking about ten years to complete. Robert Hooke may have been responsible for the design, as his diary mentions thirty-one visits to the site. The south front, built of Portland stone, faces Ludgate Hill: at street level it is three bays wide, with three doorways below large windows with curved tops. The stage above is a square bell tower, with louvred openings beneath garlands of fruit and flowers, similar to St Benet Paul's Wharf. The transition from the lower three bays to the single bay above is softened by large volutes, or scrolled buttresses, in a style typical of Italian church facades, such as Santa Maria Novella in Florence and Giacomo della Porta's influential Gesú in Rome. They are also very similar to those at Lemercier's façade of the Sorbonne in Paris which Wren would have seen during his visit in 1665. There are smaller volutes on the next stage where it narrows to support an octagonal spire of lead-covered timber. This starts with a concave domed section, like an octagonal bell; above this an iron balcony leads to an open arcade, connected by yet more volutes to a tall spirelet. Like the spire of the nearby St Augustine, it can be seen against St Paul's, and its tall tapering outline forms an elegant foil to the rotundity of the cathedral's dome (see page 60).

The design of St Martin's was clearly influenced by Giacomo della Porta's church of the Gesú in Rome (1573–5). St Martin's side buttresses have scrolls very similar to those of the Gesú; they even have the same recessed panel, shaped like a keystone. The three doors at street level are also common to both churches.

Four large Composite
columns create a Greek
cross within the square
body of the church.
The octagonal plinths of
the columns are encased
by panelling, echoed in
the wainscoting round
the walls. In the 1890s
the level of the chancel
was raised, and it is now
approached by a series
of steps. At the same
time the enclosed box
pews were cut down and
converted to open pews.

The four columns support a roof with barrel vaults which intersect to create groin vaulting.

The street doors open into a lobby or vestibule below a gallery, which was converted in 2012 to accommodate church offices and a counselling centre. The vestibule leads into the church proper through three lavishly carved wooden doorcases; the central one has cherubs holding a crown and floral garlands. As the site is longer on the north-south axis the natural orientation would be to the north, but the space taken by the vestibule leaves a square which could therefore be oriented to the east, as required by the Anglican liturgy. The design is a square containing a Greek cross defined by four large free-standing Composite columns; these support a roof with cross barrel vaulting and a large central plaster rose (St Anne and St Agnes, built in the same period, has a similar 'cross in a square' design; see page 84). In the chancel is an elegantly carved and gilded reredos, with flat pilasters and scrolled volutes (recalling the exterior) between the outer and central sections. The pulpit has inlaid geometric panels surrounded by garlands of fruits and flowers; the pulpit stairs have very slender twisted balusters.

St Martin's escaped serious damage in the war, and with its fine furnishing and original wainscoting, it retains more of the feel of the late seventeenth century than many City churches, and is a joy to visit.

RIGHT A carved wooden doorcase with cherubs holding a crown and floral garlands.

BELOW LEFT The glorious 1770s brass chandelier, still lit by candles, was brought here from the Cathedral of St Vincent in the West Indies.

BELOW RIGHT The pulpit is typical of the late seventeenth century, with oval marquetry panels between garlands of leaves and flowers.

St Mary Abchurch

TUCKED AWAY down Abchurch Lane, north of Cannon Street, is Abchurch Yard, a small courtyard that was once the burial ground and churchyard of St Mary Abchurch. The derivation of the name Abchurch is unclear, but there was a church here in the late twelfth century. The medieval church, restored in 1611, was destroyed in the Great Fire. Wren began rebuilding St Mary's fifteen years later in 1681, and it was finished within five or six years.

Looking across Abchurch Yard, paved with circular patterns of inlaid stones and cobbles in 1877, we see the south front: an exterior of warm red brick with stone quoins and dressings. A large central window stands between pairs of smaller windows, the upper ones are circular like portholes. The door to the church is on the left, beneath the western windows. Above the brick parapet is a hipped roof with an oval dormer window jutting forward. There is a tower on the north-west corner, also of brick with stone dressings. This leads to a square lead-covered ogee dome, and an open lantern beneath an elegant tapering spire. The weathervane, a gilded pelican feeding her young with her own blood, was removed in 1764 and is now inside the church.

An aerial view shows the hipped roof has oval dormer windows on all four sides. Entering the church we see why: the hipped roof contains a dome, lit by these windows. Unlike Wren's other domes at St Stephen Walbrook and St Mary-at-Hill, which are supported on columns set in the nave, here the dome rises from a cornice supported on eight arches, created by an ingenious system of groin vaults and pendentives springing directly from the external walls, with flat Corinthian capitals serving as corbels. The only free-standing column is on the west side, and this is as much to support the organ gallery as the dome. The dome covers almost all the internal space, and the effect is to make this small church seem much larger than it really is. The dome is unique amongst the City churches in being painted; the work was carried out in about 1708 by William Snow. It shows the Hebrew name of God against a sun surrounded by sunbeams, clouds and a heavenly choir of angels. A painted *trompe l'œil* cornice runs between the tops of the window openings; below this are seated female figures, representing the Virtues. On the left of the east window, above the reredos, is Hope with an anchor, while Charity suckles an infant on the right.

OPPOSITE The south front of warm red brick with stone quoins and window surrounds, seen across Abchurch Yard (which was paved with circular patterns of inlaid stones and cobbles in 1877).

BELOW The former weathervane, a Pelican in her Piety, is now inside the church.

The dome rises from a
cornice supported on
eight arches; the painting
was carried out in about
1708 by William Snow.

162

The Rector and Field Marshal Lord Wavell inspect some carving damaged during the Blitz.

The magnificent reredos is the only authenticated piece of carving by Grinling Gibbons in all the City churches; in the vestry accounts for 1686 there is a bill in his handwriting, demanding payment for his work on the 'olter pees'. Apparently not all the parishioners were happy with what he had provided, as Gibbons sees the need to insist that it was 'folle Anof of work'.[1] The carving includes festoons of garlands of fruit and flowers including corn, hops, grapes, apples, pears and pea pods. The top is decorated with four flaming urns, perhaps symbolizing the Great Fire, and in the middle two cherubs hold the emblem of the Order of the Garter, inscribed 'HONI SOIT QUI MAL Y PENSE' and encircling the royal cypher AR, standing for Anna Regina. So this must be a later addition, as Queen Anne did not come to the throne until 1702, sixteen years after the date of Gibbons's bill. Several authorities, including Bradley and Pevsner as well as the *Encyclopaedia of London*, say the altarpiece was smashed into two thousand pieces in the Blitz and reassembled after the war. Recently a report by the wartime Rector, the splendidly named Rev Reginald Merac LaPorte-Payne, has come to light telling a different story. During an attack on the second night of the Blitz, 8 September 1940, the windows were blown out and a hole made in the domed ceiling. Before further bombardments could cause more damage the reredos and 'other treasures' were removed to safety. In the church archives is a photograph of the Rector and Field-Marshal Lord Wavell inspecting some damaged carving; the date isn't recorded, but it was perhaps after the first attack, leading to the decision to move the reredos out of harm's way. Although it's not apparent today, by the end of the war St Mary's had been badly damaged by enemy bombing; it suffered at least six indirect hits, including three V-1 flying bombs in the final year of the war. It was repaired between 1945 and 1957, including the restoration of the dome painting.

St Mary's is fortunate in having many of its original furnishings, which the Victorian alterations carried out by Edward l'Anson in the 1870s (when the courtyard was paved), left largely unchanged. In front of the reredos is a small Communion Table, made in 1675 for the 'tabernacle', the temporary wooden church which had to serve the parishioners until the church was rebuilt after the Fire. Costing £265, St Mary's tabernacle was one of the more expensive, compared to some which cost as little as £50.

The 1685 pulpit is the work of William Grey and has kept its original sounding board, or tester, supported on a square Ionic pillar.

[1] Signe Hoffos in *City Events published by the Friends of the City Churches, Feb 2014.* This also tells the story of the survival of the reredos in the war.

ABOVE Grinling Gibbons's superb altarpiece: there is a bill in his handwriting for the 'olter pees'.

LEFT The underside of the tester is inlaid with geometric marquetry, while the side panels with their wavy tops are filled with elegant carving of fruit and flowers. In one panel the Holy Ghost is represented in the form of a dove.

St Mary Aldermary

THE NAME ALDERMARY probably means the Elder Mary, suggesting this was the oldest of the seven City churches dedicated to St Mary the Virgin. First mentioned in the late eleventh century, the Gothic church and tower were not finished until 1626. St Mary's was badly damaged in the Great Fire, but enough of the building was left for the local parish to decide the church should be repaired rather than totally rebuilt. At first they undertook the work at their own expense; but in 1675 the Commissioners for rebuilding the City Churches took over the financing, and Wren's office became responsible for the work. In 1677 the parish received a large bequest from Henry Rogers, a resident of Westminster. After an unsuccessful legal challenge from disappointed relatives, his estate paid £5000 into the Chamber of London to pay for the repairs and rebuilding. St Mary's reopened in 1682, having been rebuilt in the Gothic style of the original, and incorporating much of the pre-Fire structure.

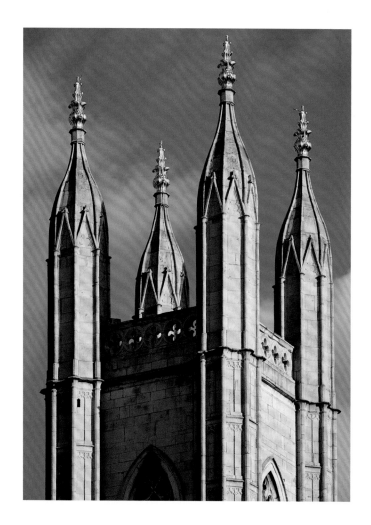

The south-west tower was extensively rebuilt in 1701–4, after the original tower had been repaired in the 1670s. It may incorporate some of the earlier work, such as the polygonal corner buttresses divided into small panels, but the distinctive pinnacles are probably the work of William Dickinson, who by 1701 had become one of Wren's assistants at the City churches office. Today the view of the church from the south and east owes a lot to the refacing in stone carried out in 1876–7 by Charles Innes, after the opening of Queen Victoria Street had exposed this view.

LEFT The Gothic pinnacles attributed to William Dickinson, Wren's assistant who also worked on the Gothic tower of St Michael on Cornhill. Their distinctive shape follows that of an ogee, or ogival arch.

OPPOSITE View from the south and east showing Wren and Dickinson's Gothic tower, with the body of the church as refaced in stone in 1876-7 by Charles Innes. His alterations include the octagonal corner buttresses on the east end.

RIGHT Wren's Gothic interior has elegant piers between the nave and the aisles. The three-light windows of the clerestory and aisles have the typical flattened profile of the Perpendicular phase of English Gothic.

OPPOSITE The ceiling is an extravaganza of Perpendicular Gothic fan vaulting, made from moulded plasterwork.

THE CHURCHES 1666–1711

The chancel ceiling is a barrel vault divided into small panels all picked out in red, black and gold. My photograph, taken looking straight up into the chancel roof, shows the irregular plan, with the east wall at a skewed angle to the rest of the church.

St Mary's is the only surviving City church interior by Wren in the late Gothic Perpendicular style, a choice probably dictated by the opportunity to reuse some of the surviving fabric, as at St Alban Wood Street. The plan follows the pre-Fire layout of six bays, divided into nave and aisles by elegant piers rising to broad Tudor or flattened pointed arches. The three light windows of the clerestory and aisles have the same profile, typical of the Perpendicular phase of English Gothic. But Wren gives the spandrels between the arches a very different character, with their Baroque scrolls enclosing the coats of arms of Henry Rogers and the Archbishop of Canterbury. The ceiling is an extravaganza of Gothic fan vaulting of moulded plasterwork, in the aisles as well as the nave. Wren's fan vaulting has large central roundels, similar to the shallow saucer domes he uses in the nave and aisles of St Paul's. In genuine Perpendicular Gothic, as at King's College Cambridge, fan vaulting serves a structural as well as a decorative function, but here it is purely decorative. At the east end, above the chancel,

THE CHURCHES 1666–1711

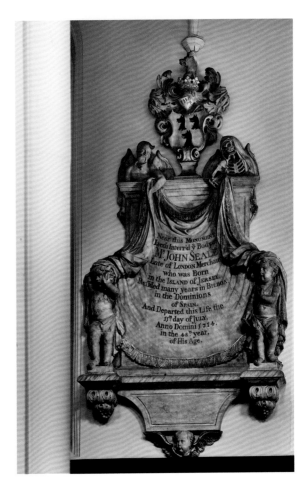

he changes the vaulting to a barrel vault divided into small ogival panels and a large central oval, all picked out in red black and gold. Looking up at the chancel roof shows it is severely skewed: the east wall is far from being at a true right angle to the north and south walls.

Many of the original furnishings, including the reredos, altar rails, pews, screens and stalls were removed and replaced with Gothic substitutes during the 1870s restoration. One of the few original fittings to survive is a sword rest of 1682; this example in oak is unique amongst Wren's City churches: elsewhere they are of wrought iron. Above a lion's head is the emblem of the Order of the Garter flanked by fluttering cherubs holding a crown, all beautifully carved. In the north aisle is a monument to Mr John Seale, who died in 1714, with the inscription written on a draped curtain held up by a bearded and winged Father Time and a skeletal figure of Death.

ABOVE LEFT The oak sword rest of 1682.

ABOVE RIGHT John Seale's monument, with the inscription on a draped curtain held up by Father Time and Death.

St Mary-at-Hill

THE ENTRANCE to St Mary-at-Hill is tucked away in Lovat Lane, an ancient cobbled alleyway that gives a good impression of what many of the narrow streets of the City were like before the Great Fire. Since at least the late eleventh century there has been a church on this site, serving the parish of Billingsgate with its bustling fish market. The Fire, which started in nearby Pudding Lane, destroyed the medieval church except for some of the walls and parts of the west tower. The parish was the first to make the deposit of £500 to the Chamber of London under the scheme for allocating priority for church rebuilding, and St Mary's was also one of the first to be rebuilt, being completed by 1674. Wren and Hooke reused as much of the surviving work as possible, and extended the building to the east. This new front, on the street called St Mary at Hill, originally had three windows, although the central one has since been blocked. There is a large projecting double-faced clock on the south-east corner. The new skyscraper known as the Walkie-Talkie towers above the church.

Along with St Mary Abchurch and St Stephen Walbrook, this is one of the three surviving churches Wren built with a dome, a form of church design he was particularly interested in and was determined to use at St Paul's Cathedral. Although the dome of St Paul's took decades to complete, St Mary-at-Hill was

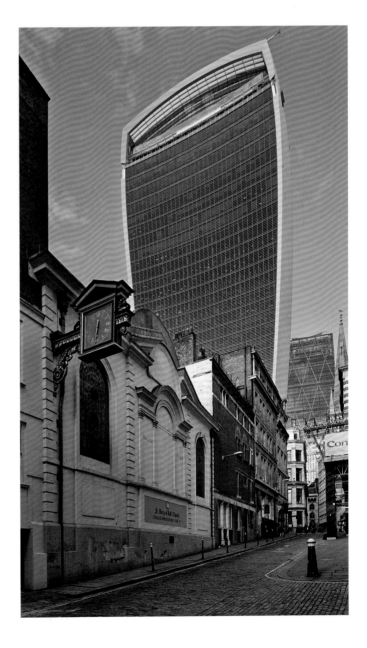

OPPOSITE The west entrance of St Mary-at-Hill is through the brick tower in Lovat Lane, a narrow alleyway in the east of the City.

RIGHT The east front of St Mary-at-Hill, with its large clock projecting into the street, is dwarfed by the Walkie-Talkie skyscraper.

RIGHT The cross-in-square plan shows clearly in this bird's-eye view, with the lantern in the centre above the dome.

OPPOSITE The bird's-eye view inverted: the inside of the dome seen from below. The decorative plasterwork was added in the 1820s by James Savage, who also inserted windows into the barrel vault of the chancel (at the bottom of the picture).

[1] Paul Jeffery: *The City Churches of Sir Christopher Wren*

finished at about the same time as the domed Great Model. Originally a large lantern rose above a shallow saucer dome, resting on four fluted columns. The dome rises from four arches, which in turn rest on four fluted columns, to form a cross-in-square design (technically a 'quincunx' plan, as in the five spot of six-sided dice). Other examples of the cross-in-square design are St Martin Ludgate and St Anne and St Agnes, but only St Mary combines this with a dome. In the 1820s James Savage made extensive alterations to the church, including the dome we see today. Paul Jeffery writes: 'The intersecting barrel vaulting with semicircular dome, described in some books as by Wren, was by Savage.'[1] Savage installed the ornate plasterwork and the cupola above the dome, as well as the windows cutting through the barrel vault in the chancel. He also replaced doors on the north and south axes with metal-framed round-headed windows and coloured glass borders, as shown in the north transept. Today the only entrance is through the yellow brick west tower, rebuilt by George Gwilt in the 1780s.

THE CHURCHES 1666–1711

I photographed the interior before the fire of 1988 when the pews, were still in place and the reredos filled the chancel.

[2] John Betjeman: *The City of London Churches*

The interior seventeenth-century furnishings, including reredos, pulpit and box pews, were by William Cleere. These were added to as part of the nineteenth-century alterations by William Gibbs Rogers (who made a special study of the work of Grinling Gibbons) and all these were of very high quality. The church escaped serious damage in the Blitz, and John Betjeman described it as 'the least spoiled and the most gorgeous interior in the City, all the more exciting by being hidden away among cobbled alleys'.[2] But this

THE CHURCHES 1666–1711

was before a disastrous fire in 1988 which seriously damaged the roof. Although the pulpit, reredos and some of the box pews were undamaged, they were removed so the roof and dome could be repaired, and have been in storage ever since. Only the organ and the wainscoting of the original woodwork remain to show how the church used to look. I was lucky enough to photograph the interior in 1987, so my views here show the church before and after the fire.

The interior in 2015, with the woodwork removed after the fire of 1988. The bases of the columns are bare and a large curtain hangs in place of the reredos.

THE CHURCHES 1666–1711

The organ was installed by William Hill in 1848, and the case carved by Gibbs Rogers in the late Stuart style. Three hundred years earlier, in the 1530s, the organist here was the great Renaissance composer Thomas Tallis.

In the lobby to the north of the entrance porch is an unusual Resurrection Panel: a seventeenth-century relief carving of the Last Judgement. A (headless) figure of Christ waves a banner as he tramples Satan, shown with gigantic claws. Below them the winged figure of the Archangel Michael helps the dead climb out of their tombs.

St Mary's connection with the fish market at Billingsgate continues with an annual festival celebrating the Harvest of the Sea. Wilson Carlile, the Evangelist and founder of the Church Army, was the Rector between 1892 and 1926 – a colourful character who played his trombone from the pulpit and encouraged the fish porters of Billingsgate to come to the church to take part in the services.

OPPOSITE William Hill's organ of 1848. In the fire of 1988 the barrel-vaulted ceiling above the organ collapsed; photographs taken after the fire show the organ case was badly damaged. It was fully restored in 2000 by the London firm of Mander Organs.

ABOVE The dead climb out of their tombs on the Resurrection Panel.

St Mary-le-Bow, the first of the City church steeples to be rebuilt, is also the most complex. On the corners of the square tower are finials of curved strapwork (resembling an archery bow, as in the church's name), topped by flaming urns. The next section is circular, with a central core surrounded by a ring of sixteen free-standing Corinthian columns. These support a balustrade and more bow-like scrolls leading to the next stage. Here the plan reverts from circular to square with a section of twelve smaller Composite columns, of dark granite. The spire, a slender obelisk, is topped by a splendid dragon weathervane.

St Mary-le-Bow

St Mary-le-Bow's steeple, housing the famous Bow Bells, was the first to be built by Wren after the Great Fire. The steeple cost £7,388, almost as much as the £8,033 spent on the rest of the church. The medieval name of the church was Mary atte Bowe; it was also known as St Mary Arcubus – St Mary of the Arches – which probably comes from the arches in the eleventh-century crypt, where they can still be seen. The rest of the church was destroyed in the Great Fire of 1666, and rebuilt by Wren between 1670 and 1675, with the tower taking until 1680. Early attempts to rebuild the old tower, much of which had survived the Fire, were abandoned when the Rebuilding Commissioners found that there were no 'hopes of making it firme' and the 'foundacons are naught, and the Core of the Wall so Crushed and weakened that . . . the Tower will be very dangerous.'[1] So a new site for the tower was chosen to the north of the old one. According to *Parentalia*, when the foundations were dug down to 18 feet Wren was surprised to find an old Roman causeway 4 feet thick, which he used to provide a firm basis for the new structure. The tower went through a number of versions at the design stage, but the final form is one of Wren's masterpieces. It stands 224 feet tall – only St Bride's has a taller steeple. At ground level there are doorways on the west

[1] Paul Jeffery: *The City Churches of Sir Christopher Wren*, page 280

St Mary-le-Bow was also known as St Mary of the Arches, after the arches in the eleventh-century crypt.

The rusticated west doorway, with cherubs and garlands of flowers.

and north based on an engraving by François Mansart for the Hôtel de Conti in Paris. Within a rusticated surround, two cherubs sit either side of an oval window draped with garlands of flowers. Below this is a Doric entablature with more cherubs in the metopes, the spaces between the grooved triglyphs.

On the second storey facing Cheapside to the north (below the clock), is an open balcony apparently built to commemorate the Royal Sild, a temporary grandstand used for viewing jousting and other tournaments taking place in Cheapside, which, as one of the widest streets in medieval London, was suited to such entertainments. In 1331 Queen Philippa of Hainault, wife of Edward III, was watching a tournament here to celebrate the birth of her son, the Black Prince, when the wooden structure collapsed under her and her courtiers. She had to intercede with her husband on behalf of the carpenters whose careless work had caused the accident. In 1702 Queen Anne used Wren's safer iron balcony to watch the Lord Mayor's Pageant.

Above the clock is the bell loft with louvred openings, housing the City of London's twelve most famous bells. The largest bell, in the centre, is the tenor featured in the rhyme:

THE CHURCHES 1666–1711

The tower and church from the north-west. The iron balcony below the clock is a reference to the medieval Royal Sild, a temporary grandstand for viewing tournaments on Cheapside.

Bow Bells, with the Great
Bell of Bow in the centre.

Oranges and lemons, Say the bells of St Clement's.
You owe me five farthings, Say the bells of St Martin's.
When will you pay me? Say the bells of Old Bailey.
When I grow rich, Say the bells of Shoreditch.
When will that be? Say the bells of Stepney.
I do not know, Says the Great Bell of Bow.
Here comes a candle to light you to bed,
And here comes a chopper to chop off your head.

According to legend it was the sound of Bow Bells calling him to 'turn again'
that persuaded the young Dick Whittington to turn back from Highgate as he
was leaving London for ever. He went back to the City to become Lord Mayor
of London and one of the richest merchants of the early fifteenth century. Bow
Bells are also associated with being a genuine Cockney: Londoners have to be
born 'within the sound of Bow Bells' to qualify. This association with the Bells
was noted as long ago as 1617, when the travel writer Fynes Moryson wrote in

his *Itinerary*[2] that 'Londoners, and all [born] within the sound of Bow Bells, are in reproach called Cockneys.'

At the top of the steeple is a weathervane, a great gilt dragon, symbol of the City of London, with a red cross on its wings representing the Arms of the City. The church accounts record a payment of £4 'To Edward Pearce, Mason, for carving of a wooden Dragon for a modell'. We get a glimpse into Wren's working methods, and his empirical approach to design, from the fact that he had Pearce make a cut-out model 'in board to be proferred up to discern the right bigness'. As finished the dragon's 'bigness' is nearly 9 feet long. Its construction shows up in the 1679 accounts: 'To Robert Bird Coppersmith for work done by him . . . about and in ye Neck Ball & Dragon £60.13.9'. On the day the dragon was finally installed a famous tightrope walker called Jacob Hall climbed on its back, to the delight of the crowds below.

In 1818–1820 George Gwilt Junior carried out extensive repairs to the upper sections, which had been damaged by the corrosion of the iron cramps used by Wren to tie the stonework together. Gwilt slightly shortened the spire, and

The weathervane, a magnificent gilt dragon almost 9 feet in length, symbol of the City of London, with a red cross on its wings representing the Arms of the City.

[2] *An Itinerary Written by Fynes Moryson Gent First in the Latine Tongue, and Then Translated by Him Into English* 1617

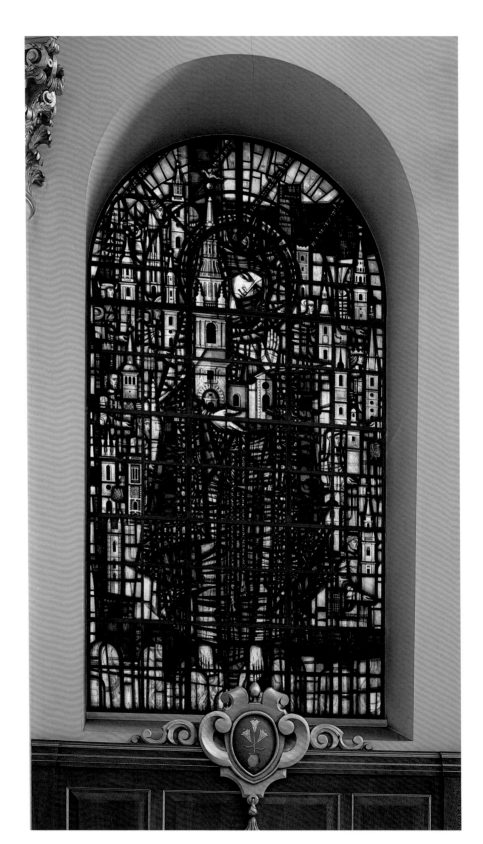

John Hayward's window
shows St Mary embracing
a model of the church.

replaced the original Portland stone of the upper columns with dark-coloured granite to provide better protection against the weather. On 10 May 1941 St Mary's was hit by incendiary bombs. The tower acted like a chimney and the heat sent the bells crashing to the ground, although the stonework survived. The rest of the church was gutted, leaving only the outer walls standing. The church and tower were rebuilt in 1956–64 by Laurence King, whose face looks out from one of the keystones in the nave. The interior of the church followed Wren's original design of a nearly square plan, with three wide arches creating aisles to north and south. The centre of the nave has a barrel-vaulted ceiling, lit by clerestory windows. The large rood cross hanging from the ceiling was designed by John Hayward in the 1960s and carved in the Bavarian town of Oberammergau, a gift of the German people in a gesture of reconciliation after the war. John Hayward also designed the 1960s stained glass windows at the east end. The one on the left shows St Mary embracing a model of the church, surrounded by the towers of other Wren churches damaged by wartime bombing.

The face of architect Laurence King in the nave. He rebuilt the church after the war.

St Mary's is unusual in having two pulpits facing each other across the nave, which provide a platform for dialogues or debates between the rector and distinguished guests on topics of social and political interest from a Christian perspective. From the ceiling hangs a large rood cross, designed in the early 1960s by John Hayward, who also designed the stained glass windows at the east end.

St Mary Somerset

Although the rest of
St Mary Somerset was
demolished in the 1860s,
the tower was saved after
a campaign to prevent its
destruction. The young
Nicholas Hawksmoor may
have had a hand in the
design of the tower, with
its distinctive silhouette
of tapering obelisks and
pinnacles.

A LONDON GUIDEBOOK of 1810 says the name St Mary Somerset is a corruption of 'St. Mary Somers Hythe or Wharf, belonging to a person named Somers. It has no monuments worthy of notice.'[1] St Mary's dates from the reign of Richard I, and the medieval building was destroyed in the Great Fire. Nearly twenty years passed before rebuilding began in 1685; the church was finished in 1694. The parish was one of the poorest in the City and, with St Andrew-by-the-Wardrobe, one of only two where the cost of the furnishings was paid for by Wren out of Coal Tax money. The building was a plain rectangle with no aisles, a flat roof and round-headed windows. Today all that is left is the tower standing on an island in the traffic near Upper Thames Street. It is between two small gardens laid out with blocks of shaped hedging; the one in front to the east shows roughly the site of the nave of the church, the one to the west is in part of the old churchyard.

The church was never prosperous, and by 1803 was in 'a trampled and dirty state'.[2] In 1866 an Act of Parliament authorized the destruction of St Mary's to allow for the widening of Upper Thames Street. Following a campaign to save the tower, led by the architect Ewan Christian, in 1868 a second Act was passed preventing its removal: 'it is expedient that the Tower . . . should be preserved and maintained as a feature of Architectural Interest.' The proceeds of the sale were used to build a new church of St Mary at Hoxton, and some of the church furnishings were transferred there in due course. The Act authorized the City to use the site and the tower 'for such purposes as they may think fit', which apparently included using it for a ladies' public lavatory between the wars.[3]

The tower has four stages with alternating circular and round headed windows, and grotesque masks as keystones on the louvred bell-chamber. The top stage is a lively composition of eight pinnacles set on panelled pedestals. The corner pedestals support fluted urns tapering outwards, while those in between, in the middle of each face, have taller obelisks tapering inwards. The contrast between the two sets of pinnacles, with their differing heights and alternately tapering profiles, makes for a very Baroque effect, suggesting that Hawksmoor could have had a hand in the design. The grotesque keystone masks are also typical of him. Although there is no evidence for his contribution, Hawksmoor had joined Wren's City churches office by 1687, in time to be involved with St Mary's. Paul Jeffery supports this view: 'Here for the first time, one can sense an input from the fledgeling but precocious Nicholas Hawksmoor.'[4]

[1] John Wallis: *London Being a Complete Guide to the British Capital*, page 422
[2] Malcolm: *London Redivivum*, vol. IV, page 428
[3] Mervyn Blatch: *A Guide to London Churches*
[4] Paul Jeffery: *The City Churches of Sir Christopher Wren*, page 136

THE CHURCHES 1666–1711

St Michael on Cornhill

The lower stages of the tower, with plain surfaces and simple octagonal corner buttresses, are the work of William Dickinson. The upper stages, where the surfaces have a complex series of grooves and recesses, are the later work of Nicholas Hawksmoor.

NEITHER WREN NOR HOOKE seems to have had much to do with designing St Michael on Cornhill. The medieval church, one of the oldest foundations in the City, was destroyed in the Great Fire, although the walls of the tower, dating back to the 1420s, remained standing. On their own initiative and using their own money, the local parish embarked on repairing the tower in 1668, only two years after the Fire. The following year they started rebuilding the church and within four years this too was complete. The work was directed by the churchwardens and the Rector, employing their own 'skilful workmen' outside the control of Wren's office for rebuilding the City churches, although in 1670 Coal Tax money was provided by the rebuilding Commissioners to help meet the cost.

By 1703 it was apparent that the repaired tower had started to develop structural problems, and the vestry successfully petitioned the City Churches Commissioners for approval to rebuild the tower. However they had to wait until 1715 for the work to start, as money from the Coal Tax was running out. The first phase of rebuilding the tower lasted from 1715 until 1717, and carried the work up to the large cornice below the bell-chamber. William Dickinson, Wren's assistant in the City Churches Office, was probably responsible for the design, which may include elements of the original tower in the lower stages, for example the large octagonal buttresses on the corners may have existed in the pre-Fire tower. In 1717 progress stopped, and the churchwardens noted that 'the workmen had left off going on with the steeple'. The following year the vestry applied to the new Commission for Building Fifty New Churches, with a separate allocation of Coal Tax money, for help with finishing the tower. The petition was successful and an Act of Parliament was passed approving this use of public money. Hawksmoor then took over the project, and designed the two upper stages of the tower; in a letter to the Dean of Westminster Abbey he talks about using the Gothic style when he 'built that noble Tower of St Michaels Cornhill.'[1]

In Dickinson's lower section the wall surfaces are plain, and the corner buttresses are straightforwardly octagonal. Hawksmoor's upper section has more depth, more light and shade, achieved by recessing the walls between the buttresses, and introducing a slender central buttress on each wall; the result is that Hawksmoor's cornice weaves in and out as it follows these contours, unlike Dickinson's much straighter cornice.

The corner buttresses themselves are different in complexity and profile: Dickinson's are simple octagons, while Hawksmoor's have elongated niches hollowed out of the stone: in cross-section they look like cogwheels. Hawksmoor

[1] Vaughan Hart, *Nicholas Hawksmoor: Rebuilding Ancient Wonders*, page 80

THE CHURCHES 1666–1711

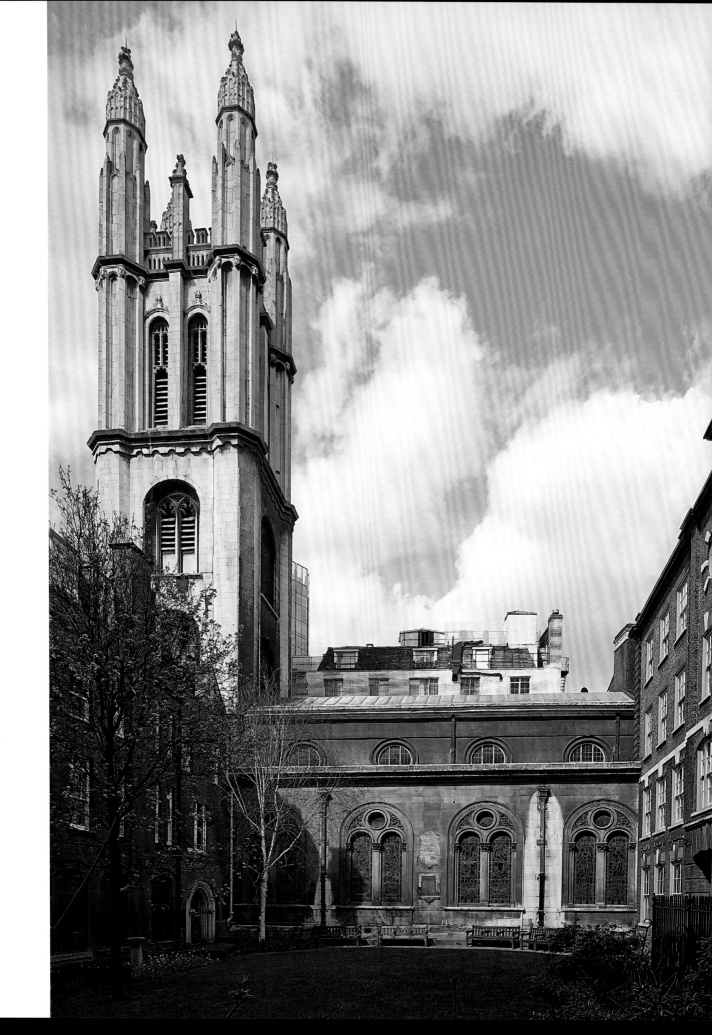

OPPOSITE George Gilbert
Scott refashioned the
south aisle windows in
the style of the Italian
Romanesque, and filled
them with stained glass.

LEFT Young faces look
out from just below the
upper cornice: a typical
Hawksmoor touch.

sets masks of old and young faces below the cornice; above the cornice the cogwheel buttresses become tall pinnacles, tapering off into crocket-like finials. Lower pinnacles are set in the middle of each face (above the slender buttresses); the contrast in height with the tall corner pinnacles gives the top of the tower a lively silhouette, in a style typical of Hawksmoor (compare St Mary Somerset; see page 190).

The church itself underwent a dramatic transformation in the late 1850s, when George Gilbert Scott remodelled St Michael's. In conformity with High Victorian taste, most of the seventeenth-century classical fittings were swept away. Scott said that by using 'a sort of early Basilican style' he attempted 'to give a tone to the existing classical architecture; and it struck me that not wholly alien to this was the Byzantine of the early Venetian palaces.'[2] So the great Gothic Revival architect, rather than using the pointed arch of the French Gothic Revival, chose the round-headed arches and windows of the Byzantine, or Italian Romanesque, style as being more compatible with the round arches of the 'existing classical architecture'. In this spirit, he divided each of the south-aisle windows into three parts: a round window above a pair of narrow arched windows divided by a column.[3] And in the nave the arcades of Tuscan columns supporting the groin-vaulted ceiling were left in place, even if the arches of the vaulting have been given gilded angels as corbels. But the original pews, reredos and pulpit all made way for Scott's replacements. As at St Mary-at-Hill, W. Gibbs Rogers was responsible for much of the

[2] G.G. Scott, *Personal and Professional Recollections*, page 192
[3] The fenestration is strikingly similar to the late fifteenth-century Palazzo Vendramin Calergi on the Grand Canal in Venice (now the Casino). But Scott goes his own way in filling the windows with stained glass.

excellent carving of the new work, including the pews and pulpit. Scott also changed the round-headed east window by making it circular, and filling it with stained glass showing Christ in Glory, designed by Clayton and Bell. In his new Italianate reredos below the window, Scott has kept two fine late seventeenth-century paintings of Moses and Aaron, by Robert Streeter.

One of the few early fittings to survive the changes is the alarming wooden sculpture of a Pelican in her Piety, carved by Joseph Glazely in 1775. The bird has plucked her own breast to produce drops of blood to feed her young, symbolizing Christ's Sacrament of his Body and Blood to save the world.

OPPOSITE Although Scott left the classical columns in the nave, he installed Gothic angels as corbels.

ABOVE LEFT Robert Streeter's painting of Aaron.

ABOVE RIGHT Glazeley's Pelican in her Piety.

St Michael Paternoster Royal

THE NAME COMES FROM nearby Paternoster Lane, where paternosters, or rosaries, were made: the beads in the rosary were used to keep count as worshippers recited the Pater Noster (Our Father) and other prayers. Royal refers to a nearby street, known for its wine merchants, called Le Ryole, itself a corruption of La Reole, a wine-producing town in Bordeaux. In 1361 the church is referred to as 'St. Michael in the Riole', and the connections with wine importing continue: the church is opposite Vintners' Hall, in Upper Thames Street.

Dick Whittington, four times Lord Mayor of London, lived next door and in 1409 paid for the church to be rebuilt. In 1423 he was buried here, but the church and his monument were destroyed in the Great Fire of 1666. In the 1960s he was commemorated in a vigorous portrait in stained glass by John Hayward, which shows him with his cat at his feet and his possessions wrapped in a red and white scarf. St Michael's was one of the last of the City churches to be rebuilt: work did not begin until 1685. In 1688, in the difficult days of the Glorious Revolution, work stopped briefly but it was resumed in 1689. By 1694 the church, including the tower, was finished except for a spire. Work began on the spire in 1713, by which time Hawksmoor had been Wren's assistant at the City Churches office for over twenty years. St Michael's beautiful spire has similarities with those at St Stephen Walbrook and the nearby St James Garlickhythe, both thought to be by Hawksmoor.

St Michael's stands on College Hill; the tower at the south-west corner rises above the trees which block a clear view of the nave. Each face has a rectangular louvred opening for the bell chamber; and below this a circular window. The next stage down has an arched, or round-headed, window. Here we are level with the nave of the church; the nave itself has five similar arched windows; the one in

OPPOSITE St Michael's stands close to the narrow alleyway of College Street. On the left is the Hall of the Worshipful Company of Innholders.

BELOW View north from Upper Thames Street.

ABOVE LEFT Windows in the
nave and the tower have
cherubs for keystones.

ABOVE RIGHT The weather-
vane is an example of the
arrow and pennant design,
topped by a plain cross.

OPPOSITE The spire,
attributed to Hawksmoor.
A complex design
enlivened by the use of
square urns, which appear
at three different levels.

[1] See page 50.

the tower continues the sequence. These arched windows, in both the nave and the tower, have charming cherubs for keystones.

The central section of the spire is an octagon, encircled by eight detached Ionic columns: above each column the entablature breaks forward in the manner of Borromini's Sant'Ivo della Sapienza,[1] and is capped by a square urn. The silhouette is all projection and recession, creating a varied play of light and shade. The stage above is a narrower octagonal open arcade leading to a cornice with more, but smaller, square urns; above this is a slender solid stage with long concave grooves cut into the stone. At the very top is an elegant weathervane in the form of an arrow and pennant.

The church interior is a plain rectangle, with a flat ceiling. On the exterior Wren's original nave was five bays long, but in 1944 St Michael's fell victim to a V1 flying bomb, which left only the tower and walls standing. Internally the nave was reduced to four bays when St Michael's was rebuilt in the late 1960s, the last of the City churches to be restored. The tower and entrance vestibule, as well as one bay at the west end, were converted to offices for the charity

Missions to Seafarers, which has taken over the church. The pulpit and reredos[1] survived the bombing. The fine chandelier marked 'Birmingham 1644' comes from All Hallows the Great, demolished in 1894, as do the Baroque sculptures of Moses and Aaron either side of the reredos.[2]

In 1700 there were no less than six churches dedicated to St Michael; this is one of only two survivors. They are named after the Archangel Michael, who leads the forces of good against the fallen Angel Lucifer. The rebuilt church includes impressive stained glass by the English artist John Hayward; the central window shows Michael triumphing over Lucifer. Lucifer, all in hellish red, lies on the floor helpless against Michael in gleaming white. The window on the left shows the Madonna; in the right-hand window Adam and Eve are tempted by the red Serpent in the Garden of Eden, with the Archangel Gabriel in green above. On the south wall another John Hayward window shows Dick Whittington and his cat.

[1] The pediment had already been removed in the early nineteenth century.
[2] The hands of both statues were damaged in the bombing. Moses on the left used to hold a rod pointing to the Ten Commandments; the turbaned Aaron, who once held an incense burner, now raises his hands in blessing.

OPPOSITE LEFT Sculpture of Aaron, from All Hallows the Great. His hands once held an incencse burner.

OPPOSITE RIGHT Chandelier, dated 1644, from All Hallows the Great.

LEFT Dick Whittington with his cat at his feet and his possessions wrapped in a red and white scarf: a 1960s stained glass window by John Hayward.

OVERLEAF Badly damaged in the war, St Michael's was rebuilt in the late 1960s, with stained glass windows by John Hayward. The centre window shows St Michael trampling Lucifer.

St Nicholas Cole Abbey

The windows of the south front are high off the ground to clear the shops that once blocked the south wall. The creation of Queen Victoria Street in the 1860s opened up this view.

ST NICHOLAS, better known as Santa Claus, was Bishop of Myra in Asia Minor in the fourth century. Besides being the patron saint of children, he is also invoked by students, sailors, merchants, archers, brewers and pawnbrokers. Cole Abbey is thought to be a corruption of Cold Harbour, a medieval hostel offering shelter from the cold. Perhaps one of these refuges existed nearby. There was a church here by the middle of the twelfth century; it was renovated in the early seventeenth century but destroyed in the Great Fire. In the 1667 proposals for reducing the number of London parishes after the Fire, St Nicholas failed to make it on to the list for early rebuilding. But this decision was reversed and instead St Nicholas became one of the first churches to be rebuilt. Work started in 1672, within six years of the Fire.

Before Queen Victoria Street was opened up to the south of the site in the 1860s, St Nicholas was hemmed in by narrow streets and the entrance was on the north. Because the city churches were often built on cramped sites, and one or more fronts were obscured by other buildings, Wren sometimes left these exteriors relatively plain. We see this in the west wall of St Nicholas which, facing a narrow alley, is of rubble and brick. But the towers and steeples, conspicuously rising above the lower buildings in the vicinity, are more ornate and detailed. As Wren wrote in his *Tracts on Architecture*, quoted in *Parentalia*, churches 'should be adorn'd with . . . handsome Spires, or Lanterns, rising in good Proportion above the neighbouring Houses (of which I have given several Examples in the City of different Forms).' Today the situation has sometimes been reversed: the towers and steeples are dwarfed by high-rise office buildings, but some of the exteriors have been opened up and made more visible by road-widening schemes.

St Nicholas is a case in point. Today we have an unobstructed view from the south-east across Queen Victoria Street, and we see that St Nicholas is built on sloping ground, between St Paul's (whose cross can be glimpsed in the background, just above the balustrade to the right of St Nicholas's tower) and the Thames. Originally there were shops built right up against the south wall, which explains why the windows are so high off the ground; those on the east and north front are longer, and reach lower down.

The church is a simple rectangular box; six bays long and three bays wide, with arched, or round-headed, windows beneath straight cornices supported on brackets, a favourite Wren motif. An elegant balustrade runs round the top. The tower ends with a small pediment on each face and urns on the corners. Above this is the lead-covered spire, whose design has been attributed to Robert Hooke. It is a charming octagonal cone, slightly concave like a trumpet, with

ST NICHOLAS COLE ABBEY

ABOVE This three-masted
galleon was originally
the weathervane of
St Michael Queenhithe
(demolished 1876). It was
installed here in 1962
when St Nicholas was
rebuilt after the war.

OPPOSITE The interior in
use as a café, looking
east towards Keith New's
stained glass windows,
installed in 1962.

two sets of small oval windows leading to an iron gallery with balcony railings. In 1678 the City Churches Commissioners, anxious to save Coal Tax money, imposed a ban on work on towers and steeples, but as St Nicholas was near completion it was specifically exempted. The parish accounts give an insight into how they kept Wren's interest in their church: 'Dinner for Dr Wren and other Company - £2 14*s* 0*d*', and 'Half a pint of canary [wine] for Dr Wren's coachmen – 6*d*'.

At the top of the spire is one of London's most striking weathervanes; a three-masted ship with fluttering pennants, intricate rigging and guns ready to fire a broadside. St Nicholas was gutted on 10 May 1941, in the worst air raid of the war. The bombed-out shell appears in the 1951 Ealing comedy *The Lavender Hill Mob*, where it is the location for a gold bullion heist.

The interior is a simple rectangle with a flat panelled ceiling, without coving, and with Corinthian pilasters between the windows. The swags over the east window have been recreated to Wren's, or Hooke's, designs, and looking east

[1] 'All our fathers . . . ate the same spiritual food, and all drank the same spiritual drink. For they drank of that spiritual Rock that followed them, and that Rock was Christ.' St Paul, 1 Corinthians 10:4

we can appreciate how the windows on the north wall are longer than those on the south. The three east windows have stained glass by Keith New, installed in the early 1960s as part of the post-war rebuilding. The central panel depicts *The Rock of Christ*.[1] The west end has three large arches, with a high screen incorporating remnants of the original woodwork. Also surviving from the seventeenth century is Richard Kedge's original font cover resembling a crown. Having been closed for several years, St Nicholas has recently opened as a café, with religious services in the middle of the week. The café provides a welcome, and welcoming, retreat when walking round the City churches. In doing so it reminds us of the origins of its name: a place offering a harbour, or refuge.

OPPOSITE LEFT The
seventeenth-century
font cover resembling a
crown; in the background
is the screen at the
west end.

OPPOSITE RIGHT A garland of
fruit and flowers, original
carving on an Ionic
pilaster on the screen.

LEFT *The Rock of Christ*
by Keith New, installed
in 1962.

St Olave Old Jewry

THIS IS ONE OF SEVERAL London churches dedicated to St Olaf, or Olave, the King of Norway who was canonized in 1164. He is venerated by the English for helping Ethelred the Unready defeat the Danes led by Swein Forkbeard, son of King Harold Bluetooth. In 1014 the Danes, who had attacked and taken over London and Southwark, were defending their positions from London Bridge when Olaf's men defeated them by pulling the bridge down, allowing Ethelred to return to his throne.

Although excavations have revealed the presence of an earlier building, perhaps as old as the ninth century, the Church of St Olave was first mentioned in 1181. It was also known as St Olave Upwell, after a well under the east end of the church. It was destroyed in the Great Fire of 1666. Rebuilding seems to have started as early as 1671, and was complete by 1679.

The unusual tapering plan of Wren's church resembled a coffin, following the original foundations which he reused. The main east façade, with a grand Venetian window, was on the street of Old Jewry. The church was demolished in 1887 under the Union of Benefices Act, although the beautiful marble font can still be seen in St Margaret's Lothbury. Today all that is left is the tower standing in tiny St Olave's Court, accessible through Ironmonger Lane to the west. It has a Doric doorcase with a curved segmental arch, below an arched window. The stage above has a clock in an elegant stone surround, and the top section has tall pinnacles on the four corners. This is the only Wren tower which is battered, getting slightly narrower from bottom to top. Because of trees growing up against it, and its cramped position in a small courtyard, it is hard to see properly from street level. But it is possible to catch a glimpse of the weathervane showing a ship in full sail, which comes from the demolished St Mildred Poultry. St Olave's tower is now used for offices.

OPPOSITE The tower of St Olave Old Jewry stands in the cramped St Olave's Court. The rest of the church was demolished in 1877.

BELOW The weathervane shows a square-rigged ship in full sail with the wind behind her.

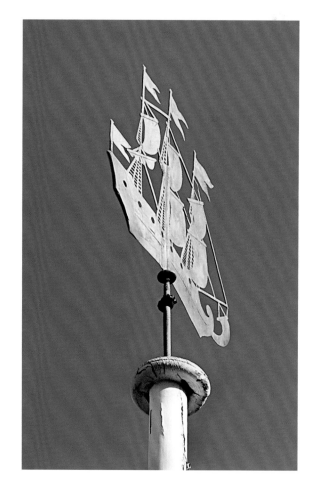

St Peter upon Cornhill

CORNHILL, the former site of a medieval corn market, is the highest point in the City of London, and the hill upon which the Romans built their Forum and Basilica. Stow, in his *Survey of London*, records the medieval church had a plaque declaring that St Peter's had been founded in AD 179, by 'Lucius the fyrst christen kyng of this land, then callyd Brytayne'. It was the see of an archbishopric, and 'the cheef Chirch of this kingdom'.

Whether St Peter's really goes back to the second century cannot be verified. The medieval church, first mentioned in 1040, was badly damaged in the Fire.

The east front on Gracechurch Street.

The parish's early attempts to patch it up were unsuccessful and Wren took over the rebuilding, which was carried out between 1677 and 1684. Wren reused some of the original foundations and structure, and the columns dividing the nave from the aisles follow the pattern of the medieval church.

Robert Hooke seems to have played a part in the design, as his diary contains several references to the church, for example in 1675, before rebuilding began, 'with Oliver and Sheldon &c. about St Peters Cornhill'; in 1672 he was 'with Sir Ch. Wren to St Peters and St Clements'; and in 1679 he records receiving a gift in gold from 'the churchwardens of St Peters one £5'.

The widening of Gracechurch Street to the east reduced the site by 10 feet and Wren designed a grand front for the church's east end, facing the newly widened street. Above a high podium is an arcade of five arched windows between Ionic pilasters, corresponding to the nave and aisles of the interior. The three central windows of the nave have cherub keystones. Above this again is an attic storey with two round windows flanking the central arched window, beneath an open pediment. Curved side pieces (like those at St Martin-within-Ludgate and St Edmund King and Martyr) smooth the transition from the five bays of the lower storey to the three bays of the attic. Around the corner in Cornhill the north entrance is hemmed in by shops, and today the way into the church is from the small churchyard to the south. This is accessed through St Peter's Alley, a narrow alleyway that was once the site of London's first coffee house, Pasqua Rosée's Head.

The churchyard gives the best view of the tower, built of red brick. The bell chamber has three arched openings on each face; above this a small lead dome supports an octagonal copper lantern and spire. The weathervane is in the form of a key, which became the symbol of St Peter when Jesus said to him 'I will give you the keys of the kingdom of heaven' (Matthew 16:19). The ball at the base of the vane is obscured by the intrusive addition of the points of the compass, absent in early engravings and photographs.

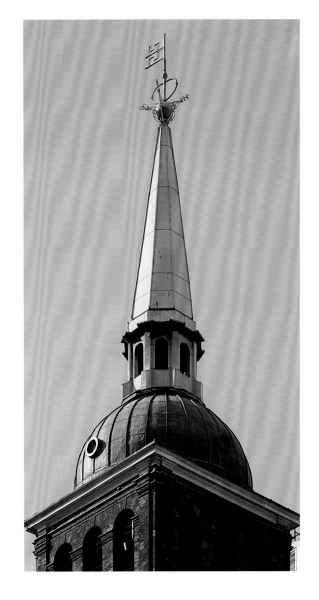

The tower and spire topped by a key weathervane.

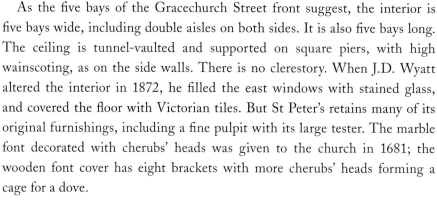

As the five bays of the Gracechurch Street front suggest, the interior is five bays wide, including double aisles on both sides. It is also five bays long. The ceiling is tunnel-vaulted and supported on square piers, with high wainscoting, as on the side walls. There is no clerestory. When J.D. Wyatt altered the interior in 1872, he filled the east windows with stained glass, and covered the floor with Victorian tiles. But St Peter's retains many of its original furnishings, including a fine pulpit with its large tester. The marble font decorated with cherubs' heads was given to the church in 1681; the wooden font cover has eight brackets with more cherubs' heads forming a cage for a dove.

The organ case dates from the 1680s, although in 1840 the organ was rebuilt by William Hill to designs by Dr Henry Gauntlett. Gauntlett persuaded Felix Mendelssohn to give a recital on the newly rebuilt instrument. 'Although this visit was not announced publicly, it became known and the church was crowded,' wrote the organist of St Peter's, Elizabeth Mounsy, in a recollection fifty years later.[1] She turned the pages for him during the performance and he gave her a souvenir by writing out the opening bars of his *Passacaglia* above his autograph. This slip of paper survives in the vestry.

The principal feature of the interior is the wooden chancel screen, one of only two in the City churches (the other is at St Margaret Lothbury). It runs right across the full width of the church, and is divided into sections by thin square shafts, and in the centre two Corinthian pilasters form a doorway into the chancel. They support a lion and a unicorn, with the Stuart royal arms in between.

The screen was introduced by the rector, William Beveridge, the author of a tract entitled *The Great Necessity of Publick Prayer and Frequent Communion*. Beveridge was very High Church: in his inaugural sermon at the reopening of St Peter's in 1681, he wrote enthusiastically how 'we of this parish have cause to be transported with joy and gladness . . . for that our church, which hath lain waste above five times three years, is now at last rebuilt and fitted again for His worship and service.' Gesturing towards the newly installed screen, he defended its presence by saying that there were historical precedents going back to 'the Apostles themselves as . . . I could easily demonstrate from the records of those times. But . . . I am loth to trouble you with it now.'

[1] William A. Little, *Mendelssohn and the Organ*, page 117

BELOW The wooden font cover: eight brackets form a cage for a dove.

OPPOSITE St Peter's has unusually high wainscoting on the plinths of the square piers and around the walls. In 1872 J.D. Wyatt filled the east windows with stained glass, and introduced Victorian floor tiles.

OVERLEAF The royal arms on the screen, installed in 1681.

St Sepulchre

When will you pay me?
Say the bells of Old Bailey.

THE BELLS IN THE NURSERY RHYME refer to the Great Bell of Bailey, the large
tenor bell in the tower of the church of St Sepulchre's. The bell was rung to
announce the execution of a prisoner at nearby Newgate Prison, which used
to stand on the street of Old Bailey. On the eve of an execution the clerk of
St Sepulchre's would ring a handbell outside the cell of the condemned, while
intoning the gruesome lines:

Examine well yourselves in time repent,
That you may not to eternal flames be sent.
And when St Sepulchre's Bell in the morning tolls
The Lord above have mercy on your souls.

A replica of this Newgate Execution Bell is kept in a glass case at the church.

St Sepulchre was probably originally a Saxon church once dedicated to
St Edmund, when it was known as St Edmund-without-Newgate. It later
became known as St Edmund and the Holy Sepulchre, or simply St Sepulchre,
apparently because of its association with the Crusades. The church was the
point of departure for Crusaders leaving for the Holy Land, and its location at
the north-west of the City, just outside Newgate, corresponded with the site of
Christ's Sepulchre outside Jerusalem.

In the middle of the fifteenth century the church was extensively rebuilt by
John Popham, the Chancellor of Normandy; at 150 feet long it was one of the
biggest churches in the City. The church was seriously damaged in the Great
Fire, and the parish was one of the first to set about rebuilding. At first this
was at their own expense, but by 1670 they were receiving funding from the
Rebuilding Commissioners. The rebuilding seems to have finished as early as
1671, when Robert Hooke and the Lord Mayor examined the accounts. The
cost was £5,276. Despite the financial involvement of the Commissioners, the
design of the rebuilt church seems to have been the responsibility of the parish,
with no architectural contributions from Wren or his office. Where possible
the surviving fabric of the walls, porch and tower was reused, and the original
Perpendicular appearance of the exterior retained. Since then St Sepulchre has
undergone a number of later rebuildings and alterations. The large pinnacles on
the tower, for example, date from a restoration by W.P. Griffith in the 1870s.
He also refaced Popham's three-storey south porch.

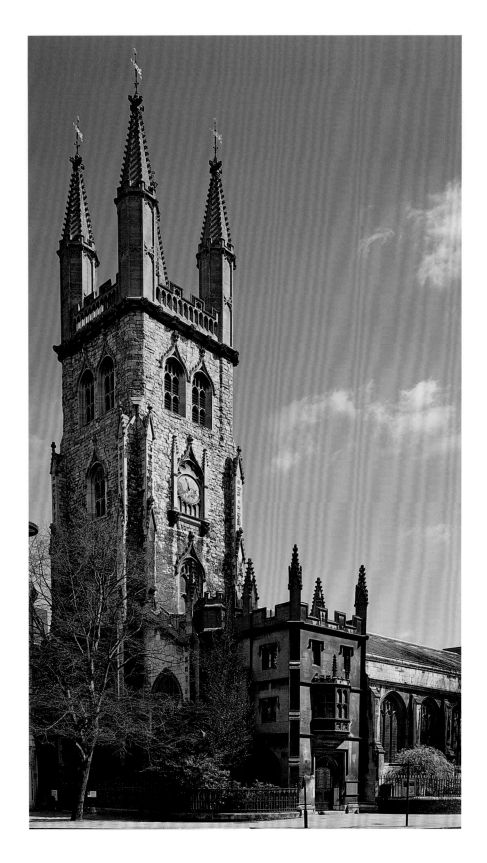

The exterior of
St Sepulchre's retains
the Perpendicular
appearance of the pre-
Fire church. The refaced
porch and the large
pinnacles on the tower
date from the 1870s.

Seven bays long,
St Sepulchre's is one
of the largest of the
City churches rebuilt
after the Fire.

The exterior is Perpendicular Gothic, so it is a surprise to find that the spacious interior is mostly classical. The largest of the City churches rebuilt after the Fire, it is seven bays long with an arcade of Doric columns on high plinths dividing the nave from the aisles. The design is likely to be by Joshua Marshall, the mason appointed by the parish; in 1668 the parish records show there were discussions with him about the twelve columns required for the nave. The deep coffering of the ceiling is from the 1830s.

St Sepulchre's has for many years been the National Musicians' Church, and in the north aisle the Musicians' Chapel contains four windows dedicated to famous musicians. One is to Sir Henry Wood, showing him conducting a Promenade Concert: he was the founder of London's Promenade Concerts which, as the window says, he conducted from 1895 to 1944. Wood learnt to play the organ at St Sepulchre's and in due course became the organist here.

He is buried in the church. Next to the chapel is the organ he played, a magnificent instrument originally built by Renatus Harris in 1670.

The font, with its carved wooden cover decorated with cherubs' heads, is from the 1670s, while the Royal Arms are those used by of the House of Hanover between 174 and 1801. The delicate wrought-iron sword rest is early eighteenth century.

ABOVE LEFT The sword rest is from the early eighteenth century.

ABOVE RIGHT The 1670s font cover is decorated with cherubs' heads.

He conducted the Promenade
Concerts from 1895 to 1944.

ABOVE Sir Henry Wood's memorial window in the Musicians' Chapel shows him conducting a Promenade Concert.

OPPOSITE The Renatus Harris organ dates from 1670. Winged angels perch on the curved pediment, and two more angels hold a crown aloft.

THE CHURCHES 1666–1711

St Stephen Walbrook

OPPOSITE ABOVE The eight red columns form an octagonal base to support the dome; the four red crosses mark the 'missing columns' where Wren breaks his rectangular grid by leaving out columns to provide space for the dome. Wren introduces a spatial ambiguity between the columns of the centrally planned dome (shown in red), and the Latin Cross design (shown in pale blue). By having two sets of aisles, he gives himself space to create 'virtual transepts' (shown in darker blue) at the crossing.

OPPOSITE BELOW The richly coffered dome rises from an octagonal base of arches supported on columns; the triangular sections between the arches form pendentives. Wren fills the spaces behind the corner arches with windows.

[1] In his *Second Tract on Architecture*, Wren writes that the architects of antiquity evolved the Corinthian order whose 'slenderer Columns would leave them more Opportunity to shew their Skill in carving and enriching their Works in the Capitals and Mouldings. Thus the Corinthian Order became the most delicate of all others.' Christopher Wren, *Parentalia*, page 242

THE WALBROOK still flows beneath the street of the same name. A tributary to the Thames, it was once an important river on whose west bank the Romans built their Temple of Mithras, which was replaced by a Christian church sometime before AD 1000. The first mention of St Stephen is in about 1090, but by the early fifteenth century the church and graveyard were too small for the parish, so a new church was built just across the river Walbrook on land given by Robert Chicheley, a member of the Worshipful Company of Grocers. This church was destroyed in the Great Fire of 1666. Rebuilding began within six years, when another Chicheley, also a Grocer and descendant of the original donor, was one of those who laid the foundation stone in 1672.

The result is Wren's masterpiece amongst the City churches. Perhaps he took a special interest in St Stephen's as this was his own parish church: he lived at No. 15 Walbrook. It is one of the few City churches where drawings by Wren survive, and the parish records show payments to Wren for his work at the church. In 1673 the churchwardens held a dinner costing nine guineas at the Swan tavern where the guests included Wren and Hooke. So even if the designs were by Wren, Hooke was also involved in the project. His diary entry for the occasion was 'Eat with great stomack'. During the meal the parish indulged in some oblique bribery of Wren by providing 'a gratuety to his Lady to incuridg and hasting ye rebuilding ye church twenty ginnes'. They must have thought they'd got their twenty guineas' worth, as in 1679 they voted to give 'Sir Christopher's Lady' a further ten pieces of gold, and held another dinner, this time at the Bull's Head Tavern, to which the principal craftsmen were invited. And in 1680 they paid nine pounds ten shillings 'for a hogshead of Claret presented to Sir Chr. Wren'.

Of the seven domed City churches built by Wren, St Stephen's is the grandest and most impressive and probably the earliest. This was also the time when he was working on the Great Model for St Paul's. This was made in 1674, a couple of years after work started at St Stephen's, which is often regarded as Wren's trial run for the dome of the cathedral.

Within the rectangular body of the church he set out rows of slender Corinthian[1] columns: four across and five down the length of the church, dividing the space into a nave and double aisles. But his problem was how to go from a rectangular base to a circular dome. He resolves this by not setting out his columns in a perfect grid of five by four: instead of twenty columns, there are only sixteen. The two inner rows along the long axis have only three columns each, rather than five. The missing ones are towards the east of the church. On the ground plan it can be seen that the space created by

CHURCH of St STEPHEN WALBROOK.

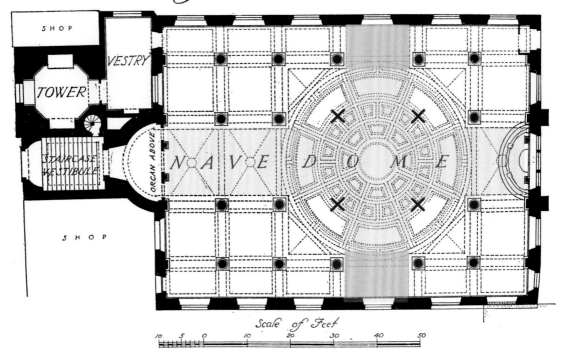

Scale of Feet

View from the nave to the dome of St Stephen Walbrook, Wren's masterpiece of church planning.

these missing columns creates an octagonal ring of eight columns. Wren uses these columns to support eight arches, which he connects with pendentives, downward-pointing triangular sections with curved sides. This creates a circular base for the richly decorated and coffered dome, with a lantern at its centre. By this means he subtly blurs the distinction between a traditional rectangular Latin Cross layout of nave and transepts on the one hand, and a centrally planned Greek Cross design on the other. The transepts are of course not real projections beyond the body of the church; instead the virtual transepts are suggested by the way Wren takes the entablature back to the outside walls under the arches at this point. This device is made possible by having double aisles in the nave, the 'virtual transepts' projecting into the outer aisles. One way to appreciate the subtlety and skill of his design is to follow the line of the entablature as it goes from column to column, weaving its way round the church as it defines the central space under the dome, and suggesting the existence of transepts where in fact there are none. Looking down the 'nave' from the west end we feel this as a longitudinal space with nave and transepts; but as we walk down the nave and look up into the dome we perceive it as a centrally planned design.

Wren's skill in creating this Baroque spatial ambiguity, with shifting perspectives as we move around the elegant columns supporting the dome, shows him as an architect of genius. 'If ever I am induced to return to England, it shall be to indulge in another view of St Stephen's Walbrook,' Antonio Canova is reported to have said of Wren's masterpiece.[2]

The original arrangement of pews facing the altar and pulpit would have stressed the longitudinal element; today the large circular altar directly under the dome, surrounded by pews in concentric rows, does the opposite. The altar, carved by Henry Moore from a monolithic block of travertine marble, was installed as part of a restoration carried out between 1978 and 1987, following subsidence caused by the river Walbrook. In an earlier restoration in the 1880s, the high pews were removed, and in May 1941 the dome was damaged in an air raid. This was repaired in the early 1950s.

Other fittings survive, including the reredos with fine carving of clusters of fruit and flowers tumbling over the entablature. The curved Communion rails are made of twisted balusters with more garlands of fruit and flowers on the panels.

One unusual furnishing for a City church is the black bakelite telephone from the 1950s, recalling the church's connection with the Samaritans, the counselling service for the despairing and suicidal. In 1953 the curate (later to become rector), Chad Varah, set up the Samaritans at St Stephen's using this telephone with the number MANsion House 9000.

[2] Canova included Waterloo Bridge as one of the two London masterpieces he wanted to revisit. Quoted in Edward Boid *Concise History and Analysis of All the Principal Styles of Architecture,* page 183

THE CHURCHES 1666–1711

THE CHURCHES 1666–1711

OPPOSITE Twisted balusters form the curved Communion rails.

LEFT ABOVE Clusters of fruit and flowers fill the curved pediment of the reredos.

LEFT BELOW The *Dance of Death* on the Lilburne monument.

Two columns at the east end, at the entrance to the chancel, have curved monuments fixed to them. The one to John Lilburne shows *The Dance of Death*: a macabre skeleton dancing with a woman. The inscription tells us he was a member of the Grocers' Company, reflecting the Company's long association with St Stephen. Sir John Vanbrugh, the great Baroque architect and Hawksmoor's collaborator on Blenheim Palace, is also buried in the church, although without a monument. This is in spite of his view, stated in his 1712 proposals for building the Fifty New Churches, that churches should be 'free'd from that Inhumane custome of being made Burial Places for the Dead. A Custome in which there is something so very barbarous in it self besides the many ill consequences that attend it; that one cannot enough wonder how it ever has prevail'd amongst the civiliz'd part of mankind.'[3]

The exterior provides a contrast between the curves of the green copper dome and the straight lines of the stone tower and spire. The body of the church was complete by 1679, but the spire, and maybe the tower as well, had to wait until about 1714, although the design may date to about 1700. The spire is square, with groups of Ionic columns breaking forward at the corners of the main stage. Above this is a smaller section, this time with clustered pilasters at the corners. In both stages the clustered corners give the entablature a dynamic projection and recession; the lower entablature supports urns at the corners, the upper one has a ball on each corner. Both sections are open, allowing the sky to be seen through them. There is another stage above, this time with a circular opening, below slender stages leading to the weathervane. This elegant design, forming a trio with the nearby spires of St James Garlickhythe and St Michael Paternoster Royal, is probably the work of Nicholas Hawksmoor.

OPPOSITE The exterior of Wren's dome is clad in green copper. The dramatic spire with its clusters of Ionic columns is attributed to Nicholas Hawksmoor.

BELOW The weathervane is of the arrow and pennant type beneath a simple cross. The long grooves in the stonework below are typical of Hawksmoor.

[3] 'Mr Van-Brugg's Proposals about Building ye New Churches', 1712, Transcribed in Kerry Downes, *Vanbrugh*, pages 257–8.

St Vedast-alias-Foster

St Vedast has London's most Baroque spire, with three stages going from concave to convex and back again. The sense of movement is enhanced by the clusters of pilasters projecting diagonally from the corners.

THIS CHURCH'S UNUSUAL NAME comes from a Frankish saint whose name in Latin was Vedastus. He became Bishop of Arras, on the border between France and Flanders, and died in 540; the church, first mentioned in 1249, may have been founded by a Flemish community. In Flemish he is called Vaast, which became corrupted into the English Foster. In time the church gave its name to the lane on which it stands, so St Vedast-alias-Foster really means St Vedast's Church on St Vedast's Lane.

The medieval building was replaced in the early sixteenth century, and enlarged in 1614. Although badly damaged in the Great Fire, enough survived for the church to be rebuilt by the parish authorities, without waiting for the Rebuilding Commission. Work started soon after the Fire, in 1669. Although the Rebuilding Commissioners took over the funding in 1672, the work was probably carried out by the churchwardens themselves rather than by Wren's City Churches office. However by the 1690s this rebuilding proved unsatisfactory and, after a visit from Hooke, it was decided to start again with a new church. This time Wren's office provided the designs, which included a tower at the south-west corner, instead of a central west tower as before. Work started in 1695, and the new church was finished in 1699. The tower was built to a height of 90 feet, but without a spire.

The mason in charge was Edward Strong, Wren's principal mason-contractor at St Paul's. Here at St Vedast's, Strong was responsible for carving the cherubs on the keystones on the west front and bell tower as well as the *Dove in Glory* in the south aisle. He received over £3000 for his work.

The church had to wait another ten years for a spire, but when built it became one of the jewels of the London skyline. This elegant Baroque design is of three stages. The lower stage, with a framed rectangular opening above an oval one, is concave. The deep cornice emphasizes the projection and recession of this section. The stage above, with a smaller plain rectangular opening, is convex, while the panelled obelisk on the top stage is in effect concave. The succession of planes going from concave to convex and back again as they taper upwards makes for a composition full of movement. This is enhanced by the clusters of triple pilasters projecting diagonally at the corners of the lower stages, whose edges catch the light and increase the verticality of the design. The work was carried out by William Dickinson, but the Baroque quality of the designs suggests they may be by Hawksmoor, who was well established as Wren's assistant by 1709. The spire was finished by 1712. As the churchyard was too small for the work to be carried out on site, the spire was prefabricated at Greenwich and brought here by river. The mason in charge of the spire was Edward Strong junior, whose father, also Edward, had earlier built the body of the church.

THE CHURCHES 1666–1711

OPPOSITE The lower stages of Wren's tower are much plainer than the ornate Baroque spire, built thirteen years later in 1712, probably by Hawksmoor who by then had become established as Wren's assistant.

LEFT Edward Strong's carving *Dove in Glory*, representing the Holy Spirit, surrounded by cherubs' heads.

The tower below is a simpler affair. The bell chamber has louvred openings with curved tops. Below this are circular windows with keystones, and Edward Strong's keystones can be seen on the arched windows of the lower stage. On the south wall of the church, and part of the base of the tower, the surface is coarser than the ashlar-faced stone elsewhere. This wall incorporates some of the fabric of the medieval building, and as it faced a very narrow alley Wren has left it as unfaced ragstone.

The doorway leads into the church interior through a vestibule. The church was hit by incendiary bombs on 29 December 1940, one of the worst nights of the Blitz, when nine of Wren's City churches suffered major damage. The interior was gutted but the walls and tower were left standing. The church was restored in the early 1950s by Stephen Dykes Bower, who arranged the seating in the style of an Oxford or Cambridge college chapel, with benches facing each other across the nave. He also installed the geometric black and white marble floor, and screened off the south aisle. The result is a harmonious and intimate interior. The stained glass east windows of 1961 are by Brian Thomas and illustrate scenes from the life of St Vedast. Most of the furnishings come from other City churches: the reredos comes from St Christopher-le-Stocks, demolished in the 1780s, and the pulpit from All Hallows, Bread Street, demolished in 1877. The marble font and wooden font cover come from St Anne and St Agnes; the font cover has elegant carvings of swags and garlands of fruit. In the south aisle is an impressive wood carving of 1697, all gilt, which survived the bombing. It is by Edward Strong, one of Wren's favourite craftsmen, and shows a group of cherubs' head surrounding a Dove in Glory representing the Holy Spirit.

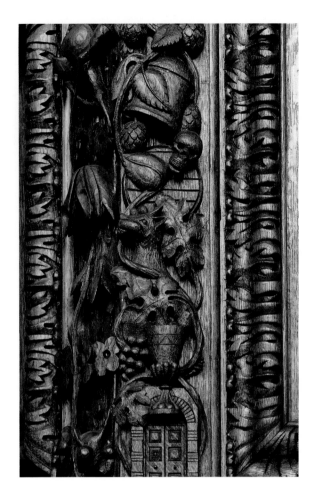

OPPOSITE The post-war restoration was carried out in the early 1950s by Stephen Dykes Bower, who arranged the seating with pews facing each other across the nave. The stained glass windows by Brian Thomas show scenes from the life of St Vedast.

ABOVE LEFT The pulpit from All Hallows, Bread Street is decorated with carvings of flowers and foliage entwined around a doorway, a chalice and even a small skull.

ABOVE RIGHT The font cover from St Anne and St Agnes.

Temple Church

THE TEMPLE CHURCH is a Peculiar, in the church's legal language, meaning it is outside the jurisdiction of the Bishop of London; instead it serves as a private chapel for the lawyers of the Inner and Middle Temples. It was built by the Crusading Order of Knights Templar from about 1160 and consecrated in 1185. The nave of the Temple is circular, like other churches built by the Order, following the model of the Church of the Holy Sepulchre in Jerusalem. Some sixty years later the rectangular chancel was added to the east. The round nave, with its six piers of Purbeck marble supporting pointed arches, is one of the earliest Gothic buildings in England. The later chancel also has Purbeck marble columns creating a nave and two aisles, with delicate rib vaulting above. Even after all the restorations that have taken place, the result is an interior of perfectly proportioned elegance.

The Temple survived the Great Fire, and in 1669 it was here that Wren chose to be married to Faith Coghill, perhaps because it was one of the few churches left standing so soon after the Fire. Thirteen years later in 1682 Wren came back to the Temple and refitted the interior with an organ, box pews, pulpit and screen, as well as an altarpiece or reredos made by William Rounthwaite, and carved by William Emmett. The reredos was removed during a Victorian restoration of the 1840s, and was for years on show at the Bowes Museum in County Durham. The Temple fell victim to the Blitz in May 1941, and much of the fabric had to be replaced, including the Purbeck marble columns in the chancel and nave. Walter Godfrey, who carried out the post-war rebuilding in the 1950s, wrote of the Victorian restorers that their methods had been so thorough that they had effectively reduced the ancient fabric to 'a complete modern simulacrum of this superb monument'. But during his restoration work after the bombing of 1941, he found that 'behind the restorer's veneer there is sufficient of the old fabric remaining to make one one feel there is still a life to be prolonged and much that is significant to be preserved.'[1]

During the restoration Wren's reredos was brought back and installed again at the east end of the chancel. As usual with Wren's altarpieces, there are finely carved garlands of flowers and cherubs' heads above the Ten Commandments, the Creed and the Lord's Prayer; a form which contains direct references to the Old Testament and Solomon's original Temple of Jerusalem, much discussed by Wren and Hooke. The Book of Exodus tells us that God gave Moses two stone Tablets on which the Ten Commandments were inscribed. Almost five hundred years later the Book of Kings describes 'the house which king Solomon built for the LORD' where these Tablets were to be kept safely in the Ark of the Covenant, itself lodged in the Holy of Holies. The Ark also served as

[1] Walter Godfrey, *Archaeologia: Or Miscellaneous Tracts Relating to Antiquity*, page 123

Wren's reredos was carved by William Emmett in the 1680s. It was removed from the Temple in the 1840s and reinstated in the post-war reconstruction.

the base for the altar or 'mercy seat' which was sprinkled with sacrificial blood on the Day of Atonement. Here in the Temple Church the Tablets with the Commandments are protected, not by being placed within the Ark, but by Wren's overhanging curved pediment. The sacrificial blood of the mercy seat is replaced by the bloodless sacrifice of the Christian sacrament that takes place on the altar or Communion table. Wren's swags of flowers, fruit and wheat recall Solomon's decoration of the doors of the Holy of Holies: 'He carved thereon cherubims and palm trees and open flowers' (1 Kings 6:35). Similarly Wren's cherubs' heads with outstretched wings above the Commandments refer to God's instructions to Moses, albeit without the gold: 'You shall make two cherubim of gold, of hammered work shall you make them . . . the cherubim shall spread out their wings above, overshadowing the mercy seat with their wings, their faces one to another' (Exodus 25:17–22).

Bevis Marks Synagogue

A SURVEY OF THE CITY CHURCHES is incomplete without the Bevis Marks Synagogue, which is better preserved than most of the churches, and retains much of the feel of the early eighteenth century. It was built by Sephardic Jews from Spain and Portugal who had been officially allowed to return to England by Oliver Cromwell in 1657 for the first time since their expulsion by Edward I in 1290. As Jews were not yet allowed to build in a prominent position, the synagogue is discreetly tucked away off the thoroughfare of Bevis Marks, near Aldgate. The Jewish community soon outgrew their first synagogue in nearby Creechurch Lane, and in 1699 signed a contract with Joseph Avis, a Quaker builder, for a new and larger building. The ceiling is said to contain an oak beam from a Royal Navy ship, given by Queen Anne as a gesture of approval. Another story is that Avis returned to the community his profits from the contract, saying he did not want to make money out of building a House of God.

The synagogue is approached through a stone arch inscribed with the year 1701, and above this 'A.M. 5461', meaning '5461 years after the beginning of

The Jewish synagogue of Bevis Marks has much in common with the City churches. A notable difference, however, is marked by the raised Reading Desk, surrounded by four large candlesticks. There are six more candlesticks in front of the Ark of the Covenant; the total of ten represents the Ten Commandments.

the world', the date of the building in the Hebrew calendar. On entering the synagogue we see many features shared with the churches. There are round-headed windows, the walls are lined with wainscoting, and there is a profusion of barley-sugar baluster rails around the Reading Desk. The upright oak seats are like pews, and the Ark of the Covenant resembles a Christian reredos. Other features are more specifically Jewish: the seven hanging candelabra represent the days of the week, with the large central one representing the Sabbath. This was the gift of the Sephardi Congregation of Amsterdam to their fellow Jews in London. As with many City churches, there are galleries supported on columns; the difference here is that the galleries are exclusively for women, and the twelve columns represent the Twelve Tribes of Israel.

The synagogue, which came through both World Wars without harm, was badly damaged in 1992 in the IRA terrorist bombing of the Baltic Exchange. Within a year of repairs being completed, including a new ceiling and roof, another IRA bomb caused further damage. This has now been repaired, and the synagogue has kept its very special atmosphere, with a quality of timeless spirituality unique in the City of London.

The candles of the seven hanging candelabra and ten large candlesticks lit for a traditional Jewish wedding.

ST PAUL'S CATHEDRAL

WHILE THE CITY CHURCHES were a collaborative effort, Wren could claim St Paul's Cathedral as his personal creation. Below the centre of the dome, brass letters set in the marble floor spell out his epitaph as 'The Architect of this Church and City' (HUIUS ECCLESIÆ ET VRBIS CONDITOR) and invite the reader: 'If you seek his monument, look around you' (SI MONUMENTUM REQUIRIS CIRCUMSPICE).

Wren's involvement with St Paul's dates back to before the Fire, when Dean William Sancroft consulted him about the condition of the cathedral after the Civil War and Commonwealth. William Dugdale, in his *History of St Paul's Cathedral*, describes how 'The stalls in the Quire were all taken away' and 'The body of the Church hath been frequently converted to a *Horse quarter* for Soldiers.' The south transept roof had fallen in, and Dugdale laments 'that so glorious a structure . . . beautified by the piety of our deceased Ancestors, should be utterly destroyed and become a woful spectacle of ruin.'[1]

Before the Fire, St Paul's was a Gothic cathedral beneath a classical exterior. In the 1630s Inigo Jones had refaced the walls of the cathedral with Portland stone, and completely encased the west front in a huge Corinthian portico of ten columns connected to the upper storey with scroll buttresses. This too had suffered during the years of conflict, when 'the beautiful Pillars of Inigo Jones's Portico were shamefully hew'd and defaced' (*Parentalia*).

By the spring of 1666 the old cathedral was in a parlous state, with the tower threatening to collapse and the walls bulging under the weight of the roof.

Charles II set up a commission, led by Dean Sancroft, to invite proposals for the repair of the old cathedral. Christopher Wren, recently returned from his Paris visit, and the two more established architects Hugh May and Roger Pratt were all asked for their opinions. John Evelyn, one of the Commissioners, gives an account of a site meeting in August 1666. Pratt proposed patching up the old tower 'to repair it onely on its old foundation', even suggesting that the reason for the 'maine building to leane outwards' was that 'it had been so built *ab origine* for an effect in perspective'. Wren disagreed, with Evelyn's support: 'we totally rejected it, and persisted that it requir'd a new foundation . . . and we had a mind to built it with a noble cupola, a forme of church-building not as yet known in England, but of wonderfull grace.'[2]

[1] William Dugdale, edited by Henry Ellis, *History of Saint Paul's Cathedral, in London, from Its Foundation Etc.*, page 110
[2] John Evelyn, *Diary*, 27 August 1666
[3] Letter from Dean Sancroft, published in *Wren Society Volume XIII*, page 44
[4] Letter to Dean Sancroft, ibid., page 45

Old St Paul's with Inigo
Jones's classical portico.

Wren suggested to the Commission that the 'Gothick rudeness of the old design' should be replaced by a 'good Roman manner', and the central tower by a dome of 'incomparable more Grace' than the 'Lean Shaft of a Steeple'.[3]

But within days the Great Fire put an end to this argument, when parts of the tower collapsed into the burning cathedral.

Although old St Paul's was badly damaged in the Fire, the church authorities initially hoped to be able to rebuild at least some parts of it. But by 1668 it was clear that this was impossible. Dean Sancroft wrote to Wren telling him there was no chance of saving Jones's portico, as they had found: 'great Defects in Inigo Jones's Work . . . there were no Keystones at all to tie it to the old Work', and asking Wren to take on the task of providing a new design: 'you are so absolutely and indispensably necessary to us that we can do nothing, resolve on nothing, without you.' In a revealing letter to the Dean, Wren wrote that even if his designs were rejected, he had derived great pleasure from 'their contrivance, which equals that of poetry or compositions in music'.[4]

At the heart of Wren's plans for the cathedral was his determination that it should have a dome. He had already proposed replacing the steeple with a dome before the Fire. Within days of the Fire, when Wren to presented King Charles II his plan for rebuilding the City of London he put a domed St Paul's at the

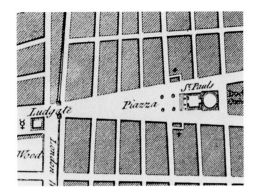

ABOVE A domed St Paul's is at the heart of Wren's plan to rebuild London, presented to the King within days of the Fire.

OPPOSITE Caius Gabriel Cibber's phoenix rises from the flames above the word RESURGAM.

centre of the design. And every design he put forward for the cathedral had a dome over the crossing.

Realizing that finance was the crux of the project, Wren wrote to Sancroft: 'I think it is silver upon which the foundation of any work must be first layed, lest it sink whilst it is yet rising.' As with the City churches, funding for the new cathedral came from the Coal Tax, as authorized by the 1670 Rebuilding Act. This instructed the Commissioners to use 'One fourth part of the money by this Act given . . . [to] the Parish Churches' for the 'building, or repaireing the Cathedrall Church of Saint Paul'. In the event, by 1710, as St Paul's was nearing completion, the Coal Tax had provided some £810,000, more than 90 per cent of the total amount of about £878,500. The rest came from gifts and benefactions.[5]

Before rebuilding could begin the site had to be cleared and the ruins of the old cathedral removed. This was dangerous work. Peyps wrote 'The very sight of the stones falling from the top of the steeple do make me sea-sick!'[6] *Parentalia* tells how 'The remains of the tower being near 200 feet high, the Labourers were afraid to work above, thereupon he concluded to facilitate this work by the Use of Gunpowder.' This was effective: a small charge brought down the 'whole Angle of the Tower, with two great Arches that rested upon it'. 'By this . . . may be observ'd the incredible Force of Powder: 18 pounds only of which lifted up above 3000 tun, and saved the Work of 1000 Labourers.'

But one explosion went wrong, sending stone fragments flying round the churchyard, to the alarm of the local population. So Wren 'turned his thoughts to another Method . . . and that was, to make an Experiment of that ancient Engine in War, the Battering-Ram.' Wren devised an iron-tipped battering ram suspended from a giant cradle; thirty men were needed to operate it, but it eventually did the trick, and by 1675, nine years after the Fire, the site was clear and rebuilding could begin.

A story in *Parentalia* is that one day, as the site was being cleared, Wren ordered 'a common Labourer . . . to bring a flat Stone from the Heaps of Rubbish' to use as a marker for where the centre of the dome would be. The stone he brought 'happened to be a piece of a Grave-stone with nothing remaining of the Inscription but this single Word in large Capitals: RESURGAM.' This claim, 'I will rise again', struck Wren as symbolic of the whole rebuilding effort, and when it came to deciding what to put in the south transept pediment he commissioned Caius Gabriel Cibber to produce a carving of a phoenix, above the word 'RESURGAM'. The phoenix is the mythical bird that dies by fire only to rise again from its own ashes, symbolizing continuity through renewal:

[5] Lecture given at Gresham College on 18 June 2008 by Dr Negley Harte, 'God Meets Mammon: the Financing of the New Cathedral'
[6] Peyps, *Diary,* 14 September 1668

AFTER THE FIRE

[7] Thomas Tickell, 'A description of the Phoenix'
[8] Wren Society, Vol. XXX, page 29
[9] Professor Vaughan Hart writes (page 34) that 'the steeple appears to be based on the exotic model of a Chinese pagoda.' Maybe Wren had in mind the Porcelain Pagoda at Nanjing, one of the pagodas illustrated by Johan Nieuhof in his accounts of his travels in China, published in 1665. In 1669 John Ogilby published an English edition: *An Embassy from the East India Company*. Ogilby knew both Wren and Hooke, and collaborated with them over his *Large and Accurate Map of the City of London* as rebuilt after the Fire.

A god-like Bird! whose endless round of years,
Outlasts the stars, and tires the circling Spheres . . .

Begot by none himself, begetting none,
Sire of himself he is, and of himself the son;
His life in fruitful death renews his date,
And kind destruction but prolongs his fate
Ev'n in the grave new strength his limbs receive,
And on the fun'ral pile begin to live.[7]

Building St Paul's was a long-drawn-out process, lasting from 1675 until 1711. During this time the design underwent important changes. There was a fundamental tension between Wren's plan for a classical, centrally planned, church with a dome, and the clergy's desire for a more traditional cathedral divided into a nave for the congregation and a choir for the celebration of religious services. The clergy were anxious to get a choir finished so they could start to hold services as soon as possible. Wren was concerned that once a choir had been built, the nave and dome might be delayed indefinitely, so he was keen to work on all sections simultaneously, and in particular to provide piers that would be strong enough to support a grand dome when the time came.

The Great Model, with two domes and a grand portico of Corinthian columns.

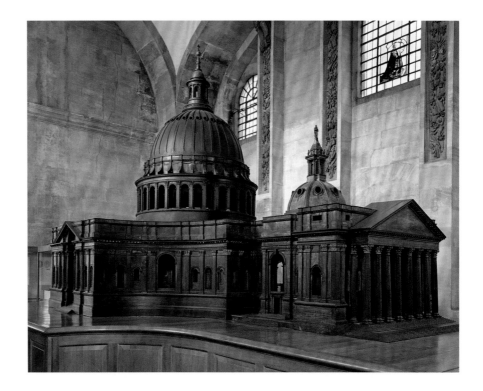

AFTER THE FIRE

Wren's initial plan, known as the Greek Cross design, was for a cathedral with four equal arms and a large dome over the central space. Wren then altered this design by extending the west end with a grand portico consisting of a pediment supported by eight pairs of giant columns, and another, smaller, dome over the nave. This design, known as the Great Model Design, was approved by the King, who commanded Wren to make a 'model thereof . . . after so large and exact a manner that it may remain as a perpetual and unchangeable rule and direction for the conduct of the whole work.'[8] It was at this time that Wren received his knighthood from the King. As Hooke notes in his diary for 14 November 1673, 'Dr Wren knighted and gone to Oxford'.

The Great Model was built during 1674. On 8 August Hooke writes: 'To Paules saw Module finished painting and guilding'. The finished model cost about £600, as much as one of the new houses of the better sort being built in the City. It stands over 13 feet high, large enough for the viewer to stand inside and get an accurate impression of Wren's plans. Unfortunately for Wren, the clergy were not happy with what they saw. *Parentalia* says: 'The Chapter, and some others of the Clergy, thought the Model not enough of a Cathedral fashion; to instance particularly, in that, the Quire was design'd Circular.' Wren, greatly disappointed, 'turn'd his Thoughts to a Cathedral-form (as they call'd it)' but adapted 'to reconcile, as near as possible the Gothick to a better Manner of Architecture; with a Cupola, and above that, instead of a Lantern a lofty Spire, and large Porticoes.' The spire, with octagonal stages getting smaller towards the top, is similar to the 'wedding-cake' design later built for St Bride's. It also resembles a Chinese pagoda, a form of 'Chapel of Idols' that recent visitors to China had described and illustrated.[9]

This design got the approval of the clergy, and received the Royal Warrant. The Warrant Design, as it is known, is a strange hybrid – in particular, the pagoda-like steeple sits uncomfortably above the dome. Wren, bruised by the rejection of the Great Model, 'resolved to make no more Models, or publickly expose his Drawings, which . . . subjected his Business many Times, to incompetent Judges.' Once St Paul's was under way Wren arranged for large wattle screens to surround the building site to prevent 'incompetent Judges' from seeing what he was doing. *Parentalia* also reports that the King 'was pleas'd to allow him the Liberty . . . to make some Variations, rather ornamental, than essential' to the design, at his own discretion.

ABOVE The Warrant Design, with a strange steeple rising out of the dome.

OVERLEAF I took this shot from a helicopter in the 1980s, when pollution had taken its toll, especially on the lower storeys, and the cathedral had yet to be cleaned. Wren achieves a unified treatment of the exterior walls by raising a screen on the upper storey, so there is no setback for the clerestory, as there would be in a Gothic cathedral. This aerial view reveals the gap between the outer screen and the inner walls, making it seem there is almost a cathedral within the cathedral.

The ball and cross stand 23 feet high and weigh approximately 7 tons. Although C.R. Cockerell replaced the weather-beaten originals with a new ball and cross in 1821, these faithfully follow a drawing of 1708 by William Dickinson, preserved in the cathedral's archives.

Wren made generous use of this 'Liberty', taking the opportunity to change the design yet again. The resulting Definitive Design is more or less as built.

One of the biggest changes was to replace the spire above the dome with a lantern and cross, as originally planned. The other change was to the exterior walls. The Warrant Design had a conventional clerestory, or upper range of windows above the aisles, set back from the walls of the ground floor of the nave and choir, and supported by flying buttresses.

The new design raised the height of the exterior walls to two storeys with a screen. This allowed Wren to hide the flying buttresses, and play down their associations with Gothic cathedrals. He announces in his *First Tract on Architecture* that 'Gothick Buttresses are ill-favoured, and were avoided by the Ancients.' The screen had another important visual purpose: it allowed for a unified treatment of the exterior walls, which wrap round the cathedral on a single plane, broken only by porticoes on the west, north and south. The lower round-headed windows light the aisles, while on the upper storey there are blind pedimented recesses above small windows. These windows serve only to light the empty space between the outer screen and the inner walls. On the interior this disconnect between the external screen and the inner walls is not apparent, as the outer screen is not visible from the church floor. Internally the layout is like a typical Gothic cathedral. At ground level the nave has aisles on either side, while the upper clerestory is only the width of the nave on its own. My aerial view shows how the upper storey sits within the outer screen. Externally the screen gives the impression they are all the same width. This skilful device shows Wren's mastery of form to create the desired visual impact.

His designs for the dome show the same attention to visual effect. Twenty-one years after the foundation stone had been laid in 1675, the eight great piers that would support the dome were ready and work could start on the drum of the dome itself. From the outside the dome needed to be tall enough to dominate the skyline, and to soar above the rest of the cathedral. As *Parentalia* puts it, 'St Paul's is lofty enough to be discerned at Sea Eastward, and at Windsor Westward.' From the inside this would mean an uncomfortably elongated dome: it needed to be much shallower to fit harmoniously with the nave and choir. Wren's solution was to build two domes, connected by a tall brick cone. The difference in height is about 65 feet, out of a total height of 365 feet. The inner dome is masonry, while the outer dome is lead-covered timber. This device was attacked in the 1840s by Augustus Welby Pugin, the Gothic Revival architect of Birmingham's Catholic Cathedral, as 'a fictitious dome . . . the dome that is seen is not the dome of the church, but a mere construction for effect . . . at vast expense without any legitimate reason.'[10]

When Wren designed the domes, both internal and external, he applied the principle that for an arch to be stable and not buckle under stress its profile should follow the curve of a chain hanging from two points. In 1671 Hooke had demonstrated to the Royal Society that inverting this curve gave the strongest profile for an arch: 'As hangs the flexible line, so, inverted, will stand the rigid arch.' He and Wren discussed this in June 1675: 'He was making up of my principle about arches and altered his module by it.' Whether or not Wren needed Hooke's advice, the cross-section of the dome shows Wren's use of the principle of the upside-down hanging chain by making the internal drum with its pilasters lean in at an angle. Externally this is disguised by the columns surrounding the drum, which are completely vertical.

The brick cone, reinforced with a continuous wrought iron chain at its base, is only 18 inches thick. The cone and the canted inner drum together support the 850-ton weight of the stone lantern and gold cross. From the outside these appear to be supported by the outer dome, but in fact it is the other way round: the weight of the lantern helps stabilize the relatively light structure of the timber and lead dome below. The brick cone is hidden on the outside, but clearly visible in the space between the two domes, which you go through when climbing to the viewing platform on the lantern. During the construction of the dome Wren would regularly inspect the work in person; as time went on he became too old to climb the scaffolding, and was instead hauled up in a basket. Work on the dome was finished by 1708, with a topping-out ceremony carried out by Wren's son Christopher, the author of *Parentalia*. He tells us that Wren's plan was to have the interior covered with mosaics, 'as is nobly executed in the Cupola of St Peter's in Rome', but this was rejected by the Dean and Chapter, who instead insisted on having eight painted panels by Sir James Thornhill showing scenes from the life of St Paul.

[10] Augustus Welby Northmore Pugin, *The True Principles of Pointed Or Christian Architecture*, pages 8–9

In cross-section the two domes are connected by a tall brick cone. Hooke had suggested that the strongest arch will follow the curvature of an inverted hanging chain. I photographed a red chain hanging against the upside down cross-section; seen the right way round this shows how closely Wren followed this 'catenary arch' principle, and made the internal pilasters lean inwards at an angle to follow the line of the chain.

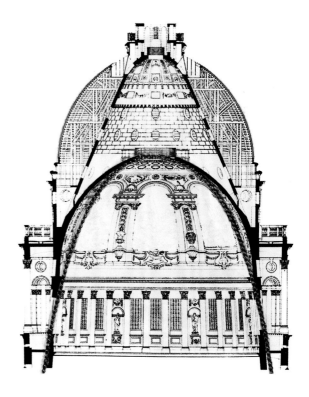

OPPOSITE The dome is divided into thirty-two bays. The lower section is a ring of thirty-two Corinthian columns; here Wren fills every fourth bay with a solid niche. This sets up a different rhythm to that of the upper sections where the thirty-two bays are uninterrupted.

LEFT Sir James Thornhill's monochrome paintings of scenes from the life of St Paul fill the interior of the dome. This panel depicts the incident, related in the Acts of the Apostles, when Paul was bitten by a viper. The Apostle shakes the snake off and is miraculously unharmed.

BELOW A view of the
crossing towards the choir.
In the corners Wren used
smaller elliptical arches
below the main arches to
disguise the narrowness
of the aisles, after he
increased the thickness of
the outer walls. Similarly,
the panels at the sides of
the four main arches mask
the unequal spacing.

OPPOSITE William
Richmond's mosaics in
the choir.

In the 1890s William Richmond was commissioned to fill the eastern end of the cathedral with colourful mosaics: the ceiling of the choir illustrates the *Benedicite*, or *Song of Creation*, with the three saucer domes divided into depictions of the animals of the land, the sea and the air. In the context of Salisbury Cathedral Wren had observed 'that nothing could add beauty to light', and these mosaics, although splendid in their own right, are hardly consistent with what Wren had in mind for his cathedral.

Wren made frequent changes to the design as building progressed, as can be seen in the piers supporting the dome. At one stage he increased the thickness of the outer walls to make them stronger, and in doing so he reduced the width of the aisles. This in turn meant that where the aisles meet the crossing below the dome, the octagonal spacing between the dome piers was no longer equal. He solved the problem by bridging the gaps in the corners with four smaller elliptical arches just below the main arches, which now appear symmetrical.

AFTER THE FIRE

The choir stalls decorated with winged cherubs and garlands of fruit and flowers, carved in limewood by Grinling Gibbons. In the 1980s, when I took this photograph, the carvings had just been restored: the brighter areas of wood show where the cathedral's craftsmen needed to restore the work.

259

A lack of suitable stone
forced Wren to abandon
his plans for a single
portico with one giant
order.

OVERLEAF The pediment
on the west front, with a
relief carving by Francis
Bird showing the central
moment in the life of
St Paul, when he is
struck blind on the road
to Damascus, whose
buildings are on the left.
In the centre St Paul,
surrounded by Roman
soldiers, looks up at the
sun as his horse collapses
beneath him.

But the four main arches in the corners are not open to their full width – they have panels at the sides to mask the unequal spacing.

A constant problem facing Wren during the construction of St Paul's was the shortage of suitable stone. His favourite material was Portland stone. This oolitic Jurassic limestone came from quarries on the Isle of Portland, a peninsula off the Dorset coast. But getting the large blocks of stone from Portland to London was no easy task. The stone had to be loaded on carts, which were dragged from the quarries to a pier on the south side of the peninsula. As the pier could not accommodate large ships, the stone had to be loaded on to small boats and then transferred at sea on to larger vessels – a precarious business, with the stone at risk of staining if immersed in salt water. The larger ships sometimes had to run the gauntlet of enemy shipping (England was sporadically at war with the Dutch or the French, and sometimes both at once, during the rebuilding) as they sailed round the coast into the Thames, and up to the quays near St Paul's. Problems became worse when a landslide carried away the pier on Portland, and supplies of stone stopped for a while. When the quarrymen tried to take advantage of the situation they were rebuked by Wren: 'Though 'tis in your power to be as ungrateful as you will, yet you must not think that your insolence will be always borne with.' He made it clear that they would only be employed if they would 'work regularly and quietly, and submit to proper and reasonable directions'.[11]

The shortage of large blocks of stone had a direct effect on the design of the cathedral. In 1685 Wren's plan was for the west end to have a single portico with a giant order of Corinthian columns, along the lines of the Great Model. But, according to Roger North, Wren claimed 'They could not have materialls to make good single Columnes.'[12] Instead the west front has two smaller porticoes, one above the other, with six pairs of Corinthian columns on the lower portico, and four pairs of Composite columns on the upper. Above this is a pediment, with a relief carving by Francis Bird showing the central moment in the life of St Paul, when he is struck blind on the road to Damascus.

In 1711, forty-five years after the Fire, the cathedral was declared finished. At the time it was the only major cathedral in the world to have been built by a single architect who carried the project through from beginning to end. The last few years of the project had been difficult for Wren, as the new Dean of St Paul's, Henry Godolphin, wanted to exercise more control over the building. It was he who had insisted on having the interior of the dome painted by Thornhill, and there were unseemly rows over the railings to go round the cathedral. When Queen Anne died, Godolphin effectively sidelined Wren. Godolphin and the other clergy overruled his wishes by installing a balustrade running around the top of the exterior walls, prompting him to comment that 'ladies think nothing well without an edging'.

[11] Letter from Wren, dated 12 May 1705, printed in *Notes & Queries*, 3rd Series, Vol. IV, 8 August 1863, page 103
[12] *Roger North's writings on architecture*, edited by H.M. Colvin and John Newman, page 22

OPPOSITE ABOVE

On 29 December 1940 an incendiary bomb crashed through the dome of St Paul's, but was extinguished by the fire crews of the St Paul's Watch without major harm. Dean Matthews wrote that St Paul's was left 'conspicuous and isolated among the ruins'.

OPPOSITE BELOW

The heroes of St Paul's Watch, a voluntary organization known as 'the best club in London': it included academics, architects, civil servants, businessmen and members of the clergy.

OVERLEAF A night-time view of St Paul's and the City.

The rebuilding happened during a period of great political change. When Charles II died in 1685 he was succeeded by his brother, James II. James was deposed, as a Roman Catholic, in the Glorious Revolution of 1688. His Protestant daughter Mary and her husband, William of Orange, took the throne. At William's death in 1702 Mary's sister, Anne, became Queen. Wren survived all these changes, and had a good relationship with all the Stuart monarchs he served. He approved of royal patronage, writing 'Great Monarchs are ambitious to leave great Monuments behind them, and this occasions great Inventions in Mechanick Arts' (*Parentalia*). But with the arrival of George I and the Hanoverians, new factions at court were jealous of Wren and in 1718 he was dismissed from the Surveyor Generalship of the King's Works, a post he had held since 1669. His replacement was William Benson, who was inept and possibly dishonest. He lasted little more than a year. Nicholas Hawksmoor observed that Benson 'got more in one year (for confusing the King's Works) than Sir Chris Wren did in 40 years for his honest endeavours.'[13]

Wren died in 1723 at the age of ninety-one. Despite his insistence that burials should not take place in churches, he was buried in the crypt of his own cathedral under a simple stone inscribed

Here Lieth SIR CHRISTOPHER WREN Kt
The Builder of this Cathedral Church of St PAUL & c.
who Dyed in the Year of our LORD MDCCXXIII
And of his Age XCI

He was the first national hero to be buried in the crypt. In 1806 he was joined by Lord Nelson, whose body was brought back from the Battle of Trafalgar to be given a state funeral. Nelson is buried directly beneath the centre of the dome in the crypt, in an imposing sixteenth-century sarcophagus originally intended for Cardinal Wolsey. Nearby is the impressive tomb of his fellow warrior the Duke of Wellington, who was buried at St Paul's in 1852. Both Nelson and Wellington also have monuments on the main church floor, among those of many other heroes of the Napoleonic wars. But it is not only warriors who are commemorated here: fine statues of Doctor Johnson and of John Howard, the great prison reformer, face each other across the open space beneath the dome. In the last century Winston Churchill's funeral service was held at St Paul's, a fitting tribute to the wartime leader who, at the height of the Blitz, ordered the Fire Service to 'save St Paul's Cathedral . . . at all costs'.

[13] H.M. Colvin, *A Biographical Dictionary of British Architects 1600–1840*, page 73

FIFTY NEW CHURCHES

A detail of the tower of St George–in-the-East, 1714–1729, by Nicholas Hawksmoor.
The 'sacrificial altars', decorated with swags and garlands, are connected by short sections
of balustrade. These incorporate Hawksmoor's trademark device of long rectangular
openings, with rounded ends, linked together with interlocking strapwork.

In November 1710 a violent storm swept across England. The 'Great infamous Wind' caused damage throughout the country, not least in London where the roof of St Alfege's church in Greenwich collapsed. This coincided with a general election which brought the Tories to power with a landslide victory, routing their Whig opponents who had held office since 1695. The parishioners of Greenwich appealed to the new Tory government for Coal Tax money to help rebuild their church. The Tories, traditional supporters of the Church of England, were worried about the rapidly growing populations in new areas around London with no Anglican churches to minister to their spiritual needs. In 1711 the Church of England published a pamphlet entitled 'A Representation of the Present State of Religion, with regard to the late excessive Growth of Infidelity, Heresy, and Profaneness'.

The author of *Gulliver's Travels* Jonathan Swift, himself an Anglican clergyman, regretted that:

> so little care should be taken for the building of churches, that five parts in six of the people are absolutely hindered from hearing divine service. Particularly here in London, where a single minister, with one or two sorry curates, hath the care sometimes of above twenty thousand souls incumbent on him.[1]

The Vicar of Deptford petitioned Parliament about the state of his church, claiming his:

> 12,000 souls cannot possibly be accommodated in the said church [leading many to] go to meeting houses . . . of Dissenters . . . Quakers . . . Presbyterians, and . . . Anabaptists.[2]

The Vicar's '12,000 souls' included many men working in the Royal Dockyards at Deptford – just the sort of literate skilled workers who were inclined to be Dissenters.

The result of these pressures was the Act of 1711 which established a 'Commission for Building Fifty New Churches'. It also provided money for the new churches by extending the Coal Tax until 1724. Besides politicians, lawyers and churchmen, the Commission included the principal officers of the Royal Works: Sir John Vanbrugh and Sir Christopher Wren, as well as the architect Thomas Archer.

Wren at the age of seventy-nine didn't design any of the New Churches, but he set out his view (discussed on page 125) that churches should be built as 'auditories'.[3] He also recommended that:

[1] *The Works of Jonathan Swift . . . in Four Volumes*, 1735, page 136, where it states in a footnote: 'This Paragraph is known to have given the first Hint to certain Bishops . . . to procure a fund for building fifty new churches in London.'
[2] *Journal of the House of Commons*, 16 (1708–11), page 581
[3] *Parentalia*, page 195, discussing the Fifty New Churches Commission, says Wren 'took occasion to impart his Thoughts . . . in a Letter to a Friend in that Commission.' (*Parentalia* incorrectly says the Act was passed in 1708.)

AFTER THE FIRE

they be brought as forward as possible into the larger and more open Streets, not in obscure Lanes, nor where Coaches will be much obstructed in the Passage.

and that the prominent fronts:

should be adorn'd with Porticos, both for Beauty and Convenience; together with handsome Spires, or Lanterns, rising in good Proportion above the neighbouring Houses (of which I have given several Examples in the City of different Forms).

He urged preachers to ensure their:

Pronunciation be distinct and equal, without losing the Voice at the last Word of the Sentence, which . . . if obscur'd spoils the whole Sense . . . I mention this as an insufferable Fault in the Pronunciation of some of our otherwise excellent Preachers; which School-masters might correct in the young, as a vicious Pronunciation.

He also condemns the practice of renting out pews to the wealthier parishioners:

It were to be wish'd there were to be no Pews, but Benches; but there is no stemming the Tide of Profit, & the Advantage of Pew-keepers.

Sir John Vanbrugh was famous as the architect of Blenheim Palace, where he had collaborated closely with Nicholas Hawksmoor. His architectural work didn't include any churches, but in 1712 he wrote about the importance of religious buildings:

Among the several kinds of Buildings by which Great Citys are Adorn'd; Churches, have in all Ages, and with all Religions been placed in the first Rank. No Expense has ever been thought too much for them; Their Magnificence has been esteem'd a pious expression of the Peoples great and profound Veneration towards their Deitys.[4]

As Controller of the Queen's Works he also made recommendations on how the New Churches should 'remain Monuments to posterity . . . & by consequence become ornaments to the Town, & a Credit to the Nation'. They should be built in a 'plain but just and noble style' and aim at the most Solemn and Awfull Appearance, within and without'. Following Wren, he then set out rules

[4] 'Mr Van-Brugg's Proposals about Building ye New Churches', 1712, transcribed in Kerry Downes, *Vanbrugh*, pages 257–8

concerning the site, how to reduce the risk of fire, the churches should be free-standing[5] and be built of stone or brick. They should also have towers or steeples.

To carry out the programme the Commission appointed two Surveyors, Nicholas Hawksmoor and William Dickinson. As we have seen, Hawksmoor had collaborated closely with both Vanbrugh and Wren on numerous projects, and they would have needed no convincing that he was the best man for the job.

Dickinson held the post of Surveyor to the Dean and Chapter of Westminster Abbey, where he had worked with Wren on the north transept and porch.[6] He also worked at St Michael Cornhill, and probably at St Mary Aldermary, two of the City churches Wren rebuilt in the Gothic idiom. Terry Friedman hails him as 'the unsung hero of this enduring style'[7] for his skill in handling

James Gibbs, as depicted in a line engraving by A. Bannerman, 1762, after William Hogarth.

the language and forms of Gothic. Although he produced a design for St Mary-le-Strand, he did not work on any of the Fifty New Churches, and resigned in 1713. At his death in 1725, his obituary describes him as a 'celebrated Architect'.

When Dickinson resigned in 1713 he was replaced by James Gibbs, who in 1716 was himself replaced by John James. Gibbs was a Catholic Scot; as a young man he had travelled to Italy, having a 'great genius to drawing and being of a rambling disposition'. He started to train as a Jesuit, but abandoned the priesthood in favour of architecture when he became a pupil of Carlo Fontana, the Papacy's chief architect. He returned to England in 1709, and could fairly claim to be the only architect with a proper training at the hands of an Italian master.

John James was a master carpenter, who when applying for a post at St Paul's claimed 'there was no person pretending to Architecture among us, Sir Chr. Wren excepted' who enjoyed 'the Advantage of a better Education in the Latin Italian and ffrench Tongues, a competent Share of Mathematicks and Ten Years Instruction in all the practical parts of Building'.[8] His masterpiece is St George's Hanover Square, but his architecture lacks the flair and genius of Hawksmoor and Gibbs. He favoured a less flamboyant style, and stated that 'the Beautys of Architecture may consist with the greatest plainness of the Structure.'

In the event only a dozen churches were actually built, and of these Hawksmoor was responsible for half. Of the six churches by Hawksmoor, two were rebuildings of existing churches: St Alfege Greenwich and St Mary Woolnoth in the City. He collaborated with his fellow Surveyor John James on two more churches, St Luke Old Street and St John Horsleydown. Besides St George's Hanover Square, John James also designed the rather tame spire at St Alfege. After Hawksmoor's death he took over the work on the west towers at Westminster Abbey, which he completed to Hawksmoor's designs. He complained that for want of clear instructions this was 'a thing of no small difficulty . . . [with] windings and turnings of so many Gothic Ornaments'.

The three other churches are the work of James Gibbs and Thomas Archer.

Gibbs's St Mary-le-Strand in Westminster sits on an island in the middle of the busy Strand, so it is almost in an 'open space'. The first of the churches to be built, he designed it in 1714, and it was completed by 1723. The richly gilded interior is influenced by the architect's recent visit to Italy. As a Scot and a Roman Catholic Gibbs was unpopular with the Whigs, and he lost his position as Surveyor when George I came to the throne. But this was not

The west towers of Westminster Abbey. After Hawksmoor's death in 1725, his designs were completed by John James.

[5] He proposes: 'Their situation may be ever Insulate. This . . . makes the Access to them easy, and is a great Security from Fire' and that towers should be 'High and Bold Structures; and so form'd as not to be subject to Ruin by fire', ibid.
[6] The porch was rebuilt by Sir George Gilbert Scott in the nineteenth century.
[7] Terry Friedman, *The Eighteenth-Century Church in Britain*, page 201
[8] H.M. Colvin, *A Biographical Dictionary of British Architects 1600-1840*, page 274

Thomas Archer, as shown in a portrait attributed to Sir Godfrey Kneller, at St John Smith Square.

[9] The Groom Porter's duties were to 'to provide Cards, Dice, &c. when there is playing at Court: To decide Disputes which arise in Gaming'. The post effectively gave Archer control over all the Court's gambling activities.
[10] H.M. Colvin, *A Biographical Dictionary of British Architects 1600-1840*
[11] Blackerby's obituary appeared in the *British Gazetteer* no. 36, March 27, 1736.

the end of his career. In the 1720s, his St Martin-in-the-Fields established a Neoclassical prototype of the Anglican church, with a pedimented portico and a steeple rising over the west end, that was widely copied in America and the other British colonies. Gibbs went on to build up a very successful practice as the architect of numerous country houses, as well as public buildings at the Universities of Oxford and Cambridge.

Thomas Archer was a gentleman architect who had obtained the lucrative court post of Groom Porter.[9] When he was appointed as one of the Commissioners, he had already built several houses and a church in Birmingham. Little is known of his architectural training: like Gibbs he was heavily influenced by the Italian Baroque, in particular the work of Borromini. He was responsible for two of the Fifty New Churches, St Paul Deptford and St John Smith Square in Westminster. Colvin describes his houses and churches as 'the most uncompromising Baroque buildings in England'.[10]

The Commission's greatest legacy is Hawksmoor's group of half a dozen churches: these are all powerfully idiosyncratic, in particular the steeples, which sometimes use classical elements to achieve an essentially Gothic form. Wren had shown one way of doing this, but Hawksmoor introduced an element of abstraction, with plain unadorned surfaces, shadowy recesses and unexpected groupings of elements, like the eight altars on the tower of St George-in-the-East. The results display the 'Solemn and Awfull Appearance' that Vanbrugh had avocated.

Of Hawksmoor's personality we know less than of Wren or Hooke. He was born in 1661, and lived to the age of seventy-five. His obituary, by his son-in-law Nathaniel Blackerby, the treasurer of the Fifty New Churches Commission, says:

In his private life he was a tender husband, a loving father, a sincere friend, and a most agreeable companion; nor could the most poignant pains of Gout, which he for many years laboured under, ever ruffle or discompose his evenness of temper.[11]

The only surviving likeness of him is a strangely gloomy bust at All Souls College in Oxford; maybe he was suffering from an attack of gout when it was made. He came from a farming family in Nottinghamshire, and Blackerby's obituary says:

His early skill in, and Genius for this noble science [architecture] recommended him, when about 18 years of age, to the favour and esteem of his great master and predecessor, Sir Christopher Wren.

He went to live in Wren's household as a member of the family, and soon joined Wren's office as a 'clerk' whose duties included copying drawings. Within a few years he had been trained in all aspects of architecture. His early interest in Gothic architecture is revealed in a youthful 'Topographical Sketchbook' which includes a drawing of the west front of Bath Abbey, dated 1683. By the late 1680s he had become Wren's official assistant in the City Churches office and was involved in designing some of the later towers and spires for the churches. He was also Wren's assistant at St Paul's from 1691 to 1712, and to begin with he was paid for making drawings of 'Designs and other necessary business for the Service of this work'. But by 1702 he was 'Giving Directions to the Masons &c'.[12] He was employed by Wren to prepare drawings for many aspects of the cathedral, including the west towers, the organ case and the interior structure of the dome, with its brick cone supporting the lantern.

Bust of Hawksmoor, attributed to Sir Henry Cheere, at All Souls College Oxford.

Glimpses of Hawksmoor's personality can be seen in the comments of his contemporaries. The famously quarrelsome Duchess of Marlborough, who dealt with him over the building of Blenheim Palace, wrote of his 'modesty and great honesty'; John Vanbrugh, his collaborator at Blenheim and Castle Howard, had written to her to ask her to find 'some opportunity to do him good, because he does not seem very solicitous to do it for himself.[13] Sir Thomas Robinson, the amateur architect who interfered with his plans for the Mausoleum at Castle Howard, said 'I never talk'd with a more reasonable man, nor with one so little prejudiced in favour of his own performances.'[14]

Blackerby's obituary talks of his other accomplishments:

Nor was Architecture the only Science he was Master of. He was bred a Scholar and knew as well the Learned as the Modern tongues. He was a very Skilful Mathematician, Geographer and Geometrician.

This scholarly approach is reflected in the contents of his library, detailed in the sale catalogue when his books were sold after his death, which gives us further insights into his character and interests. The catalogue lists many works

[12] Wren Society, vol. 13, page 33 and vol. 15, page 85
[13] *Private Correspondence of Sarah, Duchess of Marlborough* vol. I, 1838
[14] 'The Letters and Drawings of Nicholas Hawksmoor Relating to the Building of the Mausoleum at Castle Howard, 1726–1742', edited by G. Webb, published in Walpole Society vol. 19, 1930–31, page 140

in English as well as foreign languages, and the fact that he had dictionaries for these (including Minshai's *Dictionary 9 Languages*) shows how seriously he took his studies. Hawksmoor did not have a university education, nor did he ever travel abroad, unlike Wren, Archer, Vanbrugh and Gibbs. Instead he relied on books as sources of information and inspiration. His library contained works by scientists such as Isaac Newton and Robert Boyle, as well as a three-volume set of the transactions of the Royal Society, which included accounts of many exotic buildings, including the ruined temples of Palmyra in Syria and the Palace of Persepolis in Persia.

Egyptian obelisks and pyramids were of particular interest to him and he often included them in his designs; partly because they bypassed the Palladians' insistence on Ancient Rome as the only proper source for architectural authenticity, and also because obelisks were used as important landmarks in the newly Baroque Rome created by Pope Sixtus V. He owned a copy of Fontana's *Oblesco Vaticano* of 1590, and probably knew John Greaves's 1646 book on obelisks and pyramids, *Pyramidographia: or a description of the pyramids in Egypt* (see page 150). These Egyptian monuments had special significance for Freemasons, a fraternity with obvious connections to the building trades. Freemasons had grown in numbers rapidly in the early years of the eighteenth century: in 1691 Wren had joined the Freemasons, and by 1730 Hawksmoor himself had become a member of the Lodge that met at the Oxford Arms near St Paul's. Hawksmoor's son-in-law Nicholas Blackerby was Deputy Grand Master of the Grand Lodge. Sir James Thornhill and his son-in-law William Hogarth were also prominent masons; like Hawksmoor they were at odds with the forces of the new Palladianism then coming into fashion. Hawksmoor's masonic connections may have informed his architecture, as can be seen at St Mary Woolnoth, but they hardly justify the image of him as the sinister figure of the occult involved in pagan sacrifices and ritual magic, as portrayed in the popular fiction of Iain Sinclair's 1975 *Lud Heat: a Book of the Dead Hamlets*, and Peter Ackroyd's *Hawksmoor*, where the architect Nicholas Dyer is clearly modelled on Hawksmoor; he indulges in occult practices, including human sacrifice, when building his churches.

Hawksmoor's library included works on the architecture of the ancient world by Pliny the Elder, Tacitus and Caesar. He owned editions of Vitruvius by Perrault, as well as works by the modern Italians: Alberti, Palladio, Serlio and Scamozzi. Illustrations of the Roman Pantheon were to be found in his copies of engravings by Giovanni Battista Falda, and the Baroque architecture of Rome was represented by the works of Domenico and Carlo Fontana.

Wren and Hawksmoor shared a passionate interest in the buildings of the ancient world, often known only from descriptions. They discussed the Mausoleum at

Halicarnassus, which Wren had incorporated into his Great Model for St Paul's, and Hawksmoor later used as a basis for the steeple of St George's Bloomsbury. They were similarly interested in the Temple of Solomon in Jerusalem, which is of particular significance to Freemasons, who date their origins from the building of the Temple. Hooke was also involved in these archaeological debates, as shown by a diary entry for 1675: 'With Sir Chr Wren. Long Discourse with him about the Module of the Temple of Jerusalem'. Wren and Hawksmoor shared an interest in Lars Porsenna's tomb at Clusium (described by Wren as a 'stupendous fabrick' and illustrated in Greaves's *Pyramidographia*) and Hagia Sophia in Constantinople. There are a number of drawings attributed to Wren of Hagia Sophia; as one of the great domed buildings of Byzantium, Wren was particularly interested in its construction. He consulted the works of the French artist traveller

Guillaume-Joseph Grelot, who in 1680 had published his engravings of the former church which had become a mosque under the Ottomans. Grelot obtained permission to visit the interior, and describes how he went in fear of his life when he was found having a picnic by one of the guards: 'I was caught in a crime which neither the stake nor fire could expiate – that was to be in a Mosque drawing human figures, drinking wine and eating pork – three capital sins against Mahomedan law.'[15] To his relief the guard admired his drawings and left him to finish his meal in peace.

This interest in ancient buildings was an important element in the design of the Fifty New Churches. The Commissioners included clergymen like Francis Atterbury, who believed in a return to what they called the 'Primitive Christian' architecture of the early churches of Byzantium and Syria. They saw this as a way of asserting the validity of the Anglican tradition, bypassing the medieval period tainted by its associations with Catholicism. The Commission endorsed this antiquarian approach when it published a list of requirements for the new churches. These are reflected in a design by Hawksmoor for an unbuilt church at Bethnal Green, which he calls 'The Basilica after the Primitive Christians'. His plan is annotated with notes describing the 'Manner of Building the Church – as it was in ye fourth Century, in ye purest times of Christianity'.

The smaller dome of Wren's Great Model has a stepped pyramid with a statue of St Paul standing on top. Wren is drawing on ancient descriptions of the Mausoleum at Halicarnassus, which describe 'a pyramid . . . formed of twenty-four steps, which gradually taper upwards towards the summit'. At the summit were statues of King Mausolus and his wife standing in a chariot drawn by four horses.

[15] Guillaume-Joseph Grelot, *Relation nouvelle d'un voyage de Constantinople*, page 140

The church should be built in an open space and oriented towards the east; there should be no burials within or near the church; and there should be a font at the west end for 'ye Converts . . . to be immers'd'. There was to be an 'enclosure of ye Church, to keep off filth – Nastyness and Brutes'. Within the enclosure were a Minister's house and a parish vestry. The plan also shows 'The severall Approaches' allowing worshippers to enter the church on three sides. Although this Bethnal Green plan was never built, it embodied the ideal of the sort of church the Commissioners had in mind, and some of these features occur in several of Hawksmoor's churches, particularly St George-in-the-East at Wapping.

The requirement for the churches to be in open spaces contrasts with Wren's City churches, mostly built on their old medieval sites. There wasn't spare land available for those of the 'Fifty New Churches' built in the City and Westminster (St George's Bloomsbury, St George's Hanover Square, St Mary-le-Strand and St Mary Woolnoth) but those in the east had more land available. The view east from the 72nd floor of the Shard's viewing platform (at the southern end of London Bridge) shows the limestone towers of Hawksmoor's masterpieces rising from their open spaces, still dominating the local landscape. This is in stark contrast to the view north, where Wren's steeples are just visible in the densely packed City, with the majestic dome of St Paul's holding its own against the office blocks of modern London.

Like the other English Baroque architects, Hawksmoor suffered from the changes in fashion brought about by the Palladians, led by Lord Burlington. The Palladians demanded a stricter adherence to the rules of classical antique architecture, as set out by the ancient Roman writer Vitruvius in his treatise *De Architectura*, and the sixteenth-century Italian architect Andrea Palladio in his *I quattro libri dell' architettura*, published in 1570. This style, with its emphasis on proportion and symmetry, had been introduced to England by Inigo Jones in the days of James I and Charles I. Colen Campbell's *Vitruvius Britannicus*, which appeared between 1715 and 1725, backed the Palladian cause against the excesses of the Baroque, which they saw as associated with the Stuarts and their absolutist ambitions. In this climate there wasn't much opportunity for building Baroque churches. Although the Fifty New Churches Commission continued to raise and spend revenue through the 1720s, it was wound up in 1734. One of its final decisions was to grant money for rebuilding St Giles in the Fields, to designs by Henry Flitcroft in the newly fashionable Palladian style. The exterior is stone-faced (cheaper than building in stone throughout), and has a rusticated ground floor with square windows, while the upper storey is plain with round-headed windows. Their simple surrounds, and the lack of a classical order, show how the new austere style of Palladianism rejected the extravagant Baroque of

Gibbs and Hawksmoor. On the other hand the multi-stage steeple, rising from a square pilastered base to an octagonal arcade and topped with an obelisk-like spire, follows Gibbs's examples at St Martin-in-the-Fields, St Mary-le-Strand and St Clement Danes.

The Palladians contrived to get Wren and Hawksmoor dismissed from their public positions at the Office of Works, prompting Hawksmoor to complain 'I am confoundedly used for my services to ye publick' and to make sarcastic references to 'my Lord Burlington and other virtuosi' and 'that Reptile Knight' Sir Thomas Hewett, who became Surveyor General of the Office of Works in 1719.

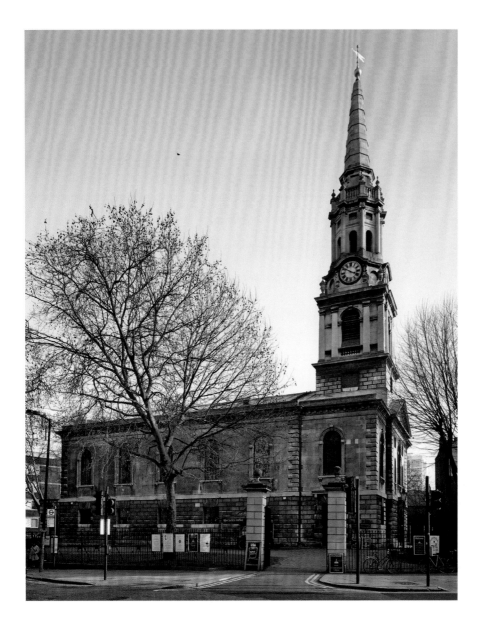

St Giles in the Fields, designed by Henry Flitcroft in the new Palladian style. The body of the church has a plain exterior free of the classical orders; while the steeple has urns, balustrades, Ionic columns and Doric pilasters, all in the manner of Wren and Gibbs.

Christ Church Spitalfields

BELOW Thomas Dunn's monument to Edward Peck, who campaigned to have the church built at Spitalfields.

OPPOSITE The spire soars to a height of 225 feet over a portico of four giant Tuscan columns supporting a a semi-circular arch. Hawksmoor uses these elements to create the effect of a colossal Venetian window.

SPITALFIELDS gets its name from St Mary Spital, a hospital or priory to the east of Bishopsgate. Today there's a good view of Christ Church from Bishopsgate: the imposing west front, capped by the soaring spire, closes the vista looking east along Brushfield Street. Christ Church, together with St George-in-the-East and St Anne's Limehouse, is one of three East End churches which Nicholas Hawksmoor built for the Commission for the Building of Fifty New Churches. All three were started in 1714. The name Christ Church was a natural choice for the members of the Commission, several of whom had been to the eponymous Oxford College, which had many links with the High Church Tory party. Indeed two of the Commissioners, Francis Atterbury and George Smalridge, succeeded each other as Dean of Christ Church.

Large numbers of Protestant Huguenot refugees from France had recently settled in Spitalfields, where they set up a prosperous silk-weaving industry. This

was just the sort of congregation the Commission wanted to encourage into the Anglican communion. The legacy of the Huguenots can be seen in the local street names: Nantes Passage, Fleur-de-Lis Street and Fournier Street, named after George Fournier, a Huguenot philanthropist. The attic storeys of some of the houses nearby still have their extra wide 'weaver's window' to provide light for the craftsmen's looms. Since then the Huguenots have moved on to be replaced by other immigrants: during the late nineteenth century many Jews settled here, fleeing the pogroms in Russia and Europe. More recently the Bengali community has brought new life to the area. In 1976 they set up a mosque, the London Jamme Masjid (Great Mosque), in a building which had previously been a Huguenot chapel, then a Methodist chapel, as well as serving as a synagogue since 1897.

One of the Commissioners for the Fifty New Churches is buried here. In the sanctuary at the east end is a fine monument to Edward Peck by Thomas Dunn, the mason who built the church. Peck was a local dyer who had been active in seeking to have a church built in the area, and his inscription reads:

He was One of the Commissioners for
Building the fifty new Churches and
in this Corner laid the first stone
of this Stately Fabrick Anno 1715.

The Stately Fabrick took fifteen years to build, with delays caused by money problems. The original estimate of just over £9,000 had risen to over £40,000 by the time the church was consecrated in 1729. Hawksmoor's powerful exterior, reaching a height of 225 feet and dominating the local area, is one of contrasts between strong geometric shapes: a triangle, a rectangle and semicircles. The tall triangular spire rises like an obelisk to a point with a gold ball and weathervane; the central section is a rectangle enclosing an arched window between round-headed niches, and at ground level the four giant Tuscan columns of the west portico jut forward below a semicircular arch to form a huge Venetian, or Serlian, window. A smaller Venetian window echoes this at the east end. There is more simple geometry in the pairs of circular porthole windows on the east end, either side of the Venetian window. These small porthole windows also run along the north and south walls as well as occurring on the west front, at the base of the middle section and on the walls flanking the portico.

Actually Hawksmoor's original spire was more medieval and less starkly geometric in appearance. In the tapering chamfered grooves on the corners there were six sets of ornaments like tongues of flame running up the spire (Hawksmoor's version of crockets, the small knobbly projections on Gothic pinnacles). On the flat surfaces between the chamfered corners he placed three sets of dormer windows, with funerary urns above. These were all removed in the 1820s.

The apparent width of the main section of the tower as it appears from the west is a typical Hawksmoor illusion. The actual width is that of the clock stage; the lower section is made to seem wider by his use of flanking buttresses, carrying pairs of blind niches, to north and south. From the sides it looks as if deep concave hollows have been scooped out of the stone. Hawksmoor does something similar at St Anne's Limehouse.

Entering the church through the giant portico we go through a vestibule and pass under the organ gallery, supported by fluted Corinthian columns, where the magnificent organ by Richard Bridge has just been reinstated. Bridge was the leading organ-maker of his day, and his organ, the largest in the country when installed in 1735, is a rare survivor from the time of Handel. Decay and neglect had made it unplayable for sixty years, but its recent restoration has restored it to its former glory. The High Church connections of Christ Church are represented by the crown over the central tower, flanked by bishops'

ABOVE LEFT The colossal 'Venetian window' portico on the west front.

ABOVE RIGHT The wide span of the middle section of the tower seen from the front is an illusion: from the sides deep concave hollows scooped out between the flanking buttresses show the central core of the tower is really square

LEFT The west front is echoed by the small Venetian window at the east end, flanked by pairs of circular porthole windows.

ABOVE The original organ, installed by Richard Bridge in 1735, has recently been restored.

OPPOSITE The massive interior has a high coffered ceiling and side aisles created by giant Composite columns in the nave.

mitres on the outer towers. The pipes are held by delicate fretwork bands of pale painted limewood, contrasting with the dark mahogany of the rest of the case.

The interior space is gigantic, with its high coffered ceiling divided into panels with plaster-work mouldings. Huge Composite columns in the nave create side aisles; these have tunnel vaults in each bay, below clerestory windows, an arrangement which Professor Vaughan Hart sees as 'as an obvious variant'[1] of Serlio's illustration of the Temple of Peace in the Roman Forum,[2] except Hawksmoor's clerestory windows have cherub keystones. The keystones on the lower nave arches are decorated alternately with more cherubs, bibles and olive branches. The columns stand on high wooden bases, with galleries running between the columns. At the east end two extra columns frame the entrance to the chancel, and support a beam, or architrave, running transversely across the nave, with the royal coat of arms in the middle.

The original galleries, along with the box pews, were removed in the 1860s by Ewan Christian (the architect who led the successful campaign to save the tower of St Mary Somerset), in an attempt 'to make the church light and cheerful instead of being dark and gloomy'. The high pulpit was also removed, and a lower one substituted. By the 1950s Spitalfields was a run-down area; the neglected church had become unsafe and was closed for worship in 1956. Twenty years later saw the formation of the Friends of Christ Church Spitalfields, who have led the campaign to save the church. Their successful fundraising has made possible the recent work on the organ as well as a major restoration, when the oak galleries were put back, between 1997 and 2004. 'The result is spectacular,' wrote Jonathan Glancy in the *Guardian* in 2004. 'For the first time in over a century, it is possible to experience this great church more or less as it looked 275 years ago.' Now the organ is back at Christ Church, this experience can be both musical and architectural.

[1] Vaughan Hart, *Nicholas Hawksmoor, Rebuilding Ancient Wonders*, page 55
[2] *Templum Pacis*, page XXIIII of *Il Terzo Libro di Sebastiano Serlio Bolognese*, first published in 1540. Wren and Hawksmoor both had copies of an edition published in 1663.

The clerestory windows have cherub keystones. The keystones on the lower nave arches are decorated alternately with bibles, olive branches and more cherubs. The side aisles have coffered tunnel vaults in each bay.

287

St Alfege Greenwich

ALFEGE, OR ÆLFHEAH, was the first Archbishop of Canterbury to be martyred. The Anglo-Saxon Chronicle tells how he was captured by Danish pirates laying siege to Canterbury after one of his own monks betrayed the city. Alfege refused to allow an enormous ransom to be paid for his release, and in 1012 his captors bludgeoned him to death at their camp in Greenwich. He was soon commemorated by the building of a church on the site. St Alfege's church was rebuilt, probably in the thirteenth century, and the tower was again rebuilt in the early seventeenth century. As a result of a violent storm in November 1710 the roof fell into the nave, and the parishioners, unable to afford the repairs, appealed to Parliament for help. Their plight

St Alfege had the largest unsupported ceiling in the country when it was built between 1712 and 1718.

helped bring about the Fifty New Churches Act of 1711. St Alfege's, started in 1712 and completed by 1718, was the earliest of these churches to be built. The architect chosen by the Commissioners was Nicholas Hawksmoor. The design is rectangular in plan, with a vast flat ceiling decorated with a simple plasterwork oval. This was the largest unsupported ceiling of its time, larger even than that of Wren's Sheldonian Theatre in Oxford. The chancel is a shallow apse at the east end, made to appear deeper than it is by illusionist *trompe l'œil* coffering. This, together with the swags and trophies, was originally carried out by Sir James Thornhill (who painted the interior of the dome of St Paul's) and restored by Glyn Jones after the war. Galleries on the other three sides allow for additional seating, and there are also vestibules and doorways on the north and south.

The chancel has illusionist *trompe l'œil* coffering, originally painted by James Thornhill. The Corinthian capitals by Grinling Gibbons survived the bombs of 1941.

FIFTY NEW CHURCHES

Although the main entrance is from the west, the east front facing the street is visually the most important. It has a pediment above a giant portico in the Doric order, with a central arch breaking through the entablature into the pediment, giving the effect of an oversized Serlian or Venetian window, a typical Hawksmoor device. The giant Tuscan pilasters running round the rest of the building are possibly the result of changes suggested to Hawksmoor by Thomas Archer, one of the Commissioners. The roofline is enlivened by monumental urns looking like detached Ionic capitals (with the scrolls facing inwards) supporting a crown, while at street level there are four bollard-like carved altars, decorated with cherubs and swags. These are Hawksmoor's interpretation of Roman sacrificial altars and reflect his interest in classical antiquity. In one of Hawksmoor's schemes for Greenwich, St Alfege's is at the end of a *Via Triumphalis* or ceremonial street leading from the grand complex of the nearby Royal Naval Hospital to the church. Vaughan Hart says this plan 'clearly explains the unorthodox sacrificial altars and eastern portico to St Alfege.'[1] In the event Romney Road was built nearer the Thames,

OPPOSITE The grand east portico takes the form of an oversized Venetian window.

BELOW LEFT A monumental urn resembling an Ionic capital with the scrolls reversed, beneath a crown.

BELOW RIGHT Four carved altars on the east front, decorated with swags and cherubs, suggesting Roman sacrificial altars.

[1] Vaughan Hart, *Nicholas Hawksmoor, Rebuilding Ancient Wonders*, page 178

so the ceremonial connection between church and Hospital was lost, but the altars remain.

Hawksmoor also designed a dramatic tower with an octagonal lantern for the west end. However as the original tower had survived the storm and could be reused, this design was not realized, although it resurfaces at St George-in-the-East. Instead the old tower was refaced by John James in 1730 in an elegant, but tamer, classical style. On 19 March 1941 incendiary bombs landed on the church and the roof collapsed into the nave, as in 1710. The walls and the tower survived, but the interior was gutted and most of the fittings destroyed, including a pulpit decorated with carvings by Grinling Gibbons of leaves, berries and grotesque faces. Sir Albert Richardson carried out a sensitive restoration of the interior in 1953, reinstating the galleries and pews. The Corinthian capitals in the apse, also attributed to Gibbons, survived the bombing, as did the Benefaction Boards on display at the east end of the galleries. These record acts of generosity by individuals, including a gift of £600 by Henry Howard, the Earl of Northampton to establish 'A Noble College for a Warden Servants and 20 old Men, 12 to be of this Parish': Trinity Hospital survives in Greenwich to this day and now provides for more than fifty residents.

Those buried in the church and its grounds include the English Renaissance composer Thomas Tallis (died 1585) and General James Wolfe, the victor (and victim) of the Battle of Quebec (died 1759).

ABOVE One of the Benefaction Boards in the galleries. Henry Howard's gift of £600 in 1613 is the seventh item down.

OPPOSITE The tower was refaced by John James in 1730 in an elegant classical style.

St Anne's Limehouse

BELOW St Anne's long links
with the Royal Navy are
enshrined in the church's
right to fly the White
Ensign at all times, a
privilege usually restricted
to Royal Naval vessels
under way at sea.

OPPOSITE The church's
200-foot tower with its
golden ball is a prominent
landmark for shipping on
the Thames. The clock is
the highest on a church
tower in London.

ST ANNE'S LIMEHOUSE is one of the trio of Hawksmoor's great Stepney churches, created following the 1711 Act which appointed the Commission for the Building of Fifty New Churches. Built between 1714 and 1727, the Limehouse church's dedication is a clear reference to Queen Anne, an enthusiastic supporter of the New Churches project. She encouraged St Anne's, built close to the Thames, to serve as a registry for the Royal Navy. This would make it easier for returning captains to register deaths, and the occasional birth, that had taken place on their ships while at sea.

The main approach to St Anne's is from the west, down a narrow alley called Three Colt Street. The contrast between the small scale of the alleyway and the imposing tower of the church makes for a dramatic effect typical of Hawksmoor. A flight of steps leads to a semicircular porch, with giant Doric pilasters projecting diagonally beneath a half dome. The semicircular theme is repeated in the lunette windows peering out from either side of the porch.

Above the roofline of the church the tower narrows to a square bell loft with louvred openings, with clusters of more giant pilasters projecting from the corners, creating deep recesses to north and south, a device Hawksmoor repeats at Christ Church Spitalfields. Above the clock is the octagonal spire, itself made up of yet more pilasters. Echoing the treatment of the porch, the clustered pilasters on the corners break forward diagonally from those on the cardinal axes, which are themselves emphasized by four small pinnacles in the shape of pyramids. Following the composition from the ground up to these pyramids the eye is unsettled by the counterpoint created as the axis shifts back and forth between the central and the diagonal. From further away the effect is of a medieval spire, achieved using classical elements.

The projecting pilasters of the spire carry finials in the form of square urns topped with fir cones. These decorative elements are rich with symbolism derived from classical antiquity. Urns suggest death and purification through cremation, (as in Thomas Browne's *Urn Buriall* of 1658), and fir cones denote fecundity and regeneration. Pyramids were

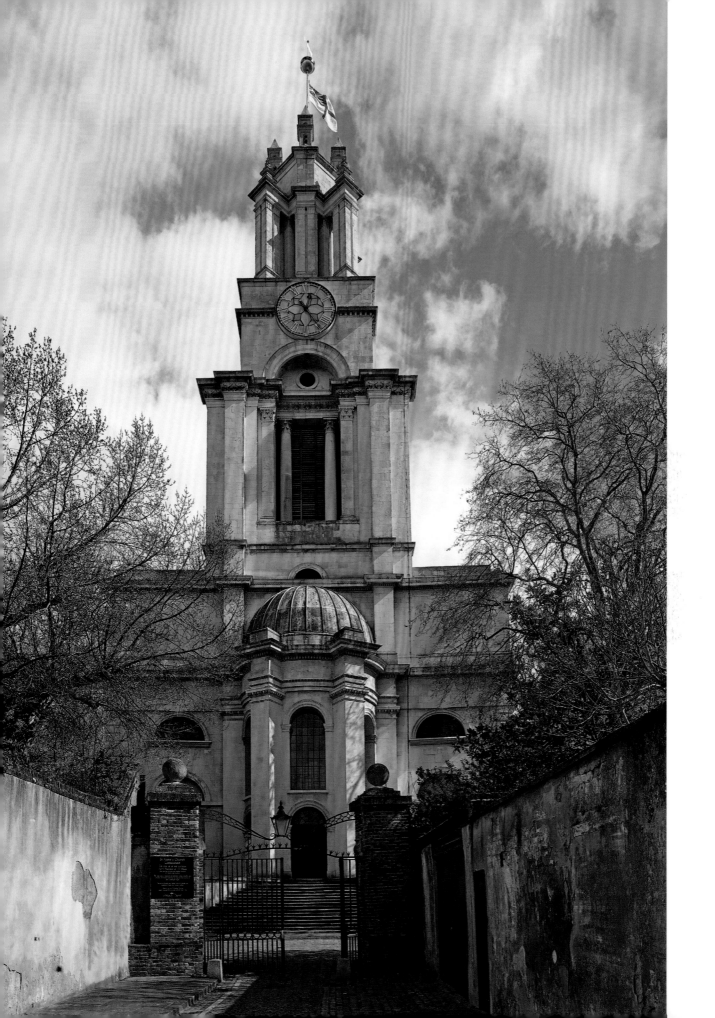

symbols of burial and the afterlife in the ancient world, as well as featuring in the masonic 'All-Seeing Eye'.

Another, much larger, pyramid sits in the north-west corner of the churchyard. This is an object of some speculation among lovers of the occult, (who seem to have it in for Hawksmoor).[1] But the prosaic explanation is that he probably intended it to go on one of the blank platforms or pedestals on the eastern façade: a drawing in the British Library of the east front shows these pedestals carrying pyramids. Another drawing shows a statue of Queen Anne between the two pyramids.[2] In the event the platforms remain as empty pedestals, while the pyramid gathers moss in the churchyard.

The view of the south front shows the empty pedestal on the right. It is decorated by three vertical panels, with Hawksmoor's trademark design of a long rectangle with rounded ends (compare St George-in-the-East and St Mary Woolnoth). On the left below the clock is the deep recess created by the projecting pilasters. The main body of the church has three tiers of seven windows and, unlike the tower, the treatment of the seven bays is plain to the point of austerity. The wall is subtly divided into three horizontal zones, the crypt, the nave and the attic storey. These horizontal divisions, which would normally be created by string courses, are here achieved by setting the middle section slightly back from the sections above and below, so there is a small projection where the different planes meet. The elegant effect is Bauhaus-like in its simplicity.

The bottom windows, which light the crypt, have tops with shallow segmental curves. The arrangement of the upper rows – small square windows beneath taller round-headed windows – suggests an interior scheme of aisles and galleries, divided into seven bays. This is confirmed on entering the nave, where square wooden piers rise from the pews to support the galleries running round three sides of the church. The piers are fluted,

BELOW The pyramid in the churchyard was probably intended to go on one of the platforms at the east end.

OPPOSITE The south front, seven bays long and devoid of decoration. On the right is one of the pedestals intended to carry a pyramid.

[1] 'We are pushed towards the notions of these churches as Temples; & as cult centres. Courts and gardens where the living communicate with the dead & receive wisdom from them.' From Iain Sinclair, *Lud Heat: a Book of the Dead Hamlets*, 1975 (the paperback edition has the St Anne's pyramid on the cover).
[2] Reproduced in Vaughan Hart, *Nicholas Hawksmoor, Rebuilding Ancient Wonders*, page 150

ST ANNE'S LIMEHOUSE   297

OPPOSITE Giant Corinthian columns rise from the gallery to support the ceiling.

LEFT Cherubs and sunbeams on the central panel of the ceiling.

OVERLEAF The nave has a flat ceiling, with ornate plasterwork. Square fluted piers with Ionic capitals support the galleries, and at the east end the reredos has been replaced by a stained glass window.

and have Ionic capitals. The large flat ceiling is characteristic of Hawksmoor (compare St Alfege Greenwich), with elaborate plasterwork surrounding the central oval panel. At the centre of the oval is a circular plaster panel with six pairs of cherubs between gilded sunbeams. In the corners the ceiling is supported by giant Corinthian columns rising from the galleries, narrowing the space at both ends of the nave. At the east this narrower space leads to an arch framing the shallow chancel with, instead of the ususal reredos, a stained glass window of the Crucifixion by Clutterbuck. This was installed as part of restorations carried out by John Morris and Philip Hardwick after a serious fire in 1850. St Anne's was damaged by bombing in 1941, and in the 1980s the roof trusses began to fail. They were repaired between 1983 and 1993 by Julian Harrap Architects. In the words of the church's own website, the interior is in a state of 'derelict chic'.

St George's Bloomsbury

Hawksmoor's St George's Bloomsbury, built between 1716 and 1731, is the strangest of the 'Fifty New Churches'. Why is a Roman emperor standing on an altar on top of the steeple ? And why are there lions and unicorns on the bottom of the spire?

The nursery rhyme provides some of the answer:

> The lion and the unicorn
> Were fighting for the crown
> The lion beat the unicorn
> All around the town

Unicorn at the base of the tower, recently replaced by stone carver Tim Crawley.

The strange heraldic beasts represent the lion of England and the unicorn of Scotland, and celebrate the defeat of the First Jacobite Rebellion at the Battle of Preston in 1715, which crushed the Jacobites' hopes of restoring the Scottish Stuarts to the British throne. The battle was a victory for the forces of the new King George I of Hanover, and not only did he lend his name to the church, he also stands on top of the steeple in the costume of a Roman emperor, as in the anonymous rhyme:

> When Harry the Eighth left the pope in the lurch
> His Parliament made him the head of the church.
> But George's good subjects, the Bloomsbury people,
> Instead of the church, made him head of the steeple

Not everyone approved of the lions and the unicorns. The Commissioners for the Fifty New Churches criticized Hawksmoor for not getting their approval for the £368 he paid Edward Strong to make the figures. 'A masterpiece of absurdity' was Horace Walpole's verdict on the tower, and the original sculptures were removed in 1871 as 'very doubtful ornaments'. In 2006, during a major restoration of the church, they were replaced by new sculptures: these lively reincarnations by the stone carver Tim Crawley are based on what is known of the originals. They cling on to the tower, a stepped pyramid designed by Hawksmoor as a reinterpretation of the Mausoleum at Halicarnassus. The Mausoleum, the tomb of King Mausolus, had lain in ruins since at least the early fifteenth century. One of the Seven Wonders of the Ancient World, it was described by Pliny the Elder as 'a pyramid . . . formed of twenty-four steps, which gradually taper upwards towards the summit'. At the top stood statues of King Mausolus and his wife in a chariot drawn by four horses.

ABOVE LEFT The Pantheon in Rome. The portico is eight columns wide, with the columns sitting directly on the ground, without a podium.

ABOVE RIGHT The Temple of Bacchus at Baalbek in Lebanon. The columns are raised on a podium.

OPPOSITE The south front has a grand pedimented portico, six columns wide and raised on a podium. The steeple is based on the Mausoleum of Halicarnassus; King George I stands on the top, in the dress of a Roman emperor.

[1] See page 276. There is a drawing by Hawksmoor showing how the Mausoleum might have looked in the Wren family copy of *Parentalia*. And Hawksmoor defended himself against criticism of his designs by invoking Wren's studies of the Mausoleum. See Du Prey, *Hawksmoor's London Churches: Architecture and Theology*.

Wren and Hawksmoor discussed the Mausoleum and speculated on its original appearance,[1] and although it only has eighteen steps, Hawksmoor's steeple is clearly based on Pliny's description, including the statue of George I dressed as a Roman emperor which takes the place of Mausolus in his chariot. Pliny says the stepped pyramid was supported on a square section of equal height, made up of thirty-six columns. Hawksmoor's version of this can be seen on the stage below the heraldic beasts: each of the four faces of the tower has a pedimented temple front of four Composite columns, with an additional column at each corner, making a total of twenty, rather than thirty-six, columns. By a quirk of history, some of the surviving pieces of Greek sculpture from the Mausoleum are now on show in the British Museum, only minutes away.

The temple fronts are smaller repetitions of the massive entrance portico with its giant Corinthian columns supporting a plain pediment. Apart from being six instead of eight columns wide, the similarity to the Pantheon in Rome is obvious. At the Pantheon the columns rise directly from ground level, but St George's follows another antique model, the Temple of Bacchus at Baalbek, in having the columns raised off the ground on a podium or base. Hawksmoor had made careful studies of both these ancient buildings.

The grand portico is on the south side, a position dictated by the cramped location chosen for the new church. The intention of the Commissioners was to locate the Fifty New Churches in open spaces with the main entrance front on the west but, unlike Hawksmoor's Stepney churches, the Bloomsbury site already had houses built on the west and east. This meant the available space was much longer on the north–south axis than the west–east, and so there was more room on the south for a grand entrance front. The easy way to handle this unequal distribution of space would be to put the altar at the north end of the church. But the Commissioners wanted altars placed at the ritually correct east,

FIFTY NEW CHURCHES

Corinthian columns support two shallow arches creating a double aisle on the north side. The gallery was removed in the 1780s to make room for the altar. This was reversed in the recent restoration, when the altar was moved back to the 'ritually correct' east wall and the north gallery reinstated.

in recognition of the practices of the Early Christians. In spite of this, both Vanbrugh and Gibbs had proposed designs oriented to the north, so following the longer north-south axis and allowing the congregation to face the altar as they entered from the south. In Vanbrugh's words, 'it cannot conveniently be built any other way'. When Hawksmoor took on the commission his 'other way' was to reduce the central area to a square by introducing galleries and aisles to the north and south. Within this square the altar could be oriented correctly to the east.

Hawksmoor left more space on the north, as shown by the double aisle on this side, allowing him to create vistas of repeated arches and columns within a small space, with a gallery running between the two sets of columns. The

second aisle, beyond the north gallery, was reserved for baptisms. The east end has a small apse with an ornate wooden altarpiece.

The flat ceiling has a smaller central square section defined by deep plaster mouldings, so the design becomes a square within a square, a device also used at St Mary Woolnoth: both churches have clerestory windows on all four sides.

Hawksmoor also provided another 'ritually correct' entrance from the west, with flights of steps either side of the tower. While retaining the grander entrance from the south portico, this western entrance through the tower allowed worshippers to face the altar at the east as they entered the church. This is how the church looks today, but in the 1780s major changes were made

Detail of the Corinthian capitals creating the double aisle on the north. Like St Mary Woolnoth, St George's has clerestory windows on all four sides.

RIGHT The Dutch chandelier, on loan from the Victoria and Albert Museum, was installed in 2009.

OPPOSITE The apse at the east end, with the altar and altarpiece reinstated in the recent restoration. The alterpiece, carved in oak and Cuban mahogany in the 1720s, has a curved and recessed niche lavishly decorated with marquetry. At the top is a sunburst pattern with groups of cherubs floating above clouds.

to St George's. The north gallery was removed, and the altar and altarpiece installed against the far north wall, beyond the double aisle. As part of the 2006 restoration the north gallery was reinstated, and the altar moved back to Hawksmoor's original position in the east. And in 2009 the completion of the restoration was marked by the installation of an elegant seventeenth-century Dutch chandelier, on loan from the Victoria and Albert Museum in London.

FIFTY NEW CHURCHES

St George's Hanover Square

ALTHOUGH THE FIFTY NEW CHURCHES ACT was passed in 1711, in the reign of Queen Anne, only one of the dozen churches actually built is dedicated to St Anne. No less than three are dedicated to St George, the dragon-slaying patron saint of England, as a gesture of loyalty to the new King George, from Hanover, who succeeded to the throne in 1714. In the case of St George's Hanover Square, the connection with the Hanoverians is spelt out in the very name of the square, developed in 1713 in the new district of Mayfair by the Earl of Scarborough. He was a powerful supporter of both the Glorious Revolution that deposed the Catholic James II, and of the Hanoverian Succession which kept the Catholic Stuarts off the throne. St George's became a fashionable square, much favoured by military grandees including at least seven generals,[1] although by the 1770s there were complaints about its condition. A contemporary wrote: 'the middle has the air of a cow-yard, where blackguards assemble in the winter to play at hustle-cap, up to the ankles in dirt.'[2]

In spite of the 'blackguards', the prosperity of the area around Mayfair has made St George's a venue for fashionable weddings, in both fact and fiction. In Sherlock Holmes's *The Adventure of the Noble Bachelor* the bride mysteriously disappears after her wedding here, and in Shaw's *Pygmalion* Eliza Doolittle's father, Alfred, gets married at St George's, as popularized in the song from *My Fair Lady* ending: 'Get me to the church on time'. The cast of real-life characters who signed the register here includes the inventor of radio Guglielmo Marconi, the clown Joseph Grimaldi, as well as the poets Percy Bysshe Shelley and Olive Eleanor Custance. She married Lord Alfred Douglas, Oscar Wilde's lover.

The growing population of the new district needed a new church, and the Commission for Building Fifty New Churches engaged John James as architect. Building took place between 1721 and 1725. The site is a block south of Hanover Square, so the monumental portico on the west front faces the narrow St George Street rather than an open space. The portico has six giant Corinthian columns supporting a large pediment, and the tower is set just behind the portico, a plan which James Gibbs also used at St Martin-in-the-Fields and which became a common feature in many classical churches built throughout the Anglican world, in particular in America. The belfry stage has projecting pilasters at the corners, topped by pairs of urns, and above this the tower rises to a cupola and lantern. The body of the church has three tiers of windows on the north and south sides. At pavement level square windows light the crypt, above are two tiers of round-headed windows, the top pedimented ones taller than the middle tier, suggesting an interior of aisles and galleries. This is confirmed on entering the church, which follows Wren's St James's Piccadilly in having square piers rising above

At St George's John James introduced the plan of setting the tower behind a large pedimented portico, which Gibbs adopted at St Martin-in-the Fields.

[1] The *Weekly Medley*, in 1717, lists: 'The Lord Cadogan, a general; also General Carpenter, General Wills, General Evans, General Pepper, the two General Stuarts, and several others whose names we have not been able to learn'.
[2] Hustle-cap was a form of dodgy street gambling, a variation of pitch-and-toss, in which coins were 'hustled' or shaken together in a cap before being tossed. William Hogarth's engraving *The Idle Prentice at Play in the Church Yard* shows the 'Prentice' lounging on a tomb, trying to cheat by using his cap to conceal the coins being gambled.

The interior looking east, with aisles, galleries and a barrel-vaulted roof.

the pews to support a gallery, from which Corinthian columns rise to support the roof. The elegant interior is in line with James's declaration that the 'Beauty's of Architecture may consist with the greatest plainness of ye Structure'.

The interior of the building is essentially as it would have been in James's day, although in 1894 Sir Arthur Blomfield made several changes to the furnishings. The pulpit lost its original canopy and base, although the main section, with its fine marquetry panels, remains. A double-deckered reading desk was removed, and the box pews on the church floor were remodelled using the original oak (they are now open-sided). However, the pews upstairs in the gallery are authentic, and some of the doors, with their scrolled tops, are curved to follow the gallery at the western corners, where it sweeps round under the organ.

FIFTY NEW CHURCHES

The three middle towers of the organ case, with the flat rows of pipes between, are part of the original organ installed by Gerald Smith in 1725; the outer sections were added by Blomfield in the 1890s. In 2008 St George's commissioned the American firm of Richards, Fowkes & Co. to build a new organ to fit inside the case. The sound was designed to suit the Baroque music which is often performed in the church, which had George Frideric Handel as a parishioner. Handel lived in nearby Brook Street, where he composed the *Messiah*, and was a regular worshipper at St George's, even when afflicted by arthritis: 'For the last two or three years of his life he was used to attend divine service in his own parish-church of St George's Hanover Square . . . expressing by his looks and gesticulations the utmost fervour of devotion.'[3]

The pews upstairs still have scroll-top doors; in the corners they follow the line of the gallery as it curves round under the organ.

[3] *Gentleman's Magazine and Historical Review*, Volume 47, 1777

ABOVE LEFT The three middle towers of the organ case are original.

ABOVE RIGHT Marquetry inlay on the pulpit.

OPPOSITE *The Last Supper*, William Kent's altarpiece painted in 1724.

OVERLEAF A performance of the *Messiah* in the nave, with Christmas decorations in the galleries. St George's was Handel's parish church.

An unusual feature is the stained glass of the east windows installed in the mid-nineteenth century. Originally from Antwerp, these depict the Tree of Jesse, and are the work of Arnold of Nijmegen (*c.*1470–1540). Equally remarkable is the altarpiece showing *The Last Supper*, painted, apparently *in situ*, by William Kent in 1724, when the church was almost finished. Christ and His Apostles are all sumptuously dressed in flowing robes of different colours, except for the dingy and barely discernible figure of Judas Iscariot as he leaves on the far left, with a guilty backward glance. The frame is exuberantly carved in the style of Grinling Gibbons, with garlands of grapes, maize, roses, pine cones, fish, cherubs, etc. In 1914 the east window suffered slight damage when a suffragette bomb left overnight in one of the pews exploded. St George's was fortunate to escape the more determined bombing of the Blitz, and is one of the least changed of the London churches. It remains wonderfully unspoilt, and is at once grand and welcoming.

St George-in-the-East

OPPOSITE St George's stands in a large open space, as the Commissioners for the Fifty New Churches intended. The east end has a projecting apse and a large pediment; beyond is the tower, flanked by 'pepper-pot' staircase turrets.

OVERLEAF The ornate plasterwork in the dome of the apse, the only part of Hawksmoor's interior to survive the bombs of 1941.

1 Du Prey, *Hawksmoor's London Churches: Architecture and Theology*, 2000
2 Charles Jarmach, the owner of the emporium, tells how the escaped tiger was approached by a young boy 'who put out his hands to stroke the beast's back, when the tiger seized him by the shoulder and run down the street with the lad hanging in his jaws'. Jarmach rushed to the boy's rescue and 'pushed my thumbs with all my strength behind his ears, trying to strangulate him thus.' But it took several 'tremendous blows over the eyes' with a crowbar before the tiger released the boy. Jarmach sold the animal to a rival menagerie, who 'exhibited him as the tiger that swallowed the child, and by all accounts made a small fortune with him.' From the *Boy's Own Paper*, vol. I, no. 3, 1 February 1879
3 From the *Eastern Times*, 4 February 1860

HAWKSMOOR'S GREAT CHURCH IN WAPPING is one of the three 'Fifty New Churches' named after St George, the patron saint of England. The dedication was a mark of loyalty to King George I, recently arrived from Hanover. St George's was hit by incendiary bombs in May 1941, when the interior was destroyed, and only the walls and the tower left standing. The church became known as St George-in-the-Ruins and in the early 1960s Arthur Bailey carried out an ingenious scheme for building a new, much smaller, church within the space. Today the only part of Hawksmoor's interior to survive is the ornate plasterwork in the dome of the apse. On the exterior the apse is a semicircular projection with five windows; the interior follows this division into five bays, with panels of elaborate gilded plasterwork. Each bay has a round-headed window; there is a pair of cherubs on the springing of each arch and another cherub at the apex.

St George's was started in 1714 but not consecrated until 1729, a lengthy process caused by financial difficulties and not helped by the constant theft of building materials and the damage done 'by the Mob to ye Building'.[1] This was in spite of an 'enclosure of ye Church, to keep off filth – Nastyness and Brutes', as Hawksmoor had suggested in his plans for a church at Bethnal Green. The site chosen for St George's was close to the river Thames, next to an old Roman road later made notorious by the Ratcliffe Highway Murders of 1811. In 1857 the Highway was once again the scene of dramatic events when a Bengal Tiger escaped from a local wild animal emporium and made off with a young boy.[2] Three years later the church itself became notorious as the scene of the St George's Riots, also known as the Ritualism Riots. The Rector tried to impose High Church rituals on his congregation: he provoked them by wearing white surplices instead of a plain black gown and placing lighted candles on the altar. Low Church opponents regularly disrupted his services, and one Sunday 'a cry arose from the centre of the Church – "Let us smash the altar!". . . Scores of vagabonds rushed at the Communion rails . . . In the midst of pushing, fighting, scuffing, singing, and shouting from all parts of the church, Bibles, Prayer Books, and hassocks were hurled at the decorated altar-piece.'[3] The trouble only ended when the Rector resigned.

In 1936 another riot took place, this time in the street running to the north of the church. The Battle of Cable Street was fought when the British Union of Fascists, led by Sir Oswald Mosley, decided to march through the East End of London, in an act of provocation against the local Jewish population. The march was resisted by local residents and left wing parties, who built barricades in Cable Street. Fighting broke out between the locals and the police who tried to clear a way for the Fascists, and Mosley was forced to cancel the march.

The victory over the Fascists is celebrated in a large mural near the church.

St George's stands in a large open space, as the Commissioners for the Fifty New Churches intended. In Hawksmoor's time the space was constrained to the south and west by a group of houses. Hawksmoor failed to get the Commissioners to buy these so they could be demolished; instead we have the Blitz to thank for their eventual removal. The tower is a dramatic composition typical of Hawksmoor. On the sides of the tall belfry stage, to the north and south, are pilasters with long incised recesses; these act as buttresses and create the hollowed-out effect at the sides of the tower Hawksmoor also used at Limehouse and Spitalfields. The tower ends in an octagonal lantern, a design originally intended by Hawksmoor for St Alfege Greenwich but reused here. Two arcades of round-headed windows are set between eight projecting buttresses, topped by fluted columns in the form of Roman sacrificial altars, with swags of drapery below flat tops (similar to the four bollard-like altars at St Alfege). Between the altars are short sections of balustrades, created using Hawksmoor's trademark device of a long rectangular opening, with rounded ends (compare St Anne's Limehouse, St Mary Woolnoth). The overall effect is of a medieval tower, with a silhouette reminiscent of the Octagon at Ely, created from classical elements.

St George's has four additional smaller towers or turrets, lower down on the roof of the nave. These octagonal 'pepper-pots', capped by shallow cupolas, stood above the staircases which gave access directly to the galleries from doors on the south and north. This fulfilled another requirement of the Commissioners that the Fifty New Churches should be accessible from as many sides as possible. Internally, these staircases, which project out from the north and south walls, form a square element, like a Greek Cross, within the longer east–west axis. Externally Hawksmoor defines this square zone by placing oversize triple keystones above the four staircase doors and the windows between them. Here is a typical Baroque ambiguity: a single keystone properly placed is enough to keep an arch from collapsing; by using a triple keystone Hawksmoor reinforces the appearance of strength while simultaneously suggesting that one on its own isn't up to the task.

ABOVE Triple keystone above a door to the gallery staircase.

OPPOSITE St George's from the south. In Hawksmoor's day this view was obstructed by a group of houses, which were cleared away in the Blitz.

RIGHT The sides of the tower have tall projecting pilasters with long incised recesses; these act as buttresses and create a hollowed-out effect: Hawksmoor also used this device at Limehouse and Spitalfields.

OPPOSITE One of the 'pepper-pot' towers above the staircases to the galleries.

FIFTY NEW CHURCHES

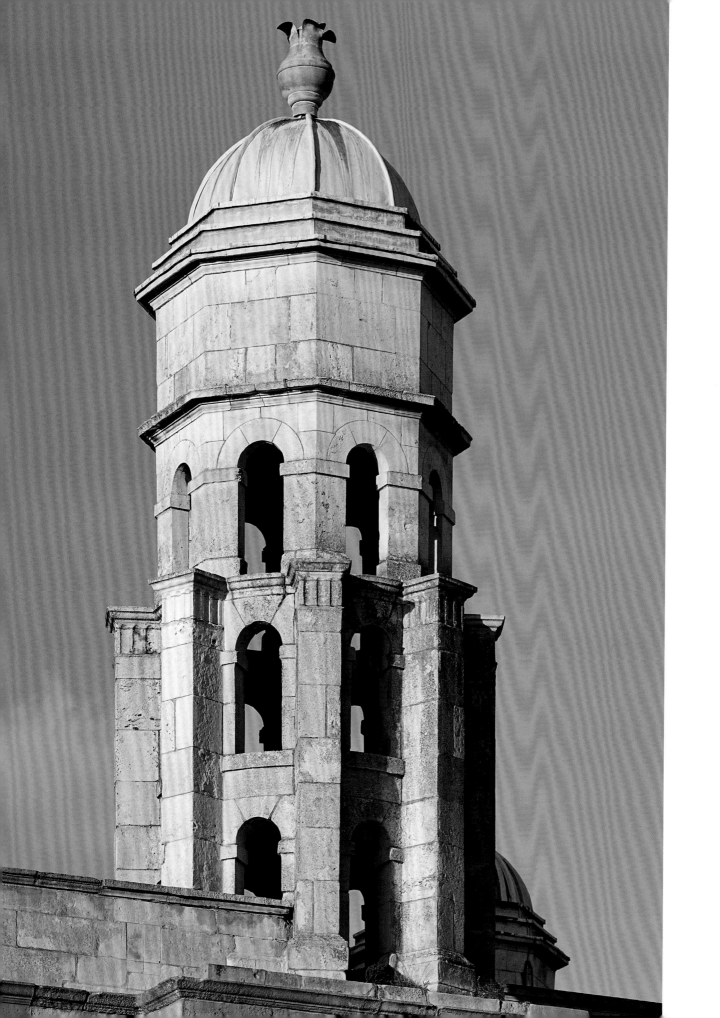

St John Smith Square

The tower at the south-west corner: the height was reduced 'without the Consent or Knowledge of Mr Archer'.

CHARLES DICKENS heartily disliked St John's: in *Our Mutual Friend* he describes it as 'a very hideous church with four towers at the four corners, generally resembling some petrified monster, frightful and gigantic, on its back with its legs in the air'. Dickens was writing in the 1860s, when architectural fashion favoured Gothic Revivalism based on the medieval churches of northern Europe rather than Thomas Archer's lavish Baroque style, inspired by the classical tradition of Rome and southern Europe.

St John's was built between 1713 and 1728, under the Fifty New Churches legislation of 1711. Costing over £40,000 it was one of the most expensive of the Queen Anne churches. With St Paul Deptford, started in the same year, it was one of the two churches built by Thomas Archer, a gentleman architect who held the court post of Groom Porter, a lucrative appointment giving him control over the court's gambling activities. As one of the Commissioners for building the New Churches it was natural that Archer should get work under the scheme. He was an enthusiastic follower of the Italian architect Francesco Borromini, whose work in Rome embodied the Baroque style, with its emphasis on curved surfaces, mass and volume, light and shade, projection and recession. These features are all in evidence at St John's, with its four identical corner towers. Each is built on an oval plan with diagonally projecting columns and ornate capitals, and capped with a fir cone, symbol of fecundity and regeneration. These corner towers house staircases which lead to the galleries.

The fir cones were not part of Archer's design submitted to the Commissioners; he originally planned these towers to be taller, rising to balustrades capped by pairs of pinnacles. Indeed he published an engraving of his original scheme showing the pinnacles, with the disclaimer that the alterations made to the design during construction, which substituted the fir cones, 'were done without the Consent or Knowledge of Mr Archer'.

The problem was that the weight of the new church was too much for the marshy ground of Millbank, close to the Thames. In spite of the foundations being reinforced in 1714, in 1719 it was found there were 'holes and Cracks within the Church occasion'd by . . . settling'. So a shorter, and lighter, version of the corner towers was built, giving the church the nickname 'Queen Anne's footstool'; the story goes that when Archer asked the Queen how she wanted the new church to look she kicked over her footstool and said 'Make me a church like that !'

Access was through the north and south fronts, where flights of steps lead to massive cavernous porticoes below broken pediments. The four fronts are connected to each other by curved sections of rusticated stonework, with elaborate window frames following the curvature of the wall. The exaggerated

The south front's cavernous portico. Archer uses the Doric order here, with a frieze of blank metopes and grooved triglyphs with hanging 'guttae'.

scale of the building is amplified by its situation in this small square, approached by terraces of domestic buildings. Photographically St John's is a challenging subject, being surrounded by large trees on all sides.

The overall plan is almost square, but the the staircase towers and deep porticoes on the north and south reduce the nave area to a longish rectangle. Within this Archer evokes a typically Baroque ambiguity of axis, which is expressed by the way the deep entablature breaks forward at the four corners, where it is supported by giant Corinthian columns, to produce a cross-in-square design, with a simple groin-vaulted ceiling. Below, the galleries running the length of the nave suggest a conventional longitudinal east–west axis, giving a Baroque feeling of ambiguous orientation. This is quite unlike Archer's other church of St Paul Deptford, where the deeply coffered ceiling runs emphatically east–west.

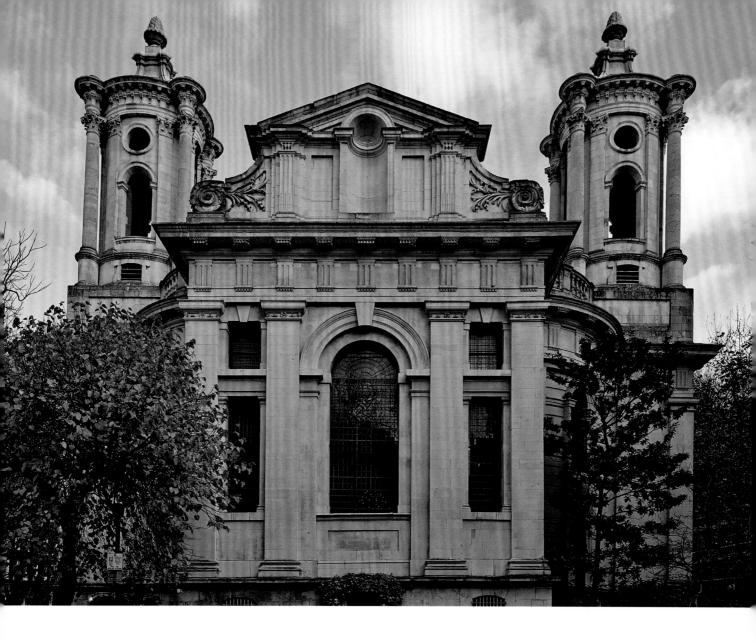

St John's has had an unlucky history. It was badly damaged by fire in 1742, when Archer was still alive, and in the rebuilding the twelve giant Corinthian columns in the nave were not replaced. It suffered a lightning strike in 1773, and in May 1941 incendiary bombs gutted the building. For twenty years the church was open to the sky, but in the 1960s money was raised by the Friends of St John's to convert the ruin into a concert hall. The reconstruction was carried out in 1965–69 by Marshall Sisson, who reinstated the Corinthian columns in the nave and installed a stage or platform for the performers at the east end, where the altar had been. The inaugural recital was given by Joan Sutherland in 1969 and it continues to hold regular concerts by distinguished performers.

The west front with giant pilasters of the Doric order, and two of the corner towers.

RIGHT An elaborate
window frame following
the curvature of the wall.
The ornaments at the
bottom have tapered
pegs, or 'guttae', hanging
down: a reference to
the Doric order on the
entablature, with guttae
below the triglyphs.

OPPOSITE View up the
south-west corner
staircase.

OVERLEAF Giant Corinthian
columns support a groin-
vaulted ceiling to produce
a cross-in-square design,
reinforced by the way the
entablature returns to the
outside walls to create
the effect of transepts to
north and south. Now
that St John's is a concert
hall, the altar at the east
end has been replaced by
a stage.

St Luke Old Street

ONE OF THE TWO LAST 'Fifty New Churches' built under the Act of 1711, St Luke's was created to provide for the overpopulated parish of St Giles-without-Cripplegate, now part of the Barbican complex. It was started in 1727 and finished in 1733, apparently to the joint designs of John James and Nicholas Hawksmoor, both Surveyors to the Fifty New Churches Commission.[1] There is no documentary evidence for who did what, but it seems that James designed the main body of the church, while Hawksmoor was responsible for the west end, including the tower and the spire. This is the reverse of their first collaboration at St Alfege Greenwich, where James provided the tower for Hawksmoor's church.

At the east end of St Luke's James follows the precedent of Wren's St James's Piccadilly and Hawksmoor's Christ Church Spitalfields by having a large Venetian window, here with elegant Ionic pilasters and square columns. All the windows on the long north and south walls have triple keystones, but their small

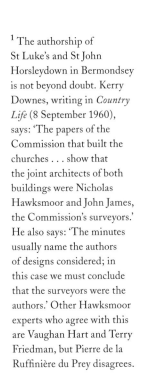

BELOW Venetian window with Ionic pilasters and columns at the east end.

OPPOSITE The south front with discreet triple keystones over the windows. The obelisk spire soars above the west end.

[1] The authorship of St Luke's and St John Horsleydown in Bermondsey is not beyond doubt. Kerry Downes, writing in *Country Life* (8 September 1960), says: 'The papers of the Commission that built the churches . . . show that the joint architects of both buildings were Nicholas Hawksmoor and John James, the Commission's surveyors.' He also says: 'The minutes usually name the authors of designs considered; in this case we must conclude that the surveyors were the authors.' Other Hawksmoor experts who agree with this are Vaughan Hart and Terry Friedman, but Pierre de la Ruffinière du Prey disagrees.

ST LUKE OLD STREET

OPPOSITE ABOVE LEFT
A flaming red-eyed
dragon serves as the
weathervane.

OPPOSITE BELOW LEFT
Doric doorway at the
west end.

OPPOSITE RIGHT The fluting
of the giant obelisk was
an afterthought.

discreet scale lacks the dramatic effect of Hawksmoor's oversized keystones at St George's Bloomsbury and St George-in-the-East.

At the west end is an elegant Doric doorway at the base of Hawksmoor's tower. Above this are the bell chamber, with round-headed louvred openings, and the clock, with dials on the north and south faces. The clock stage forms the base for the spire, a very tall fluted obelisk that soars up to a weathervane, the grooves of the fluting accentuating the vertical thrust.

The weathervane is a flaming dragon complete with a red eye, whose symbolism is unclear. Perhaps it is the Biblical fiery serpent that cures snake bites: 'And the LORD said unto Moses, Make thee a fiery serpent, and set it upon a pole . . . And Moses made a serpent of brass, and set it upon the pole; and it came to pass, that if a serpent had bitten any man, when he looked unto the serpent of brass, he lived.' (Numbers 21:8-9) Local residents thought it looked more like a louse, giving rise to the church's nickname: Lousy St Luke's.

The obelisk, with its associations with Ancient Egypt and Baroque Rome, was a form of great interest to Hawksmoor which he used repeatedly in his work, including several of his designs for church steeples.[2] But a fluted obelisk was unusual; apparently this was an afterthought, as the accounts show 'an extra allowance in changing the Scaffolds to flute the Obelisque after it was Erected'. Hawksmoor liked to be able to change his mind during the course of a project. It is also characteristic of him to use a single classical element dramatically enlarged in scale, like the keystones at St George's Bloomsbury or the giant Venetian window he used as the portico of Christ Church Spitalfields.[3]

St Luke's was built on marshy land and from the beginning suffered from severe subsidence; by 1960 it had become a dangerous structure and was closed. The parish was reunited with St Giles-without-Cripplegate and the organ, font and altar were transferred to the older church, where they can still be seen. In 1966 the roof was removed for safety reasons and for thirty years the church was a dramatic ruin, with trees growing out of the nave. In 1996 the building was taken over by the London Symphony Orchestra, based at the nearby Barbican Centre. The converted church was reopened in 2003 and is now used by the LSO as a recording space, and for rehearsals and concerts.

[2] Examples include St Augustine's, St Bride's, St Margaret Pattens, St Mary Somerset, St Vedast-alias-Foster and Christ Church Spitalfields.
[3] There is a similarity between St Luke's, with its oversized obelisk, and the giant tapering column of the spire of St John Horsleydown in Bermondsey, complete with a large Ionic capital with large scrolls or volutes. St John's was built as one of the Fifty New Churches at the same time as St Luke's. It is also thought to be a collaboration between Hawksmoor and John James. It was badly damaged in the war and largely demolished in the 1960s.

ST LUKE OLD STREET 337

St Martin-in-the-Fields

The grand portico
and south front
fromTrafalgar Square.

THE LEGEND OF SAINT MARTIN tells us he was a Roman soldier in the late fourth century. One day, near the French city of Amiens, he was moved by the plight of a freezing beggar and, using his sword, cut his cloak in two to share it with the poor vagabond. That night Jesus came to him in a vision wearing the beggar's half of the cloak. Martin converted to Christianity, and went on to become the Bishop of Tours. His humanity makes him an appropriate dedicatee of St Martin-in-the-Fields, famous for its work with the homeless of London.

There has been a small church here since the early thirteenth century. Henry VIII disliked having the bodies of plague victims carried through his Palace at Westminster for burial at nearby St Margaret's. So in 1544 he built a new church further away at St Martin's where funerals could be conducted instead, and transferred the Palace of Westminster to the newly enlarged parish. At that time St Martin's was in open country, and so literally 'in the fields'. By the early eighteenth century the population of the parish had increased to some forty thousand and the dilapidated Tudor church, although enlarged in 1607, was quite inadequate for such large numbers. In 1720 James Gibbs won the competition to design a new church, after he had taken the selection committee on a tour of Wren City churches, as well as round his own recently completed St Mary-le-Strand, one of the Fifty New Churches. Initially he wanted to build a round church with a shallow dome: Gibbs tells us that 'There were two Designs made for a Round Church which were approved by the Commissioners, but were laid aside upon account of the expensiveness of executing them.' As built, St Martin's follows St George's Hanover Square, designed by his rival John James, in having a tower built over the west end of the church, behind a large pediment above a grand Corinthian portico. By 1800 the church faced 'vile houses' at the bottom of St Martin's Lane, and it only acquired the prominent position it enjoys today with the creation of Trafalgar Square in the 1820s. As a pre-existing parish St Martin's was outside the remit of the Fifty New Churches Commission, but I include it here because stylistically it has so much in common with the New Churches that were built.

In 1728 Gibbs published his influential *A Book of Architecture*, which included a double-page 'Perspective View of St Martins Church'. The success of the publication helped establish St Martin's as the prototype for many churches in the English-speaking world. The basic plan of placing the tower behind a pedimented portico is common throughout North America; in the words of the architectural historian Calder Loth: 'nearly every major colonial American city received one or more churches inspired by Gibbs's plates of St. Martin.'

FIFTY NEW CHURCHES

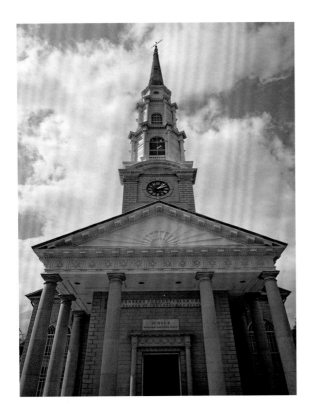

ABOVE LEFT John Holden Greene's Independent Presbyterian Church at Savannah, Georgia. A grand version of St Martin's, complete with Neoclassical sunburst in the pediment, built 1817–19.

ABOVE RIGHT First Presbyterian Church at Clarkesville, Georgia, a rudimentary clapboard version of the St Martin's plan (built in 1848 by Jarvis Van Buren).

Examples range from the grand Independent Presbyterian Church at Savannah, Georgia, to the much humbler First Presbyterian Church at Clarkesville, Georgia. It is ironic that Gibbs, a Roman Catholic, should have provided the template for so many Protestant churches.

The royal connection that started with Henry VIII continued with George I, who became a churchwarden at St Martin's and whose coat of arms is in the pediment of the west portico. Royal patronage ensured that it soon became a fashionable church, and as early as 1725 the *London Spy* announced that St Martin's 'can produce as handsome a show of white hands, diamond rings, pretty snuff-boxes, and gilt prayer-books, as any cathedral whatever.' Above the pediment is an elegant steeple in the tradition of Wren's City churches. Gibbs wrote that 'Steeples are . . . of a Gothick Extraction; but they have their beauties, when their parts are well dispos'd, and when the Plans of the several Degrees and Orders of which they are compos'd gradually diminish, and pass from one Form to another without confusion.' The steeple at St Martin's embodies these principles: a square tower rises to a clock stage, and above this an open octagonal arcade runs between Corinthian half-columns. The top section is a delicate concave spire of four octagonal stages, each with a circular opening. In Plate 30 of his *Book of Architecture* Gibbs shows three further variations on his design.

Gibbs wrote that the separate elements of a steeple should 'gradually diminish, and pass from one Form to another without confusion', as he demonstrates here.

When the steeple was finished there was an unusual topping-out ceremony involving a tightrope walker known as Signor Violante: 'Soon after the completion of St Martin's steeple, this adventurous Italian descended from the arches, head foremost, on a rope fastened across St Martin's Lane.'[1] He held a flaming torch in each hand, and wore a breastplate with a groove cut in it to 'fly' down the rope.

The royal association continues inside, with another coat of arms at the east end. The nave's barrel-vaulted ceiling is carried on Corinthian columns, with aisles and galleries on the north and south. In Gibbs's original plan the only pews were in the galleries. Gibbs, like Wren, saw pews as a necessary evil; he wrote that galleries and pews 'clog up and spoil the Inside of Churches, and take away from that right Proportion which they otherwise would have, and are only justifiable as they are necessary.' There was no permanent seating in the nave until the introduction of pews in 1799, although these were altered in 1858. The chief glory of the interior is the magnificent plasterwork ceiling, carried out by the Italian-Swiss craftsmen Artari and Bagutti, who had previously worked for Gibbs at St Mary-le-Strand. There is no clerestory, but the large windows above the gallery make up for this by flooding the church with light.

ABOVE Detail of marquetry panel on the pulpit.

OPPOSITE The curved theatre-like box on the north was for the King's use; here the royal family could attend services at their parish church in comfort.

A distinctive feature of St Martin's is at the east end, where Gibbs provides curved theatre-like boxes on the north and south, at an angle between the ends of the galleries and the shallow chancel. These boxes, with their balustrades and sash windows beneath gilded cornices, have two faces: an inward-curving section faces diagonally out on to the nave, while a flat section looks down on the shallow chancel. Above the altar in the chancel is a Venetian, or Serlian, window. A new window was installed in 2008 by the Iranian artist Shirazeh Houshiary: her design uses clear glass within a lattice of curvilinear glazing bars, subtly distorted to suggest a cross with an oval at its centre.

Celebrities buried here include Charles II's mistress Nell Gwyn in 1687, and the romantic highwayman Jack Sheppard, who escaped from prison four times before dying on the gallows in 1724.

[1] Malcolm, *Londinium Redivivum*, vol. IV, page 194

The nave is dominated
by Artari and Bagutti's
plasterwork ceiling, above
the new east window
installed in 2008.

344

St Mary-le-Strand

OPPOSITE Looking east along the Strand, with St Mary's in the foreground. In the middle distance is another steeple by Gibbs: in 1719 he used a similar design to complete Wren's St Clement Danes, which also stands on an island in the Strand.

BELOW The tail of the weathervane represents a comet.

[1] 'Pope's ironic reference to the prostitutes who worked in Drury Lane, at the heart of London's sex trade.

THERE HAS BEEN A CHURCH in the Strand since the twelfth century, when it was known as the Church of Innocents or the Church of the Nativity of the Blessed Virgin Mary. Thomas Becket was rector here before he became Archbishop of Canterbury. The Strand, which as the name suggests was the ancient riverbank of the Thames, became in time the main thoroughfare from Whitehall to the City of London, and was lined on the south with the palaces of bishops and princes, including the Palace of Savoy. The earlier church was demolished in 1549 by the Duke of Somerset, uncle of the young king Edward VI, to make way for his new mansion at Somerset House, and for over 150 years the congregation had to go to the nearby St Clement Danes or the Savoy Palace Chapel. With the passing of the Act for Building Fifty New Churches in 1711, money for a new church became available from the Coal Tax. St Mary's, built between 1714 and 1717, was one of the first of the Fifty New Churches. The Commissioners appointed James Gibbs as Surveyor, and he was given responsibility for the new St Mary-le-Strand; Gibbs was a young Scot who had studied under Carlo Fontana in Rome, and so had a first-hand knowledge of the Italian Baroque that no other British architect could offer. In a letter to the Commissioners Gibbs claimed that he had 'studied Architectur abroad for several years under the greatest masters at Rome, and especially that parte that relates to churches.' He had the support of Wren, who told his fellow Commissioners that he had 'had opportunity's to observe his knowledge in Architecture and what relates thereto; I believe him to be very well qualified.'

The site, slightly to the north of the old church, was for years occupied by a great maypole, over 130 feet tall. Taken down by the Puritans, it was re-erected at the Restoration. By the early eighteenth century storms and wind had reduced it to a height of about 20 feet, and it was finally cleared away to make way for the new church, as Pope says in the *Dunciad*:

> Where the tall maypole once o'erlooked the Strand,
> And now (so Anne and piety ordain)
> A church collects the saints[1] of Drury Lane . . .

According to John Strype's *Survey* of 1720 the remains of the maypole were 'obtained by Sir Isaac Newton and . . . carried away to Wansted in Essex . . . for the raising of a telescope, the largest in the world.'

ABOVE The projecting semicircular portico at the west end, and the north front with alternating curved and triangular pediments. The roofline is decorated with urns and a balustrade. In 1802 large numbers gathered to watch a procession celebrating peace with France; three of the crowd in the Strand were killed when a spectator on the roof of the church dislodged one of the urns, sending it crashing to the ground.

RIGHT The apse at the east end, with hanging garlands of vine leaves.

Although on a relatively cramped site, St Mary's fulfils the Commissioners' requirement that the New Churches should be in open spaces: it sits in the middle of the Strand, and Gibbs provided a free-standing design which would look good from all sides. At the east end is an apse with delicate garlands of vine leaves hanging between the windows. On the side walls Gibbs made the inner bays of the lower storey windowless 'to keep out noises from the street'; instead there is a blind arcade of five niches below alternating curved and triangular pediments, all contained between Ionic columns. This theme is repeated with three more alternating pediments on a larger scale in the upper storey, where they break into the balustrade, above a series of tall round-headed windows, here between Corinthian columns. The composition resembles a Baroque fugue in its counterpoint of contrasting rhythms. At the west end the projecting semicircular entrance porch is under a shallow dome, recalling Wren's south transept portico at St Paul's, itself derived from Pietro da Cortona's *Santa Maria della Pace* in Rome, which Gibbs would have seen when studying there. Above the porch pairs of Corinthian columns support a pediment; above this an elegant steeple rises through several stages to a little lantern, crowned by a weathervane in the form of a comet. Gibbs originally planned to have a simple bell tower at the west end, and a tall column supporting a statue of Queen Anne in front of the church, but this came to nothing. In another scheme of about 1713 Gibbs proposed placing a statue of Queen Anne above the porch, but after her death in 1714 this too was abandoned in favour of the funerary urn we see today.

Santa Maria della Pace in Rome by Pietro da Cortona: the model for Gibbs's semicircular portico.

Architecturally the interior of St Mary's is fairly plain, with no aisles, transepts, galleries or clerestory. Above the wooden panelling in the nave plain fluted pilasters decorate the blank expanses of the lower windowless walls. The east end is a more elaborate design. Two tiers of columns, Corinthian below and Composite above, support a pediment containing the Royal Arms; below this is the apse, which, unlike the nave, does have windows at the first storey. Above the blue stained glass of the windows are stone carvings of cherubs' heads amidst swirling clouds and sunbeams. The plasterwork in the nave is attributed to Wilkins: the ornate coffered ceiling is a tightly packed expanse of squares, triangles and lozenges. In 1718 the expense of the decoration so alarmed the Commisioners that they demanded a 'stop should be put to the extravagt. Carvings within'.

The interior looking east. 'To keep out noises from the street', Gibbs kept the lower storey windowless on the north and south walls.

Sir John Soane, lecturing in 1809, was scathing about Gibbs's work, saying he 'crowded together so many small parts without sense that the mind is fatigued and embarrassed by their smallness, whilst the number of them prevents the eye from resting upon any of them.'[2]

Even as St Mary's was being completed, political events brought about the removal of Gibbs from his post as Surveyor for the Fifty New Churches. In 1714 Anne died, and was succeeded by George I from Hanover. This was followed by the unsuccessful Jacobite Rising of 1715 in Scotland, whose supporters hoped to gain the crown for the Catholic James Stuart, son of the deposed James II. When the Tories lost power in the General Election of 1715 Gibbs, a Catholic Tory Scot, found himself out of favour with the new regime. He appears to blame Colen Campbell, the arch-Palladian author of *Vitruvius Britannicus* and a fellow Scot, for his dismissal: 'a false report by a countryman of mine that

[2] Lecture four. Quoted by David Watkin in *Sir John Soane: Enlightenment Thought and The Royal Academy Lectures*, 1997

misrepresented me as a Papest and a disaffected person, which I can assure you is intirly false and scandalous'.

Although he lost his Surveyorship to John James in 1716, and St Mary-le-Strand is the only one of Fifty New Churches he built, Gibbs went on to have a very successful private practice with many clients among the landowning aristocracy. He also built the Radcliffe Camera at Oxford and the Senate House at Cambridge, as well as St Martin-in-the-Fields (see page 338).

ABOVE Detail of stone carvings in the apse with cherubs' heads, clouds and a triangle containing the Hebrew letters for YAH, the first syllable of the name YAHWEH, or JEHOVAH. It's not clear why only part of the name appears.

OVERLEAF The shallow barrel-vaulted ceiling is an intricate design of plasterwork lozenges, triangles and squares.

St Mary Woolnoth

OPPOSITE The west front
has a rusticated lower
section and twin towers
above. The cylindrical
Tuscan columns are made
uncompromisingly plain
by the lack of entasis,
the subtle swelling and
tapering usually seen in
classical columns.
Hawksmoor uses the deep
grooves of the rustication
to form the keystone and
voussoirs of the arches
over the door and the half-
moon window above.

BELOW The keystones above
the doors to the crypt are
decorated with groups
of three cherubs, a motif
repeated in marquetry
on the pulpit and in the
etchings on the modern
glass doors to the church.

St Mary Woolnoth was built by Nicholas Hawksmoor between 1716 and 1727. At the heart of the City of London – the only one of Hawksmoor's churches built in the City – between Lombard Street and the Mansion House, it faces the Bank of England. Although funded by the Commission for Building Fifty New Churches, it was far from being a new church. St Mary Woolnoth is first recorded in the late twelfth century, but probably goes back to well before the Norman Conquest. The name might be a corruption of Wulfnoth, a Saxon noble credited with founding the church, or it might come from a nearby wool market. But St Mary's itself has probably been a place of worship since at least Roman times. George Godwin pointed out in his 1839 *Churches of London*: 'The discovery of many fragments of antiquity, when excavating for this church in 1716, led to the belief that a temple, probably that which was dedicated to Concord, at one time occupied the site.'

More excavations took place between 1897 and 1900, when the City and South London Railway built Bank Underground Station below St Mary's. They wanted to demolish the church, but had to make do with excavating the crypt and underpinning the walls and internal columns on huge steel girders. What is now the Northern Line has its ticket machines directly beneath the church. The bones found in the crypt were removed to Ilford cemetery.

The medieval church was damaged in the Great Fire, but enough survived to make it worth repairing. However these repairs, carried out in the 1670s, were not a success and by 1711 the building was so dilapidated that the parishioners were afraid to worship there, and petitioned the Commission for money for a new church. The Commissioners agreed and engaged Hawksmoor as architect, with his fellow Surveyor, John James, as his assistant.

Of all Hawksmoor's London churches St Mary's is the most compact, due largely to the cramped site, unlike the open spaces available to him in East London. The west front has bands of rustication running across the façade, which Hawksmoor calls 'Rusticks'. These wrap round the Tuscan columns on the corners, tying the tower into the main body of the church. The tower above, much broader than it is deep, continues at the full width of the rusticated façade. The lowest section is a shallow platform with three square unornamented windows. These correspond to the three bays framed by the Composite

ST MARY WOOLNOTH   355

[1] John Summerson, *Georgian London*

San Carlo alle Quattro Fontane (1638-41), Borromini's masterpiece of Roman Baroque church building, has a façade that undulates from concave to convex, with the entablature breaking forward to form sharp points above the columns.

columns of the main stage above. The central louvred bay is the bell chamber while the outer two bays are blank, below an entablature with a deep cornice carried on the Composite columns. Above the cornice are twin square turrets topped by elegant balustrades. The turrets are connected by another balustrade created using Hawksmoor's trademark device of a long rectangular opening, with rounded ends (compare St Anne's Limehouse, St George-in-the-East). There is an ambiguity here: the turrets evoke twin towers, as in many medieval cathedrals (compare Hawksmoor's own twin towers at Westminster Abbey), while the columns of the stage below suggest a single tower: it's as if the two towers have fused together to become a solid mass.

The effect is very different from the soaring verticality of Hawksmoor's steeples at St Anne's Limehouse or Christ Church Spitalfields, which were designed to be seen at a distance. Here the cramped site would prevent a tall steeple being seen properly; it also restricted it structurally, as Hawksmoor explains in a letter to the Commissioners: 'The steeple cannot rise high, being on ye plann but 14 ft broad one way.'

Where the west front is solidly rectangular with few curves, the Lombard Street façade on the north is all about movement, with its three large arches containing recessed niches. Each niche encloses Ionic columns with the bases and capitals set at an angle; a dramatically concave entablature breaks forward to form sharp points above the columns, in a design that recalls Borromini's façade of San Carlo alle Quattro Fontane in Rome. These in-out curves in the horizontal plane contrast with the round-headed frames and the little arches below. The combination produces a lively Baroque interplay, making up for the lack of direct light and shadow on the north-facing wall. The architectural historian Sir John Summerson, an early champion of Hawksmoor's work, described his treatment of this elevation as 'a piece of sheer architectural eloquence hard to match'.[1] The rustication of the west front is continued in the frames of the niches, although here it does not carry across the full width of the façade. The design is similar to Wren's doorway at St Mary-le-Bow (see page 180), which Hawksmoor knew well from the drawings he made of it. To reduce the noise of traffic from Lombard Street, there are no windows on this north side. In Hawksmoor's day the south side faced a narrow alleyway, and here he does provide windows; however King William Street has since been opened up, and now has even more traffic than Lombard Street.

LEFT ABOVE The twin turrets, connected by a balustrade with Hawksmoor's trademark long rectangular openings.

LEFT BELOW The Lombard Street façade has three large recessed arches, with sharply pointed entablatures above Ionic columns set at an angle, a device Hawksmoor derived from Borromini's San Carlo alle Quattro Fontane in Rome.

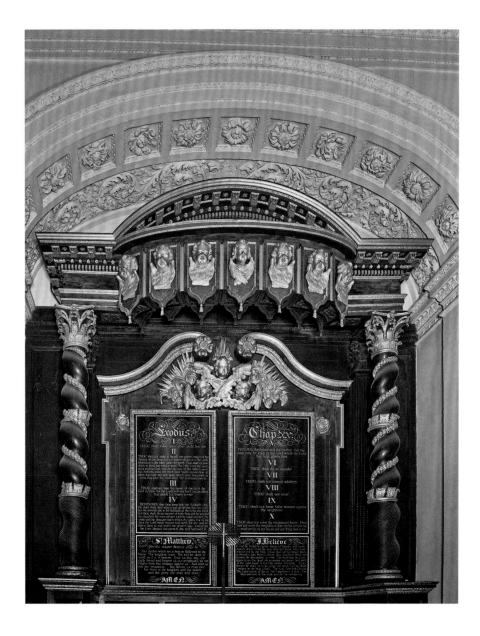

OPPOSITE The square interior is lit by four large semicircular windows in the clerestory. Hawksmoor's galleries were removed in the 1870s.

LEFT The reredos with twisted Solomonic columns. In the 1870s Butterfield raised the chancel, pushing the reredos up against the chancel arch.

OVERLEAF View into the lantern of St Mary Woolnoth: a square within a square.

The interior is square in plan, except for a shallow chancel at the east end containing a reredos. With its large twisted Solomonic columns this is a restrained Protestant version of Bernini's baldacchino at St Peter's in Rome, and similar to Wren's designs for St Paul's. These columns are a common feature in Flemish Baroque churches, such as St Paulus in Antwerp. The barley-sugar design is associated with the Temple of Solomon in Jerusalem, which Hawksmoor studied, and is significant to Freemasons, who date their origins from the building of the Temple. The square ground plan becomes essentially cubic when seen in three dimensions, and the cube also has biblical and masonic significance.

OPPOSITE TOP LEFT
Butterfield took down the
galleries, and fixed the
front panels and capitals
to the walls.

OPPOSITE TOP RIGHT
Monument to John
Newton, the writer of
the hymn 'Amazing
Grace', with an 'Epitaph
written by the Deceased'
describing himself as
'Once an Infidel and
Libertine' who 'by the Rich
Mercy of Our Lord and
Saviour' was 'Preserved,
Restored, Pardoned and
Appointed to Preach
the Faith' he had long
Laboured to Destroy'.
He died in 1807.

OPPOSITE BELOW The
bulbous pulpit, with a
marquetry sunburst
of 42 rays.

The traditional cornerstone used in some masonic foundation rituals is a cube, symbolizing truth, for at the heart of the temple of Jerusalem the Holy of Holies was a pure cube: 'And the oracle in the forepart was twenty cubits in length, and twenty cubits in breadth, and twenty cubits in the height thereof' (1 Kings 6: 20). This is carried forward in the Book of Revelation, where the cube is also the form of the New Jerusalem: 'And the city lieth foursquare, and . . . the length and the breadth and the height of it are equal' (Revelation 21:16).

In the 1870s Butterfield altered the interior arrangement of the church, including raising the chancel, with the result that the reredos is crammed up against Hawksmoor's chancel arch. As with the height of the tower, Hawksmoor's choice of lighting was dictated by the cramped site. There would not be much light from the windows, so his solution is to provide top lighting: within the outer square he raises a smaller square lantern on four clusters of Corinthian columns, with large semicircular clerestory windows on all four sides. The effect is to flood the church with reflected light from all directions, with magical results. The play of light and shade would have been still more effective and varied when Hawksmoor's galleries were in place, but Butterfield took them down as part of his alterations. He kept the gallery fronts and supporting columns by fixing them to the walls, in an oddly flattened arrangement. The pulpit, made by Hawksmoor's craftsmen, is an unusual bulbous design, with marquetry panels above bands of foliage carved in relief.

Counting the rays of the sunburst on the front panel of the pulpit reveals a total of 42, a number with profound religious and mystical significance. In the Kabbalistic tradition of Judaism 42 is the number with which God creates the Universe. And Matthew 1:17 calculates there are 42 generations from Abraham to Jesus Christ, just as Thomas Cranmer proposed 42 Articles as a summary of Anglican doctrine in 1552. More recently, Douglas Adams's *Hitchhiker's Guide to the Galaxy* tells us that 42 is the answer to the 'Ultimate Question of Life, the Universe and Everything'.

In the late 1700s this pulpit was the setting for fiery sermons preached by John Newton against the evils of the slave trade. The author of the hymn 'Amazing Grace', Newton was a former slave-trader and atheist turned fervent Christian abolitionist. He wrote a pamphlet, 'Thoughts Upon the Slave Trade', with a 'confession, which . . . will always be a subject of humiliating reflection to me, that I was once an active instrument in a business at which my heart now shudders'. He was Rector here from 1779 until his death in 1807; he became a close friend of William Wilberforce, and lived to see the British abolition of the slave trade. He is commemorated in a plaque on the north wall with an 'Epitaph written by the Deceased'.

JOHN NEWTON
CLERK.
ONCE AN INFIDEL AND LIBERTINE,
A SERVANT OF SLAVES IN AFRICA,
WAS,
BY THE RICH MERCY
OF OUR LORD AND SAVIOUR
JESUS CHRIST,
PRESERVED, RESTORED, PARDONED,
AND APPOINTED TO PREACH THE FAITH
HE HAD LONG LABOURED TO DESTROY.

HE MINISTERED
NEAR XVI YEARS AS CURATE AND VICAR
OF *OLNEY* IN *BUCKS*,
AND XXVIII YEARS AS RECTOR
OF THESE UNITED PARISHES.

ON FEB. THE FIRST MDCCL, HE MARRIED
MARY,
DAUGHTER OF THE LATE GEORGE CATLETT,
OF *CHATHAM, KENT*,
WHOM HE RESIGNED
TO THE LORD WHO GAVE HER,
ON DEC. THE XV. MDCCXC.

The above Epitaph was written by the Deceased
who directed it to be inscribed on a plain Marble Tablet.

He died on Dec. the 21. 1807. Aged 82 Years,
and his mortal Remains
are deposited in the Vault
beneath this Church.

St Paul Deptford

St Paul is raised on a platform above a crypt, and has colossal banded pilasters supporting pediments on the north and south. At the west is a cylindrical tower, around which Archer wraps a semicircular portico of four giant Tuscan columns. The graceful spire is reminiscent of Wren's St Mary-le-Bow.

ST PAUL DEPTFORD attracts superlatives: 'London's most splendiferous baroque church', says John Betjeman; 'The exterior is Baroque of astonishing vigour', according to Simon Jenkins; and 'One of the most moving eighteenth-century churches in London', says Nikolaus Pevsner. Mervyn Blatch goes further, suggesting it has a claim to be 'externally, the most outstanding [parish church] in the Metropolis of any period'.

In 1711 George Stanhope, the Vicar of Deptford, appealed to Parliament about the poor state of his existing church in which '12,000 souls cannot possibly be accommodated', leading many to 'go to meeting houses . . . of Dissenters . . . Quakers . . . Presbyterians, and . . . Anabaptists'.

Later that year the recently elected Tories, with the support of Queen Anne, passed the 'Act for Building Fifty New Churches in the cities of London and Westminster and the suburbs thereof'. One of the first suburbs chosen to receive a new Anglican church was Deptford, where a new parish, St Paul, was created on an open site. Thomas Archer, one of the Commissioners for the Fifty New Churches, took the job of architect. Work began in 1712, although it proceeded slowly and the church was not consecrated until 1730.

Archer was the most exuberantly Baroque of English architects, having spent four years in Italy where he would have seen at first hand the work of Borromini, Bernini and Pietro da Cortona. As with his other London church, St John Smith Square, the influence of the Italian Baroque is clear. This is a square church, like St John's, with entrances on three sides. Archer also provided a very Baroque rectory to the south, but this has since been demolished.

The outside is spectacular. The whole church is raised on a platform, which adds to the grandeur of the design. A circular tower stands above the main entrance on the west. Above the arched bell chamber and the clock stage, the tower rises to an octagonal arcade, and a graceful spire, reminiscent of Wren's St Mary-le-Bow. Following the line of the tower down, we see that the base of the tower, or at least one half of it, becomes the semicircular doorway into the church. It is as if the tower is a free-standing column around which Archer wraps the rest of the church. The doorway is set within another, larger, semicircle: a portico of four giant Tuscan columns approached up a flight of steps, again semicircular. The portico with its projecting semicircle of columns (like Wren's south portico at St Paul's and Gibbs's west portico at St Mary-le-Strand) is derived from Pietro da Cortona's Santa Maria della Pace in Rome (see page 349). Archer continues the giant order of the columns in a series of rusticated pilasters running round the rest of church, with tall arched windows almost the full height of the pilasters. Symmetrical balustraded staircases lead

FIFTY NEW CHURCHES

ST PAUL DEPTFORD

to the north and south entrances, both with large pediments. At the east end is a semicircular apse, corresponding to the west doorway; here it contains a Venetian window that follows the curve of the apse.

The interior is just as thrilling. Looking east we see how the curved Venetian window forms the east end of the chancel, framed by Doric pilasters and columns and *trompe l'œil* consoles and garlands. Above the gilded entablature is more *trompe l'œil*: heavy red brocade curtains part to reveal a heavenly choir of cherubim. This was the work of the painter Henry Turner, who charged £189 for '94½ Yards of Painting and Guilding about the Altar Containing the Fluting of the Columns and Pilasters, the Enrichments of their Bases & Capitals with Guilding and Ornaments in the Soffits, together wth a Large Curtain, Cherubs Heads and a Glory in the Spherical Arch'.

The square plan is not felt in the interior, thanks to giant Corinthian columns dividing the interior space longitudinally into nave and aisles, and galleries running between the columns. The deeply coffered and ornate plasterwork ceiling contains a long central panel which contributes to the feeling of length. At each end the line of columns narrows before meeting the end walls, and in the angle the galleries project forward to look like giant theatre boxes. This treatment of the internal corners is similar to Borromini's S. Agnese in Rome. Archer uses the space created by these angled sections for staircases and vestibules.

At the west end is the organ gallery, supported by two pairs of fluted mahogany Corinthian columns. The organ was installed around 1745 by Thomas Griffin, although the maker is unknown.

The nave narrows at the east end where the galleries project forward like giant theatre boxes. The shallow apse contains a curved Venetian window and is decorated with *trompe l'œil* painting by Henry Turner.

Trompe l'œil garlands hang between the columns and pilasters at the east end.

ABOVE The west end follows the same pattern as the east end: the nave narrows and the galleries project forward at an angle. The organ dates from the 1740s.

LEFT Mahogany Corinthian capitals support the organ gallery.

LOSS AND SURVIVAL

OF THE FIFTY-ONE CHURCHES built by Wren and his colleagues in the City, there are twenty-nine left in one form or another. One, St Mary Aldermanbury, has been rebuilt in Missouri in the United States. Six remain only as towers, where the body of the church was either demolished in the nineteenth century or destroyed in the intensive bombing of London by the Luftwaffe during the Second World War.

The earliest church to be demolished was St Christopher-le-Stocks, removed in 1782 to make way for an extension to the Bank of England. This was also partly to prevent rioters using the church as a platform to attack the Bank, which had been damaged during the Gordon Riots two years before. During the first half of the nineteenth century a few churches were removed to make way for civic improvements: in 1831 St Michael Crooked Lane was destroyed as part of the rebuilding of London Bridge, and in 1840 St Bartholomew-by-the-Exchange was demolished to allow the widening of Threadneedle Street.

The worst destruction of the City churches was in the second half of the nineteenth century. As those working in the City moved to the suburbs the residential population declined dramatically and many fewer churches were needed. With increasing pressure on land for new railway stations, road-widening projects and more office space, the Church of England set about selling the sites of unwanted churches. In the mid-nineteenth century, as the Gothic Revival came to dominate church architecture, the Baroque churches of Wren and Hooke had little appeal, being dismissed by Pugin as 'meagre imitations of Italian paganism'. In this climate the Church authorities met little effective opposition to the demolition of Wren's City churches.

To demolish an Anglican church requires an Act of Parliament, so in 1860 the Union of Benefices Act was passed; this allowed parishes to be amalgamated, and redundant churches demolished. Not everybody agreed with Pugin. In 1854, during a debate in the House of Commons on the subject, George Hadfield MP declared: 'he wished to preserve the noble monuments of Sir Christopher Wren's genius from the grasp and cupidity of the prelates of the Established Church.'[1]

But he was in a minority, and fifteen City churches were eventually demolished under the Act. The first to go was St Benet Gracechurch in 1867, and the last was All Hallows Lombard Street in the 1930s (see page 64). In 1943, shortly

[1] Hansard, Church Building Acts Amendment Bill, 6 July 1854
[2] G.W. Wright, 'The 1860 United Benefices Act' in Oxford Journals, Arts and Humanities, *Notes & Queries* 1943, Vol. 184, Issue 10, pages 290–291

after the Blitz, G.W. Wright wrote: 'The trail of wilful destruction that followed the Act of 1860 accounts for more City Churches . . . than the recent exploits of the alien Hun.'[2]

In 1919 another nineteen had been threatened by the proposals of Lord Phillimore and his City of London Churches Commission, but these were withdrawn after opposition from, amongst others, the Corporation of the City and the Royal Institute of British Architects. The RIBA's support for the City churches shows how Wren's architecture had come back into fashion by the early twentieth century.

In a single night of the Blitz, 29 December 1940, German bombs destroyed or caused major damage to nine City churches. St Paul's was hit by an incendiary bomb which crashed through the dome, but was extinguished by the fire crews of the St Paul's Watch without further harm. Dean Matthews wrote that St Paul's was left 'conspicuous and isolated among the ruins'. The survival of St Paul's became symbolic of the nation's struggle through the remaining years of the war.

Altogether, three churches were destroyed outright in the Blitz – St Stephen Coleman Street, St Mildred Bread Street, St Swithin London Stone – while nine others suffered substantial damage and were rebuilt in the 1950s and 1960s. The rebuildings took different forms. St Mary Abchurch was badly damaged but restored as far as possible to its original condition. St Mary-le-Bow was rebuilt by Laurence King, who reproduced Wren's design but with a colour scheme Sir Christopher would not have recognized. St Bride's Fleet Street was rebuilt without Wren's galleries, although the galleries were preserved at St James's Piccadilly in Sir Albert Richardson's sensitive restoration. Some were substantially altered before the Blitz: St Magnus the Martyr in the 1760s, St Mary-at-Hill in the 1820s, and in the 1850s Sir George Gilbert Scott remodelled St Michael on Cornhill in the High Victorian taste of his time. Among the best preserved are St Martin-within-Ludgate and St Margaret Lothbury, where the wainscoting on the lower walls retains the look of the late seventeenth century. Both churches also have very fine woodwork.

The Fifty New Churches suffered in the war, although they fared better than Wren's City churches. St Alfege Greenwich was firebombed but (like St James's Piccadilly) sympathetically restored by Richardson. St John Horsleydown, with its strange tower in the form of an Ionic column, was damaged beyond repair and has since been demolished. St George-in-the-East and St John Smith Square were both gutted during the Blitz, but the exteriors have survived. St John Smith Square was sold as a ruin and restored as a concert hall. St Luke Old Street suffered severe subsidence in the 1960s, and has also recently been rebuilt as a concert hall. Gibbs's St Mary-le-Strand and James's St George's

Hanover Square both escaped damage in the war. Hawksmoor's genius can best be appreciated at Christ Church Spitalfields, St Anne's Limehouse, St George's Bloomsbury and St Mary Woolnoth, none of which was bombed.

One solution to the problem of finding new uses for churches without a congregation has been the creation of guild churches. In 1952 the City of London (Guild Churches) Act designated sixteen guild churches to serve the non-resident population, allowing these churches to form partnerships with a number of Christian groups and civic charities. At St Clement Eastcheap, recently reopened by the Amos Trust after months of building work, the result has been to turn the nave into an open-plan office. Other examples have done more to preserve the spirit of Wren's work: St Lawrence Jewry, next to the Guildhall, became the guild church of the Corporation of London, while St Michael Paternoster Royal is home to the Mission to Seafarers. St Anne and St Agnes has recently been taken over by the Gresham Centre, a music charity. In these cases the effect has been to keep the church in use, while retaining much of the original feel and atmosphere. A recent development has seen the reopening of St Nicholas Cole Abbey as a restaurant and coffee bar, with a mid-week church service. The Wren interior has been preserved, providing a welcome retreat for the sightseer doing a round of the City churches.

Visiting the churches requires a bit of planning, as their opening hours vary. Most are closed at the weekends, although some, including St Bride's and St Sepulchre's, have regular Sunday services. Many of the churches have lunchtime concerts and organ recitals, as well as weekday services. The best source of information about the churches in general, as well as special events and opening times, is the Friends of the City Churches, a charity dedicated to promoting their protection and appreciation. Besides their informative website and regular newsletter, the Friends provide a rota of volunteer 'Church Watchers' who keep some twenty of the churches open to visitors on different days of the week – an invaluable service to those who love and value London's City churches.

A member of the St Paul's Fire Watch looking out for enemy bombers from the roof of the Cathedral.

AFTER THE FIRE

GLOSSARY

AISLE A side aisle is the space, created by columns or piers, parallel to the central body of a church. The London churches may have one or more side aisles, or none at all.

ALTARPIECE or REREDOS Panel or screen behind and above an altar, typically divided into three or more sections. An important decorative feature of the London Baroque churches. Those at *St Mary Abchurch* and *St James's Piccadilly* are decorated with carvings by Grinling Gibbons.

APSE Semicircular or polygonal projection, usually beyond the chancel at the east end. A feature of the Hawksmoor churches: *St Alfege, St George's Bloomsbury, St George-in-the East.*

ARCADE Row of arches, usually supported by columns or piers.

ARCH Curved structure connecting columns or piers. Pointed arches are a feature of Gothic architecture, while classical buildings typically have curved arches.

ARCHITRAVE In classical architecture the lowest section of the entablature, forming a lintel supported by columns, piers or pilasters.

ATTACHED Describes a column which is not free-standing, but embedded in a wall, as in the west front of *St Lawrence Jewry.*

ATTIC In a classical façade, a shallow area above the main entablature, sometimes including a pediment: *St Lawrence Jewry.*

BALDACCHINO Free-standing canopy above an altar, supported by columns: *St Paul's Cathedral.*

BALUSTERS Vertical elements, typically with bellied or bulging lower sections, supporting coping stones on a church wall or tower.

BALUSTRADE Made up of rows of short balusters, a balustrade provides a decorative top section to a tower: *St Andrew Holborn, St Andrew-by-the- Wardrobe, St Mary Woolnoth*; or church wall: *St Paul's Cathedral.*

BAROQUE The French term *baroque* comes from the Portuguese *barocco*, meaning a misshapen pearl. It describes a style in art and architecture developed in Europe, particularly in Rome, from the early seventeenth to the mid-eighteenth century. In architecture it creates a dramatic, often exaggerated effect and is characterized by bold, curving forms, elaborate ornamentation, oval plans, and contrasts between projection and recession, light and shade.

BASILICA In ancient Rome a basilica was a public court of law; in church architecture it is a type of building with an oblong plan without transepts, having a central nave and one or more aisles created by rows of columns or piers: *St Michael Cornhill, St Paul's Cathedral, Christ Church Spitalfields.*

BAY Vertical division of the interior or exterior wall of a church.

BELFRY Upper stage of a tower or steeple where church bells are hung. Often identifiable by window openings with louvres or slats which act as baffles.

BOX PEW Type of pew, or church seating, enclosed with high wooden back and ends, often with latched doors, and originally reserved for the pew-holder and his family: *St George's Hanover Square.*

BUTTRESS Vertical element projecting from a wall to counter the sideways thrust or load of an arch, roof or vault. A Gothic flying buttress uses part of an arch to transmit this load to a separate element, itself stabilized by its own weight. Wren used concealed flying buttresses at *St Paul's Cathedral.*

CAMPANILE Italian for free-standing bell tower: *All Hallows Twickenham.*

CAPITAL Top element of a column or pilaster. In the classical orders of architecture, the form of the capital varies with the order. Doric is relatively plain with a narrow band; Ionic has two scrolls or volutes like rams' horns; Corinthian has stylized acanthus leaves. A Composite capital combines Ionic scrolls above Corinthian foliage.

CARTOUCHE Carved oblong panel, representing a scroll with rolled-up ends, also an ornate frame around a design or inscription: *St Andrew Holborn.*

CHANCEL   Eastern area of a church, beyond any transepts, where the altar or Communion table is situated.

CHANCEL SCREEN   Division between the chancel and the rest of the church; the two examples in the London Baroque churches are both ornate and delicately carved: *St Margaret Lothbury, St Michael on Cornhill.*

CHOIR   The area, usually east of the crossing, of a cathedral or church where the choir sings during a service: *St Paul's Cathedral.* Also spelt Quire.

CHOIR STALLS   Seating reserved for the members of the choir, usually in two sections facing each other across the choir or quire: *St Paul's Cathedral.*

CHURCHWARDENS' PEW   A grand pew reserved for the use of the churchwardens: *St Margaret Pattens.*

CLASSICAL   Style of architecture of Ancient Greece and Rome, revived in the Renaissance by Palladio and others. The style is characterized by the use of the five classical orders: Tuscan, Doric, Ionic, Corinthian and Composite.

CLERESTORY   Upper storey of a church which is 'clear', with windows to light the interior space: *St Paul's Cathedral, St James Garlickhythe, St Mary Woolnoth.*

COLONNADE   A row, or ring, of columns carrying an entablature: steeples of *St Mary-le-Bow, Christ Church Newgate Street.*

COLUMN   A vertical element, usually in one of the classical styles, round in section and carrying a capital.

COMMUNION RAIL   Rails, often decorated with spiral twisted balusters, enclosing the area around the Communion table: *St Margaret Lothbury, St Stephen Walbrook.*

COMMUNION TABLE   The table used by Protestants for the celebration of Holy Communion. With the reredos, organ and pulpit, an opportunity for the display of skilled carving: *St Benet Paul's Wharf, St James Garlickhythe.*

COMPOSITE ORDER   One of the classical orders of architecture, with a capital combining Ionic scrolls above Corinthian foliage: *Christ Church Spitalfields.*

CONSOLE   A bracket with a curved outline: *St Paul Deptford.*

CORBEL   A projection which carries some structural element, typically an arch as at *St Michael on Cornhill*; or an entablature as at *St Anne and St Agnes.*

CORINTHIAN ORDER   One of the classical orders of architecture, with a slender shaft and a capital decorated with acanthus foliage: *St Benet Paul's Wharf, St Paul's Cathedral.*

CORNICE   A projecting ledge with a flat top, the cornice is the topmost element of an entablature: *St Mary Abchurch, St Michael on Cornhill.*

COVING   A concave moulding used in the interior of a building to bridge the gap between the outer walls and a smaller flat central panel in a ceiling: *St Margaret Lothbury.*

CROCKET   The small, leafy, knobbly projections on Gothic pinnacles: *St Alban Wood Street.*

CROSSING   The central space where transepts 'cross' the nave and divide it from the chancel: *St Paul's Cathedral.*

CRYPT   The basement of a church, either wholly or partly underground, rare in the City churches, unless they existed in the original pre-Fire church: *St Mary-le-Bow, St Bride's Fleet Street.*

CUPOLA   The Italian for dome, derived from the Latin *cupella* (a small cup), denoting a small circular, square or polygonal dome-like structure, often used by Wren and Hooke as the stage of a steeple beneath the spire: *St Benet Paul's Wharf, St Mary Abchurch.*

DORIC ORDER   One of the classical orders of architecture, the Doric has a plain or fluted shaft and a capital decorated with a narrow band. Characterized by a frieze featuring triglyphs and metopes: *St Mary-le-Bow, St Luke Old Street* doorways.

DRUM   Vertical wall supporting the curving upper portion of a dome: *St Paul's Cathedral.*

ENTABLATURE   In the classical orders the entablature is carried by columns, piers or pilasters; its principal elements are the architrave, frieze and projecting cornice.

ENTASIS   Subtle swelling and tapering seen in classical columns to counteract the optical illusion that perfectly parallel lines appear slightly concave. Hawksmoor avoids its use at *St Mary Woolnoth.*

FESTOON   A string or garland of fruit, flowers or foliage suspended in a loop or curve between two points: *St Benet Paul's Wharf, St James's Piccadilly* altarpiece.

FINIAL   The small ornament, sometimes in the shape of a ball, or leaf or flower, at the top of a tower, spire, pinnacle or cupola: *St Mary Aldermary, Christ Church Newgate Street*.

FLUTING   Series of parallel concave grooves in the shaft of a column, pier, pilaster or obelisk: *The Monument, St James Garlickhythe, St Luke Old Street*.

FONT   The bowl-shaped container that holds the water used in the service of baptism. Grinling Gibbons carved an exquisite font cover for *All Hallows by the Tower*.

FRIEZE   A horizontal band, ornamented or plain, the central element of an entablature.

GALLERY   An upper storey providing additional seating above the aisle(s). Used by Wren at *St James's Piccadilly* and *St Andrew Holborn*. And by Hawksmoor at *St Alfege Greenwich* and *Christ Church Spitalfields*.

GIANT ORDER   An order more than a single storey in height: *St Alfege Greenwich* and *Christ Church Spitalfields*.

GREEK CROSS   A type of centralized church design favoured by Italian Renaissance architects where the four arms – nave, chancel and two transepts – are all of equal length: *St Martin within Ludgate, St Anne and St Agnes*.

IONIC ORDER   One of the classical orders of architecture, the Ionic capital has two downward-curving scrolls or volutes like rams' horns: *St James Garlickhythe, St Peter upon Cornhill*.

KEYSTONE   See Arch. The keystone is the wedge-shaped block at the top of an arch, holding the other blocks in place. Often decorated by Wren with cherubs' heads: *St Michael Paternoster Royal*; and used by Hawksmoor as an occasion for Baroque exaggeration: *St George's Bloomsbury, St George-in-the-East*.

LANTERN   A round or polygonal structure with openings. On top of a cupola a glazed lantern brings light into the body of the church below: *St Mary-at-Hill, St Stephen Walbrook*. In a steeple a lantern is an open stage for bringing transparency and lightness to the design: *Christ Church Newgate Street, St Magnus the Martyr*.

LOUVRED   A shutter made of louvres – horizontal baffles or slats. Louvred windows of a belfry allow the sound of the bells out, but prevent the rain coming in. At *St Mary-le-Bow* the louvres can be adjusted to modify the sound.

LUNETTE   French for a small moon, so semicircular window or opening: *St Anne's Limehouse*.

METOPE   The spaces between the grooved triglyphs in a Doric frieze, sometimes decorated with sculpture: *St Mary-le-Bow*.

MODILLIONS   Small brackets supporting a cornice, typically at the top of the tower: *St Benet Paul's Wharf, St Michael Paternoster Royal*.

NAVE   The main area of a church reserved for the congregation. The nave can be flanked by one or more side aisles, usually lower than the nave itself. The word comes from the Latin *navis*, meaning a ship, possibly because the nave's vaulted roof in medieval churches resembles the keel of an upturned boat.

OBELISK   Originally an Ancient Egyptian monument or landmark, an obelisk is a tall tapering pillar, square in section. Much favoured by Hawksmoor as a decorative element: *St Luke Old Street, St Margaret Pattens*.

ORDERS   The five orders of classical architecture, as described by Andrea Palladio and others, are the Doric, Ionic, Corinthian, Tuscan and Composite. Each order has its own stylistic elements, as shown by the column (with its base, shaft and capital) and entablature (with its architrave, frieze and cornice).

ORIENTATION   Originally meaning to face the Orient or east, orientation is the siting of a church on an east–west axis, usually with the Communion table at the east end.

PEDIMENT   In ancient classical architecture, the triangular gable end of a temple. Pediments can also be curved (round-headed or segmental). A pediment is *open* when the some of the base is missing , or *broken* when the apex is missing.

PENDENTIVE   The triangular concave section of vaulting between arches supporting a dome. So-called because these downward-pointing sections appear to hang from the base of the dome: *St Stephen Walbrook, St Paul's Cathedral*.

PEW   Long bench with a back, usually arranged in rows in the nave and aisles, providing seating for the congregation. See also Box Pew and Churchwardens' Pew.

PIER   An upright element supporting an arch or some other superstructure, as in the massive supports for the dome of *St Paul's Cathedral*, or the slender piers carrying the galleries of *St Anne's Limehouse*.

PILASTER   A vertical element carrying a capital, usually attached to wall. It differs from a column in being flattened.

PINNACLE   Topmost decorative element of spiky or pointed design on steeples of the London churches: *St Mary Aldermary, St Mary Somerset*.

PODIUM   A platform that supports a wall while raising it off the ground: *St Peter Cornhill, St Lawrence Jewry*.

PORTICO   A porch with a roof supported by columns, sometimes with a pediment, as at the Pantheon in Rome.

PULPIT   A raised and enclosed platform where the minister stands to preach.

QUIRE   See Choir

QUOINS   Derived from the French *coin*, meaning corner, quoins are blocks of dressed stone reinforcing the outside corner, or angle, of a building.

REREDOS   See Altarpiece

ROUND-HEADED   An arch, window or pediment with a top curved in a semicircle.

RUSTICATION   Masonry where the depth of the joints between the blocks is exaggerated to give a sense of strength: *St Mary-le-Bow* porch, *St Mary Woolnoth*.

SAUCER DOME   An internal dome, or series of domes, with a shallow saucer-like profile: *St Paul's Cathedral, St Mary Aldermary*.

SEGMENTAL   A segmental element (arch, window or pediment) has a curved top, but the curve is shallower than its round-headed equivalent, as it uses only a segment of the semicircle.

SERLIAN WINDOW   See Venetian Window.

SOLOMONIC   Solomonic columns have spirally twisted shafts, like barley sugar: *St Mary Woolnoth*.

SPANDREL   A roughly triangular space between two arches and the moulding or cornice above them: *St Mary Aldermary*.

SPIRE   Tall, tapering structure on top of a church tower; so the topmost element of a steeple.

STEEPLE   The tall structure comprising a tower, belfry, lantern and spire.

STRING COURSE   A horizontal band or moulding used to divide a wall or other surface into smaller zones.

SWAG   Similar to festoon, although usually refers to drapery (rather than fruit, flowers and foliage).

TOWER   A tall structure, the section of a steeple below the spire.

TRANSEPTS   In a church that is cruciform (in the shape of a cross), transepts project beyond the main body of the church to provide the side arms of the cross.

TRIGLYPHS   Vertical grooved elements representing stylized beam ends of early wooden temples, found on the frieze of the Doric order.

TUSCAN ORDER   The simplest of the classical orders of architecture, similar to the Doric (but without Doric triglyphs and metopes) and with a simple circular base: *St Mary Woolnoth*.

VAULT   An arched roof. The simplest is the barrel or tunnel vault, (a continuous semicircular arch): *St Peter upon Cornhill*. A groin vault is where two barrel vaults intersect: *St Michael on Cornhill*. Wren uses a late Gothic fan vault at *St Mary Aldermary*.

VENETIAN WINDOW   Also known as a Serlian window. A window with three separate openings, the central one being arched and taller than the others: *St James's Piccadilly, St Martin-in- the-Fields*.

VOLUTES   Spiral scrolls, as on an Ionic capital.

WAINSCOTING   Wooden interior panelling on the lower sections of a building: *St Martin-within-Ludgate*.

BIBLIOGRAPHY

Atkinson, Frank, *St Paul's and the City*, Michael Joseph, London, 1985

Aubrey, John, *Brief Lives with An Apparatus for the Lives of our English Mathematical Writers*, edited by Kate Bennett, Oxford, 2015

Baker, T.M.M., *London: Rebuilding the City after the Great Fire*, Phillimore & Co., Chichester, 2000

Beard, Geoffrey, *The Work of Christopher Wren*, John Bartholomew & Son Ltd, Edinburgh, 1982

Betjeman, John, *The City of London Churches*, Pitkin Pictorials, London, 1965

Blatch, Mervyn, *A Guide to London's Churches*, Constable, London, 1978

Boid, Edward, *Concise History and Analysis of All the Principal Styles of Architecture*, London, 1829

Bradley, Simon and Nikolaus Pevsner, *The Buildings of England, London 1: The City of London*, Penguin Books, London, 1987
The Buildings of England, London: The City Churches, Penguin Books, London, 1998, and Yale University Press, London, 2002

Campbell, James W.P., *Building St Pauls*, Thames & Hudson, London, 2007

Cobb, Gerald and Nicholas Redman, *London City Churches*, Batsford, London, 1989

Colvin, Howard, *A Biographical Dictionary of British Architects 1600–1840*, John Murray, London, 1995

Colvin, Howard and John Newman (eds.), *Roger North's Writings on Architecture*, Clarendon Press, Oxford, 1981

Cooper, Michael, *'A More Beautiful City': Robert Hooke and the Rebuilding of London after the Great Fire*, Sutton Publishing, Stroud, 2003

Downes, Kerry, *Hawksmoor*, Thames & Hudson, London, 1969
Christopher Wren, Allen Lane The Penguin Press, London, 1971
Vanbrugh, Sidgwick & Jackson, London, 1977

Dryden, John, *Annus Mirabilis*, printed for Henry Herringman, London, 1667

Dugdale, William, *History of Saint Paul's Cathedral, in London, from Its Foundation Etc.*, edited by Henry Ellis, London, 1818

Du Prey, Pierre de la Ruffinière, *Hawksmoor's London Churches: Architecture and Theology*, University of Chicago Press, Chicago and London, 2000

Evelyn, John, *The Diary of John Evelyn Esq. F.R.S. from 1641 to 1705, With Memoir*, edited by Willam Bray Gibbings & Co., London, 1895, facsimile edition by Forgotten Books, 2012
Fumifugium or The Inconveniencie of the Aer and Smoak of London Dissipated, printed by W. Godbid, London, 1661

Friedman, Terry, *The Eighteenth-Century Church in Britain*, Yale University Press, London, 2011
James Gibbs, Yale University Press, London, 1984

Godfrey, Walter H., *IV.—Recent Discoveries at the Temple, London, and Notes on the Topography of the Site*, Archaeologia (Second Series), The Society of Antiquaries of London, Volume 95, 1953

Grelot, Guillaume-Joseph, *Relation nouvelle d'un voyage de Constantinople*, Paris, 1680

Hart, Vaughan, *Nicholas Hawksmoor: Rebuilding Ancient Wonders*, Yale University Press, London, 2002

Hibbert, Christopher, *London: The Biography of a City*, Penguin Books, London, 1980

Hollis, Leo, *The Phoenix: The Men who Made Modern London*, Weidenfeld & Nicolson, London, 2008

Hooke, Robert, *The Diary of Robert Hooke*, edited by H.W. Robinson & W. Adams, Taylor & Francis, London, 1935
Micrographia or some Physiological Descriptions of Minute Bodies made by Magnifying Glasses, The Royal Society, London, 1665

Hooke, Robert & R. Waller, *The Posthumous Works of Robert Hooke*, London, 1705

Inwood, Stephen, *The Man Who Knew Too Much: The Strange and Inventive Life of Robert Hooke*, Macmillan, London, 2002
A History of London, Macmillan, London, 1998

Jardine, Lisa *The Curious Life of Robert Hooke: The Man who Measured London*, HarperCollins, London, 2003

Jeffery, Paul, *The City Churches of Sir Christopher Wren*, Continuum Publishing, London, 1996

Jenkins, Alan, *The City: London's Square Mile*, Viking Kestrel, London, 1988

Little, William A., *Mendelssohn and the Organ*, Oxford University Press, New York, 2010

Malcolm, James Peller, *London Redivivum*, London 1807

Marlborough, Sarah, Duchess of, *Private Correspondence of Sarah, Duchess of Marlborough Illustrative of the Court and Times of Queen Anne*, Henry Colburn, London, 1838

Milward, John, *The Diary of John Milward, Esq., Member of Parliament for Derbyshire, September 1666 to May 1688,* edited by Caroline Robbins, Cambridge, 1938

Pennick, Nigel, *Sacred Architecture of London,* Aeon Books, London, 2012

Pepys, Samuel, *Diary and Correspondence of Samuel Pepys FRS . . . deciphered by the Rev. I Smith,* in 2 volumes, J.M. Dent Everyman's Library, London, *c.*1900

Pevsner, Nikolaus, *The Buildings of England, London 2,* Penguin Books, London, 1952

Pope, Alexander, *The Works of Alexander Pope Volume V containing the Three First Books of the Dunciad,* London, 1757

Pugin, Augustus Welby Northmore, *The True Principles of Pointed Or Christian Architecture set forth in Two Lectures Delivered at St Marie's, Oscott,* London, 1841

Royal Commission on Historical Monuments, *The City of London,* HMSO, London, 1929

Rushworth, John, 'A Letter Giving Account of that Stupendious Fire which consumed the Citty of London; beginning saturday Septmbr 1st . . . 1666', dated 8 September 1666, published in *Notes & Queries, A Medium of Intercommunication for Literary Men, General Readers, Etc.,* Fifth Series, Volume 5, John Francis, London, 15 April 1876, page 306

Saunders, Ann, *St Paul's Cathedral: 1400 Years at the Heart of London,* Scala Publishers, London, 2012

Summerson, John, *Georgian London,* first edition Pleiades Books, London, 1945
Architecture in Britain 1530-1830, paperback edition Penguin Books, London, 1970

Swift, Jonathan, *A Project for the Advancement of Religion, 1709,* published in *The Works of Dr Jonathan Swift in Four Volumes,* Dublin, 1735

Taswell, William, *Autobiography and Anecdotes,* edited by George Percy Elliott, Camden Society, London, 1852

Tickell, Thomas, 'A description of the Phoenix', published in *The Sixth Part of Miscellany poems, published by Mr. Dryden,* London 1716

Tinniswood, Adrian, *A Life of Christopher Wren,* Jonathan Cape, London, 2001
By Permission Of Heaven: The Story of the Great Fire of London, Jonathan Cape, London, 2003

Tucker, Tony, *The Visitor's Guide to the City of London Churches,* The Horizon Press, Ashbourne, 2010

Uglow, Jenny, *A Gambling Man: Charles II and the Restoration,* Faber & Faber, London, 2009

Verney, Margaret M., *Memoirs of the Verney Family from the Restoration to the Revolution, 1660 to 1696,* Longmans Green & Company, London, 1899

Vincent, Thomas, *God's terrible voice in the city . . . the two dreadful judgements of plague and fire, inflicted upon the city of London,* printed for George Calvert, London, 1667

Wallis, John, *London: Being a Complete Guide to the British Capital . . . Faithfully abridged from Mr Pennant's London and brought down to the present Year, Third Edition,* London, 1810

Webb, Geoffrey, *The Letters and Drawings of Nicholas Hawksmoor Relating to the Building of the Mausoleum at Castle Howard, 1726-1742,* Volume 19 of the Walpole Society, 1930-1931

Weinreb, Ben, Christopher Hibbert, Julia Keay and John Keay, *The London Encyclopaedia,* Macmillan, London, third edition 2008

Whiffen, Marcus, *Thomas Archer: Architect of the English Baroque,* Hennessey & Ingalls Inc., Los Angeles, 1973

World Monuments Fund, *St George's Bloomsbury,* Scala Publishers, London, 2008

Wren, Christopher (editor), *Parentalia, or, Memoirs of the family of the Wrens . . . Now Published by Stephen Wren,* London, 1750

Wren, Christopher, letter to Portland quarrymen, dated 12 May 1705, published in *Notes & Queries, A Medium of Intercommunication for Literary Men, General Readers, Etc.,* Third Series, Volume 4, London, 8 August 1863, page 103

ACKNOWLEDGMENTS

I am very grateful for the help and support of many people. First and foremost to my wife, Laura, who has encouraged and supported me during the three years this project has taken, and provided her expert literary agency skills without taking a percentage. Also to my editor and publisher Jo Christian for embracing the idea of a book on London's Baroque churches, and her colleagues Mirabel Cecil and Basil Postan at Pimpernel Press for their support. I am thrilled by Anne Wilson's design, which makes my photographs look better than I thought possible. She has skilfully negotiated the competing demands of the author and photographer, a task made all the more difficult when they are one and the same. I am very grateful to my friends Jonathan Keates for taking the time to read the manuscript, and Pierre de la Ruffinière du Prey for his help with the Hawksmoor churches. All errors are of course mine.

This book would not have been possible without the cooperation of the Rectors, Vicars, Churchwardens and Church Administrators who have given me permission to take photographs in their churches. I am particularly grateful to the following:

The Vicar of All Hallows by the Tower for permission to photograph the Grinling Gibbons font cover; the Synagogue Manager for permission to reproduce the photographs of Bevis Marks; the Rector of Christ Church Spitalfields; the Church Administrator of St Alfege Greenwich; the Administrator of St Andrew-by-the-Wardrobe; the Manager of St Andrew Holborn; the Director of the Gresham Centre at St Anne and St Agnes; the Rector of St Anne's Limehouse; the Guild Vicar of St Benet Paul's Wharf; the Administrator of St Bride's Fleet Street; the Resident Chaplain of St Clement Danes; the Administrator of the Amos Trust at St Clement Eastcheap; the Trustees of the London Spirituality Centre at St Edmund the King; the Events Manager of the World Monuments Fund for permission to reproduce the photos of St George's Bloomsbury; the Parish Administrator of St George's Hanover Square; the Administrator of St James Garlickhythe; the Parish Secretary of St James's Piccadilly; the Administrator of St John Smith Square Charitable Trust; the Guild Vicar of St Lawrence Jewry; the Rector of St Magnus the Martyr, who also gave me access to St Mary Abchurch; the Rector of St Margaret Lothbury, who also gave me access to St Mary Woolnoth; the Administrator of St Margaret Pattens; the Vicar of St Martin-in-the-Fields; the Administrator of the Guild Church of St Martin-within-Ludgate; the Priest in Charge of the Guild Church of St Mary Aldermary; the Churchwarden of St Mary-le-Strand; the Parish Administrator of St Mary-at-Hill; the Parish Secretary of St Mary-le-Bow; the Mission to Seafarers for access to St Michael Paternoster Royal; the Rector of St Michael Cornhill; the Manager of the Wren Coffee for permission to take photographs of St Nicholas Cole Abbey; my photographs of St Paul's Cathedral are reproduced with the permission © The Chapter of St Paul's Cathedral; the Rector of St Paul Deptford; the Facilities Manager of St Helen's Bishopsgate for access to St Peter upon Cornhill; the Priest in Charge of St Sepulchre's; the Rector of St Stephen Walbrook; the Administrator of St Vedast-alias-Foster; the Administration of the Temple Church.

The portrait of Wren by Sir Godfrey Kneller, Wren's Warrant Design for St Paul's Cathedral and my photograph of the bust of Nicholas Hawksmoor are all reproduced by permission of the Warden and Fellows of All Souls College, Oxford.

I am grateful to the British Library for permission to use *Hollar's Exact Surveigh of the Streets Lanes and Churches Contained within the Ruines of the City of London* © The British Library Board, Maps.Crace.Port.1.50; and to the Wellcome Library for permission to use historical images from their website.

TECHNICAL NOTE ON THE PHOTOGRAPHY

Most of the photographs were taken specially for this book using a digital Phase One medium format camera system, with lenses ranging from 28mm to 300mm. A few were taken with the smaller Fuji X Pro 1 camera system. For the close-ups of weathervanes and other distant details I used the Fuji camera body with an astronomical telescope (Altair Astro Wave Series 102mm) as an extreme telephoto lens. Both cameras produce RAW image files; these were all converted using Capture One image processing software, with final editing done in Photoshop. A few of the photos were taken up to forty years ago; these older photos were taken on film, using a Linhof technical camera.